WE CAN FIX IT!

A TIME TRAVEL MEMOIR

JESS FINK

Top Shelf Productions
Atlanta / Portland

More Praise for Jess Fink

"Fink deals with fearless honesty and shameless self-indulgence, and she draws it all in a loose, exuberant style that gives a nice counter-texture to the more serious, soul-searching moments (not that she doesn't handle the poop jokes with aplomb, too). Her personal journey through humiliation and acceptance should speak to anyone who's had the misfortune of being a teenager."
— Ian Chipman, *Booklist*

"*We Can Fix It* is what autobiography should be. Maybe Jess Fink didn't ACTUALLY go back in time to spy on herself, make out with herself, and give herself terrible advice, but there are different kinds of truth. And this is the awesome kind."
—Joey Comeau, author of *A Softer World*

On *Chester 5000*:

"Both sexy and charming."
—*The AV Club*

"A naughty tale of true romance."
—*io9*

"Like the works produced during the high point of the adult film industry, *Chester 5000* has both a narrative and a heart…fluid and cute."
—*Paste*

"A woman-friendly, couple-friendly book destined to become a perennial in sex-positive toy and book stores."
—*The Comics Journal*

"Delightfully playful…a genuinely beautiful piece of erotica."
—*Page 45*

"This is the kind of book that makes me ecstatic to read comics."
—Johanna Draper Carlson, *Comics Worth Reading*

For everyone whose timeline has
rubbed up next to mine.

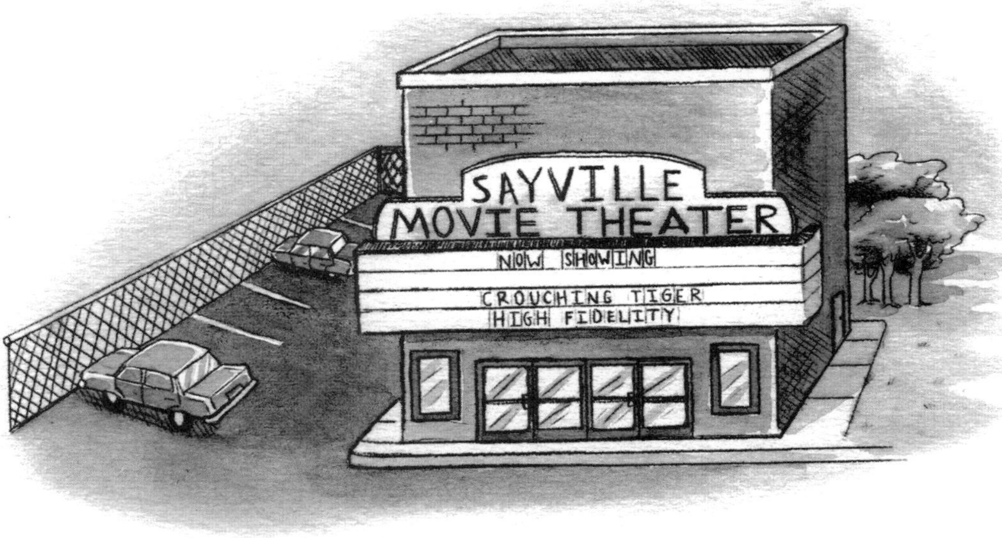
SAYVILLE
MOVIE THEATER
NOW SHOWING
CROUCHING TIGER
HIGH FIDELITY

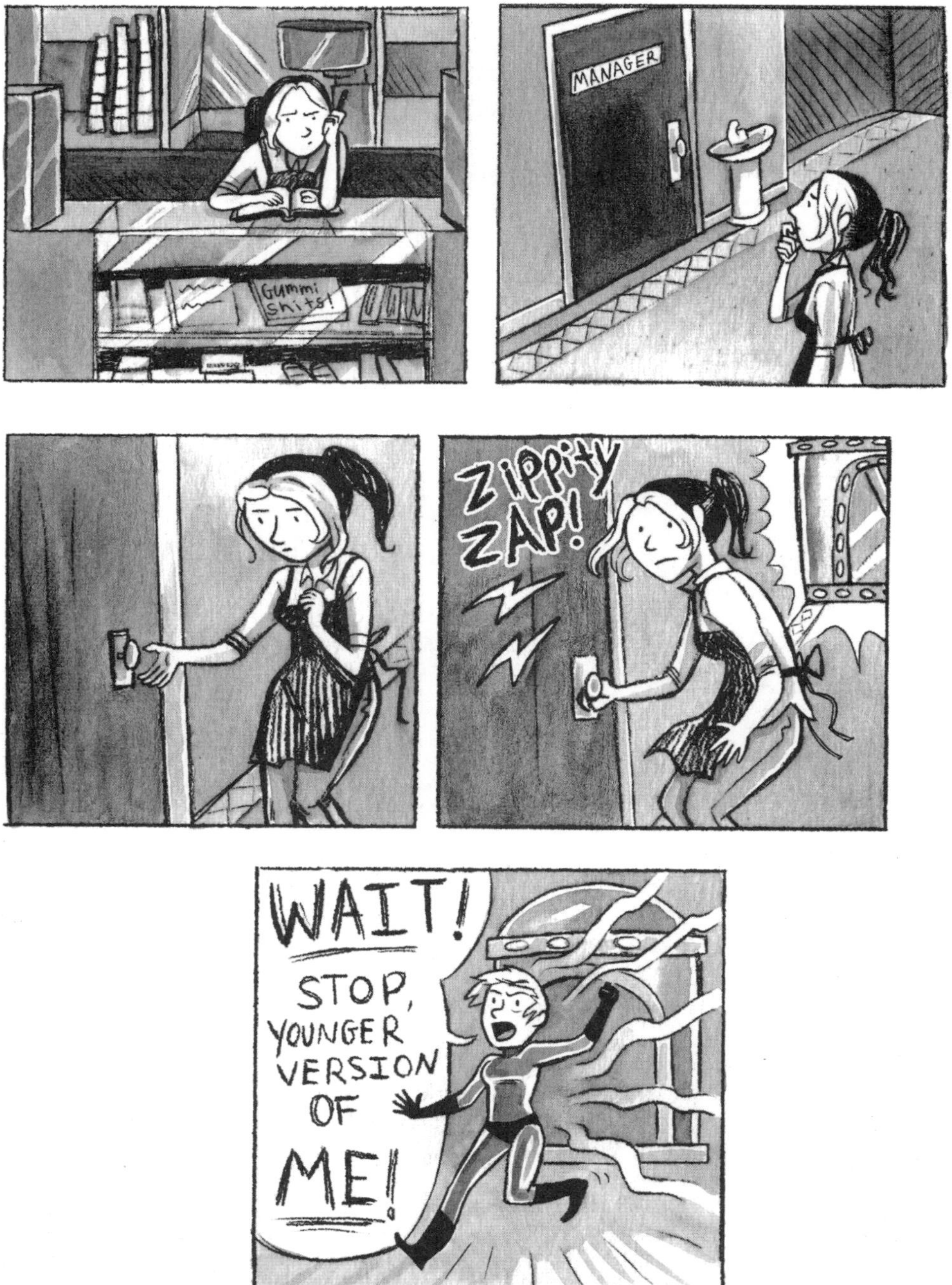
Gummi Shits!
MANAGER
Zippity ZAP!
WAIT!
STOP, YOUNGER VERSION OF ME!

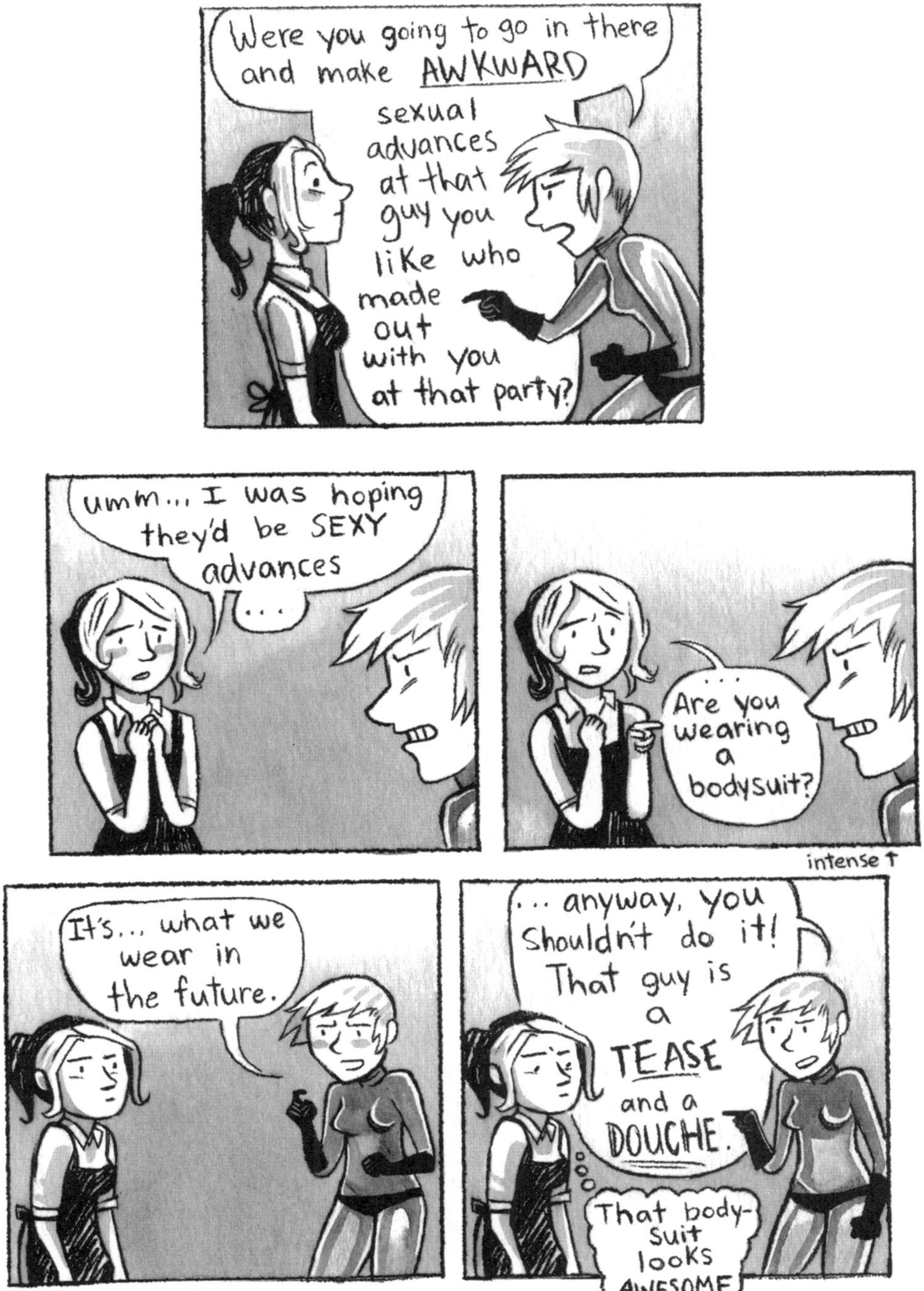
Were you going to go in there and make AWKWARD sexual advances at that guy you like who made out with you at that party?
umm... I was hoping they'd be SEXY advances
...
...
Are you wearing a bodysuit?
intense ↑
It's... what we wear in the future.
...anyway, you Shouldn't do it! That guy is a TEASE and a DOUCHE.
That body-suit looks AWESOME

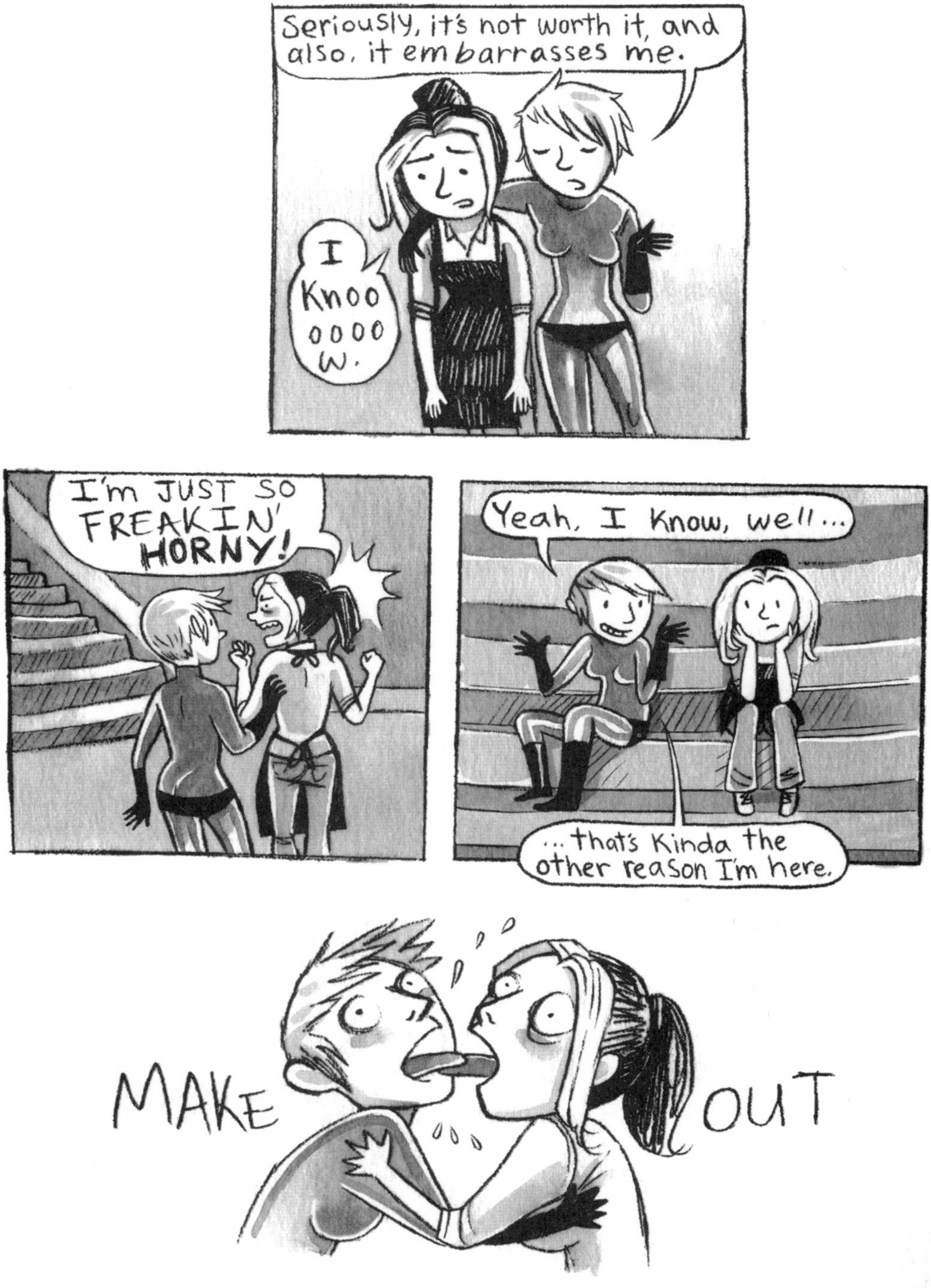
Seriously, it's not worth it, and also, it embarrasses me.
I Knoo oooo w.
I'm JUST SO FREAKIN' HORNY!
Yeah, I know, well...
... that's Kinda the other reason I'm here.
MAKE OUT

LATER:

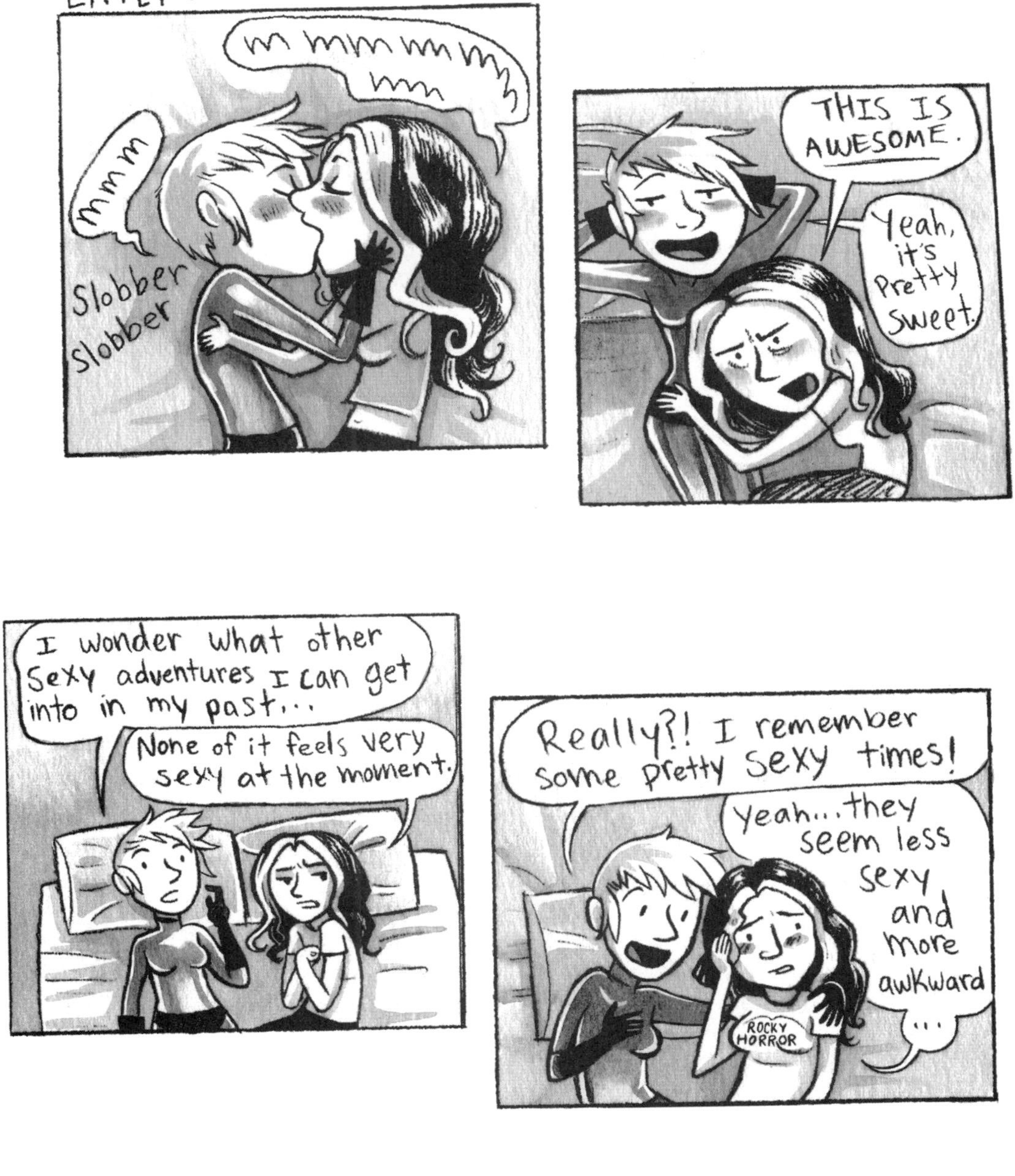
m mmmmmm mm
mmm
Slobber slobber
THIS IS AWESOME.
Yeah, it's Pretty sweet.
I wonder what other sexy adventures I can get into in my past...
None of it feels very sexy at the moment.
Really?! I remember some pretty sexy times!
yeah...they seem less sexy and more awkward
...
ROCKY HORROR

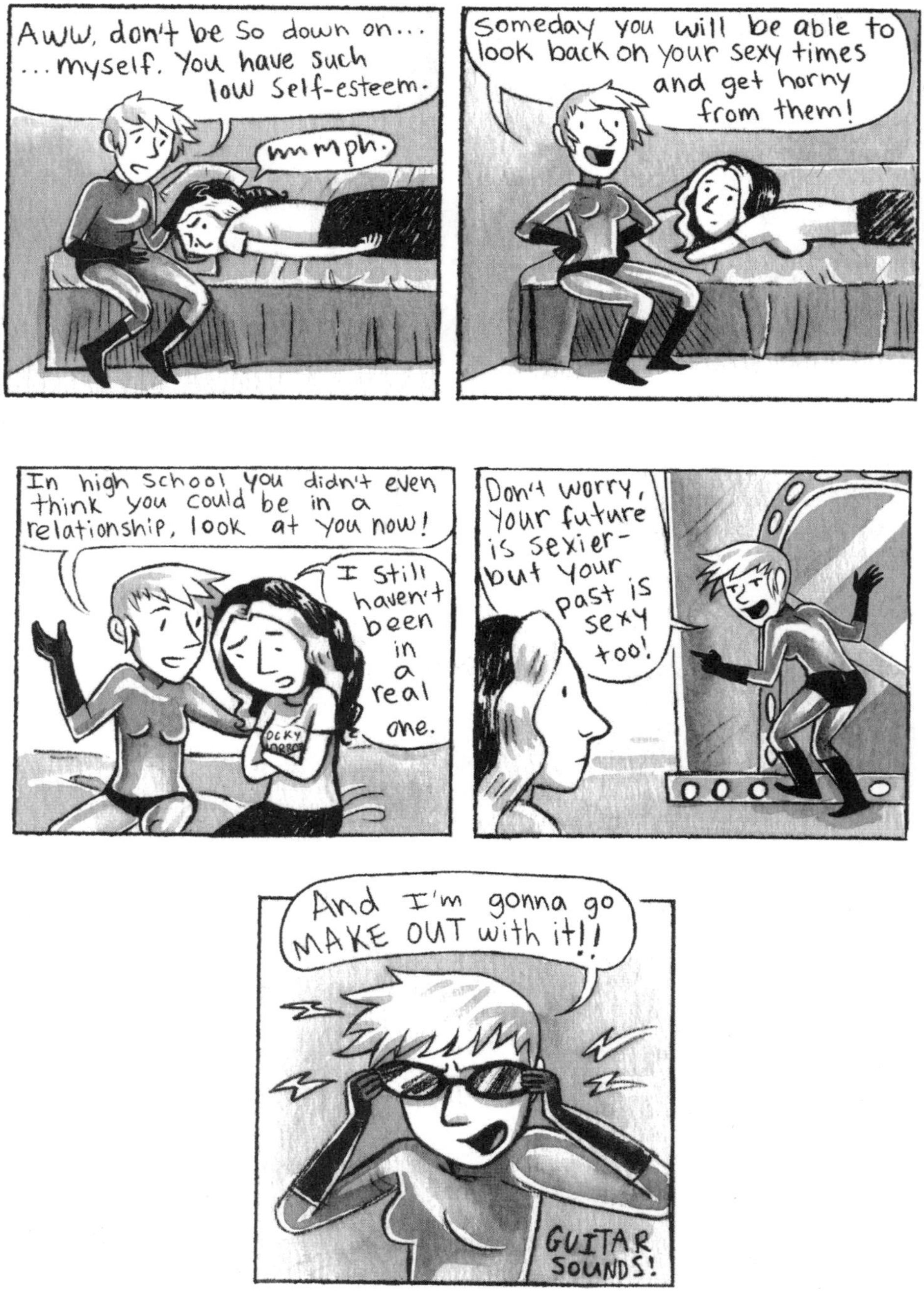
Aww, don't be so down on... ...myself. You have such low self-esteem.
mmmph.
Someday you will be able to look back on your sexy times and get horny from them!
In high school you didn't even think you could be in a relationship, look at you now!
I still haven't been in a real one.
Don't worry, your future is sexier- but your past is sexy too!
And I'm gonna go MAKE OUT with it!!
GUITAR SOUNDS!

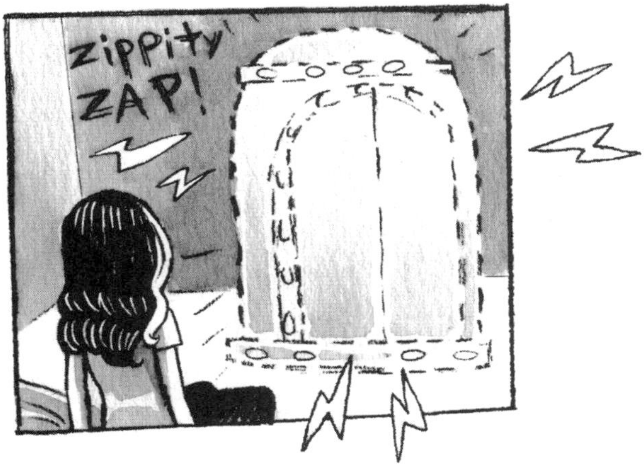
zippity ZAP!

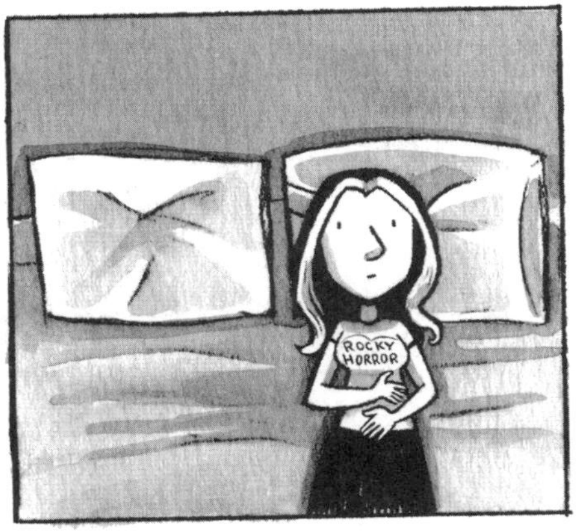
ROCKY HORROR

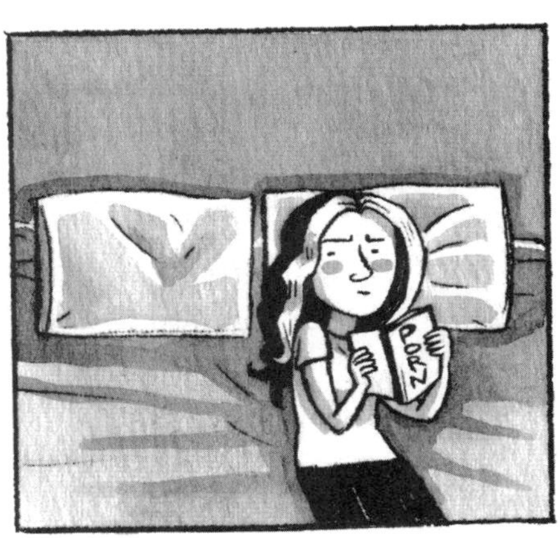
PORN

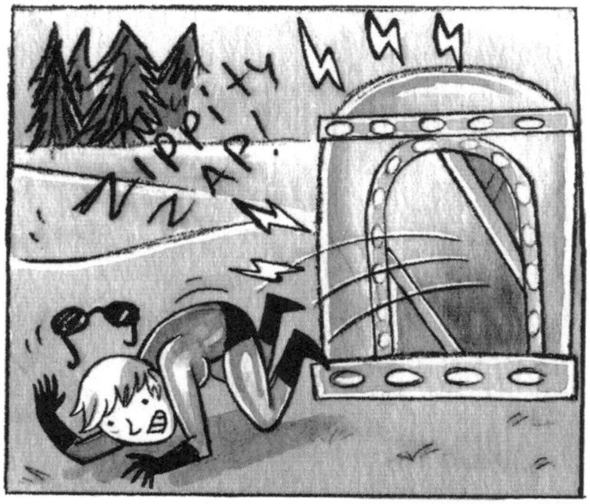
NIPPITY
NAP!

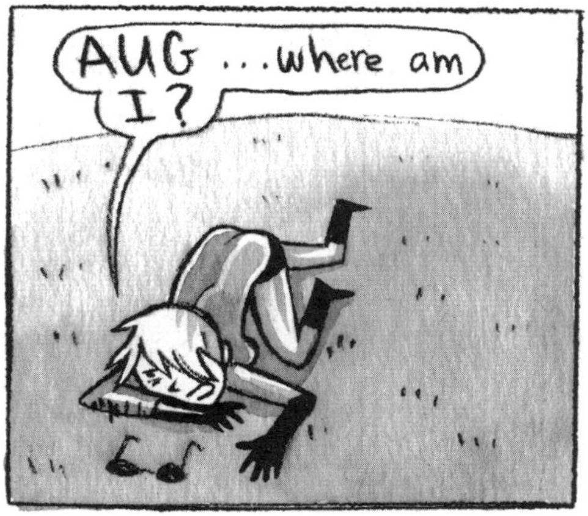
AUG ...where am I?

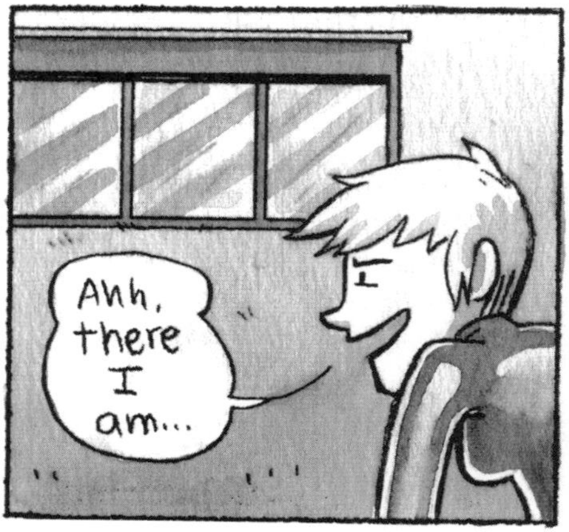
Ahh, there I am...

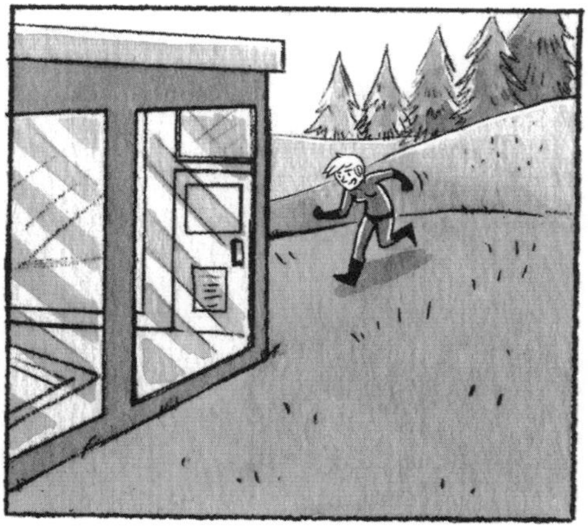

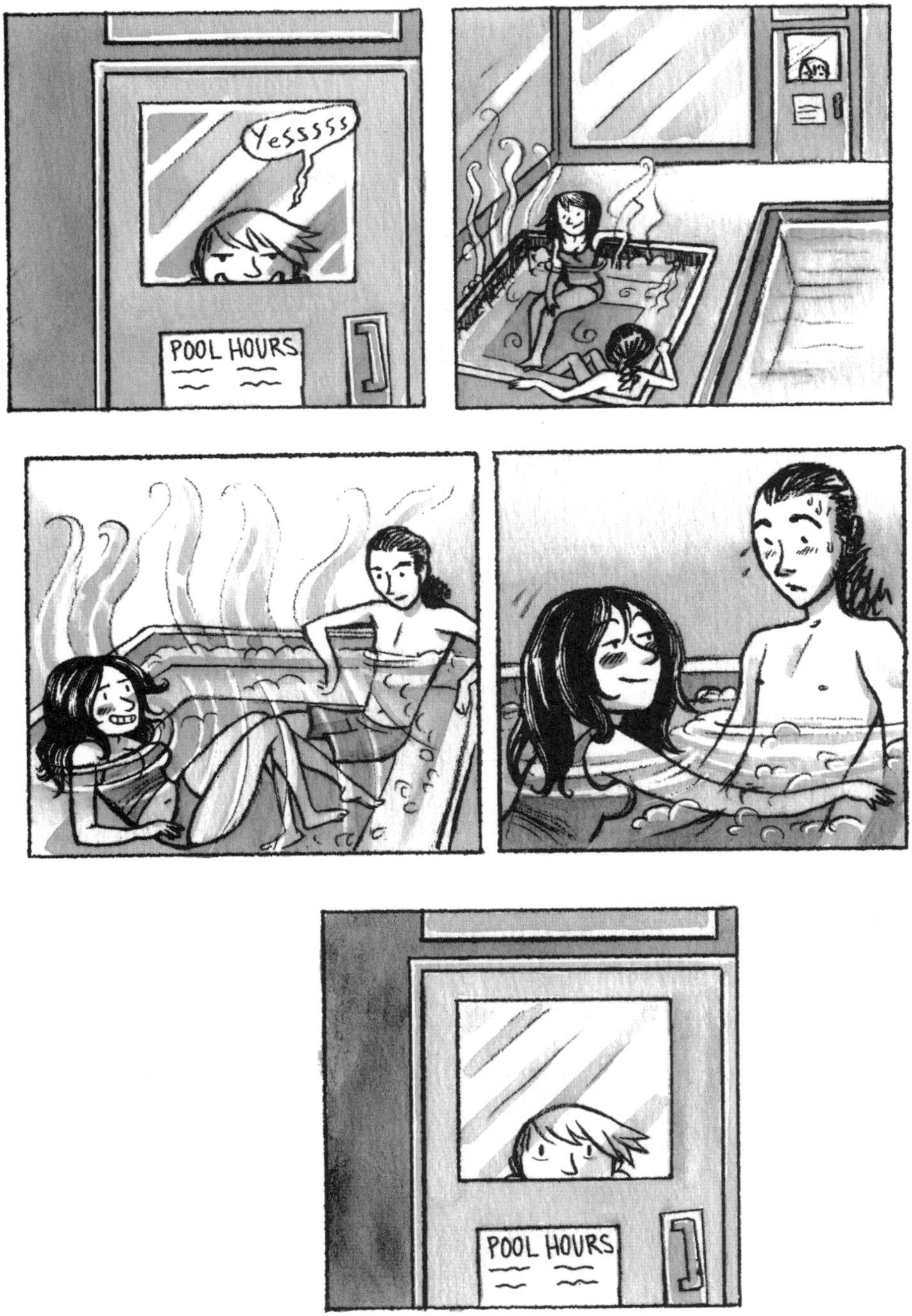
Yesssss
POOL HOURS
POOL HOURS

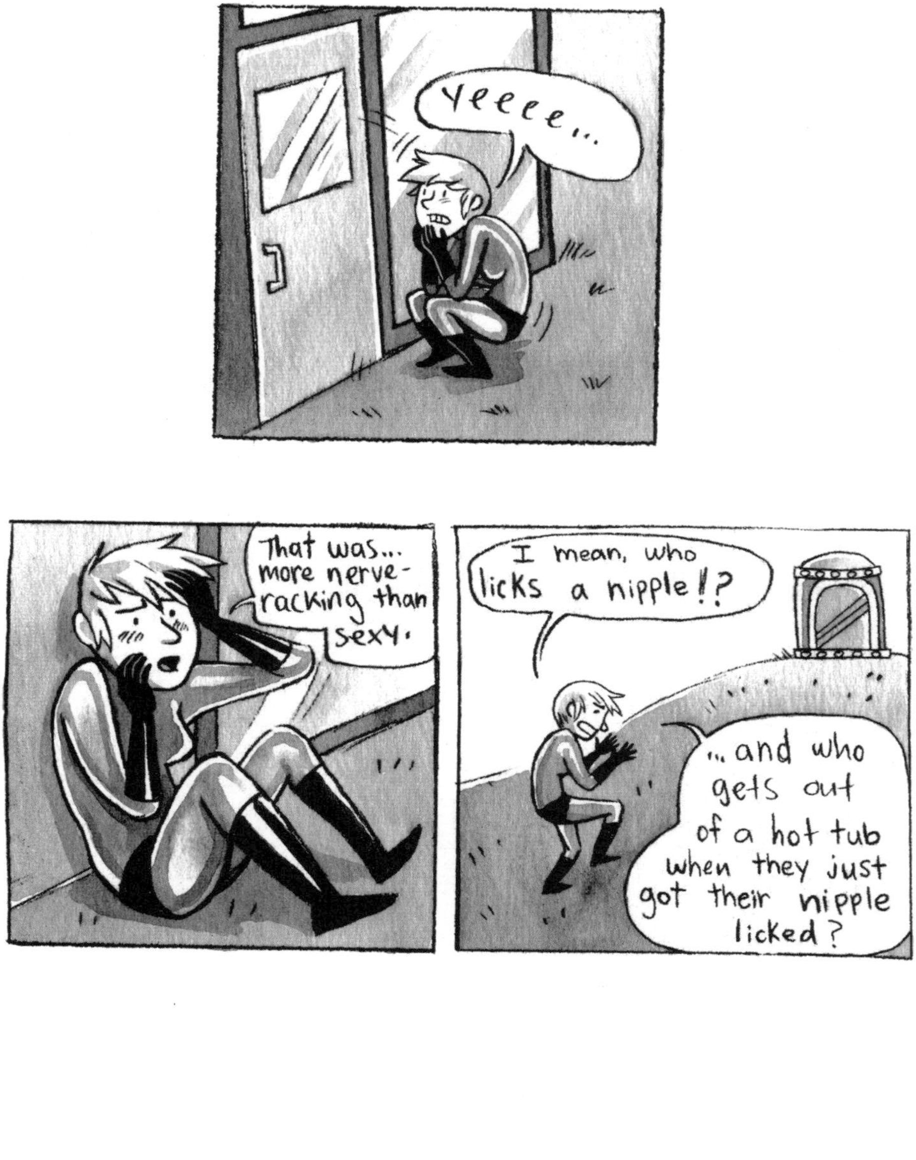
Yeeee...
That was... more nerve-racking than sexy.
I mean, who licks a nipple!?
... and who gets out of a hot tub when they just got their nipple licked?

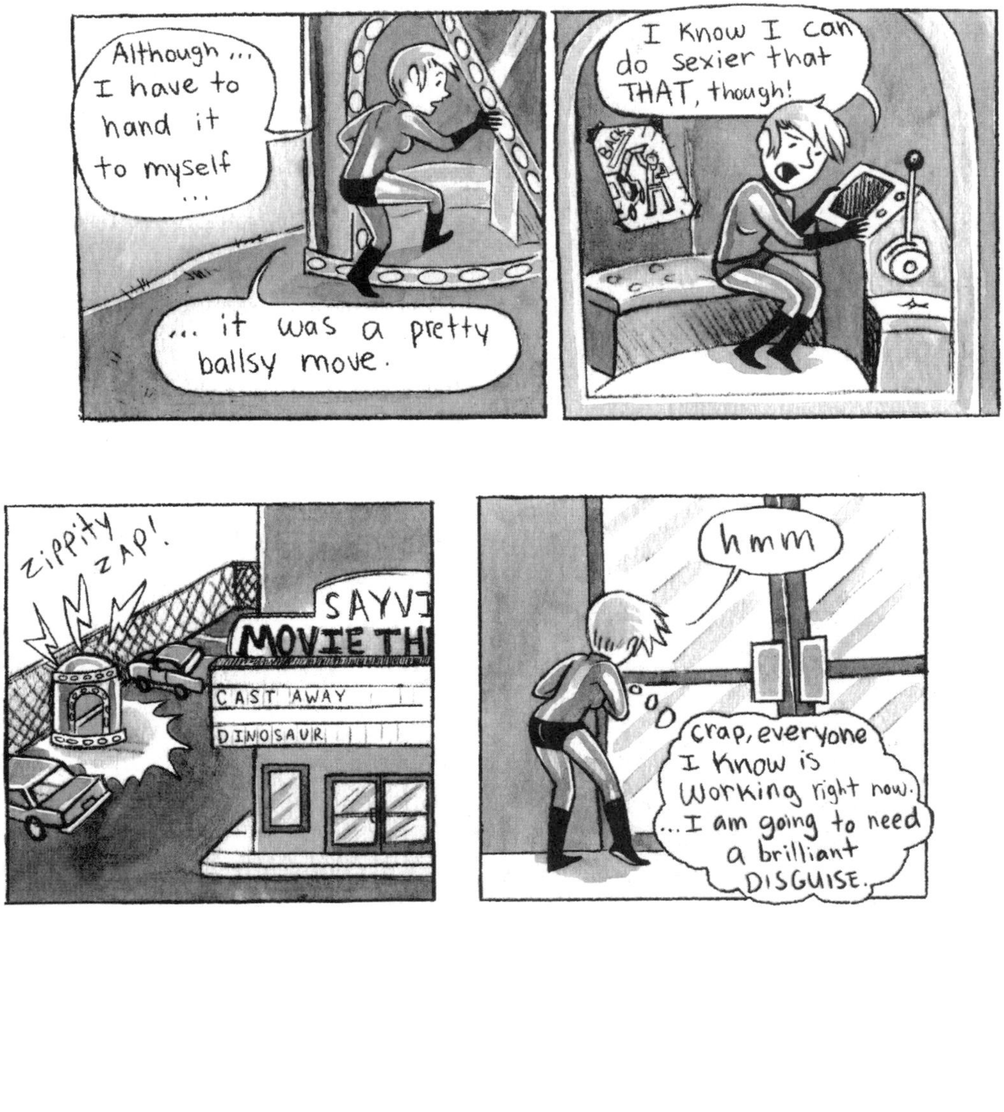

Although ... I have to hand it to myself ...
... it was a pretty ballsy move.
I Know I can do sexier that THAT, though!
BACK
zippity zap!
SAYVI
MOVIE TH
CAST AWAY
DINOSAUR
hmm
crap, everyone I Know is Working right now. ...I am going to need a brilliant DISGUISE.

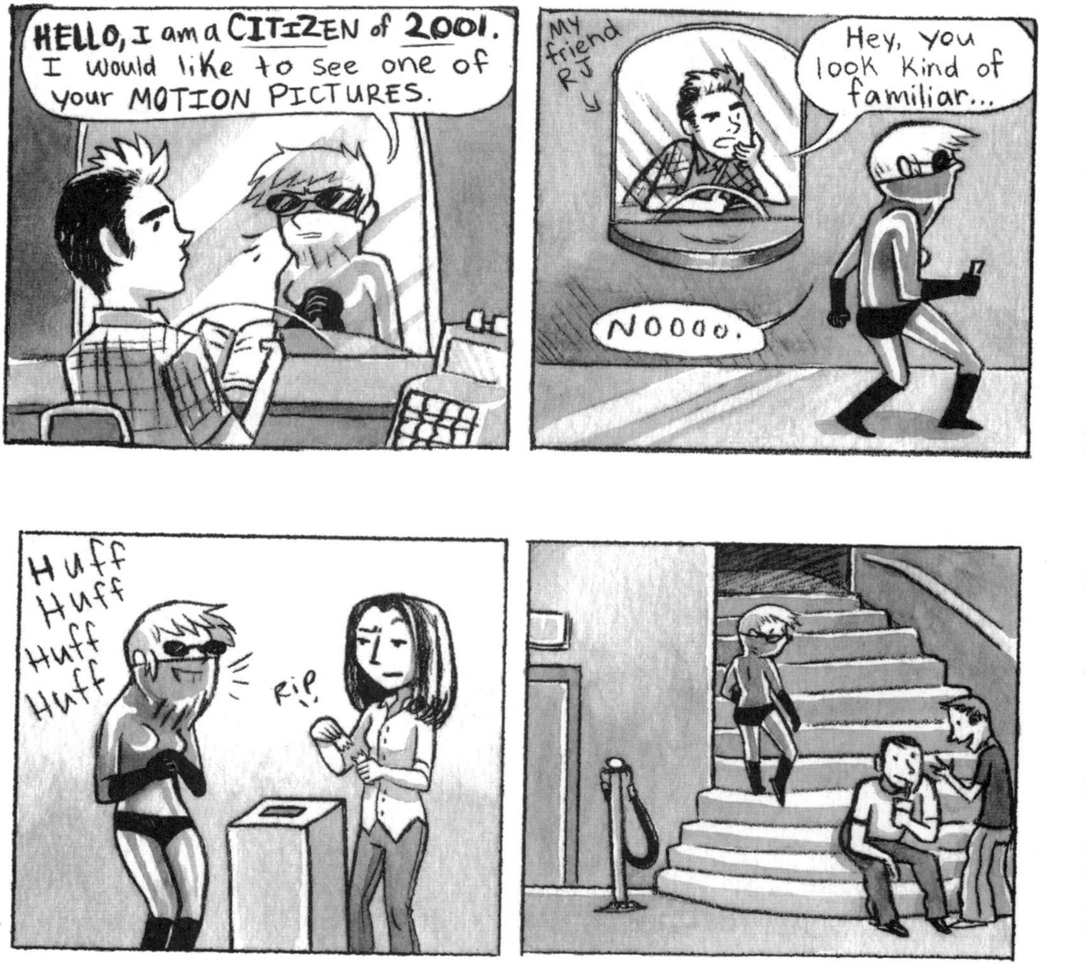
HELLO, I am a CITIZEN of 2001. I would like to see one of your MOTION PICTURES.
My friend RJ
Hey, you look kind of familiar...
Noooo.
Huff Huff Huff Huff
Rip

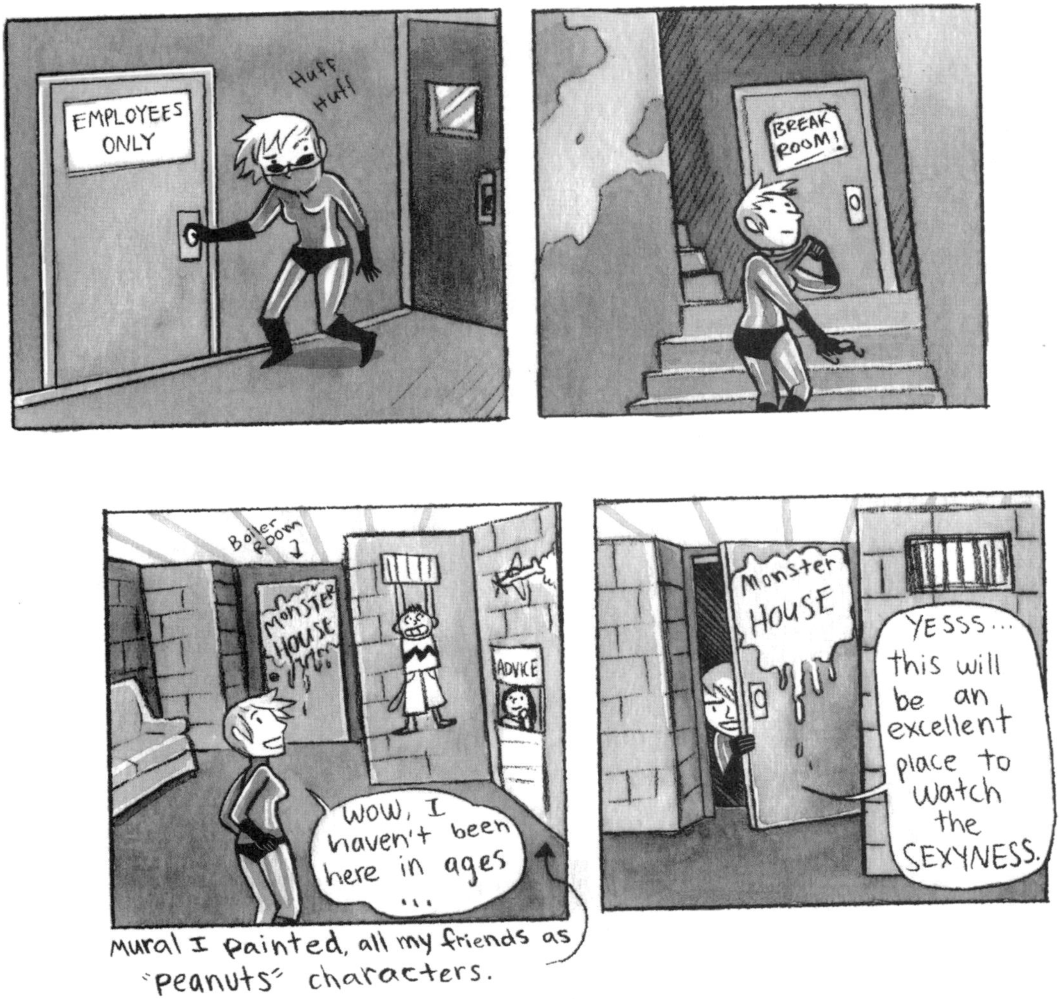

EMPLOYEES ONLY
Huff Huff
BREAK ROOM!
Boiler Room
MONSTER HOUSE
ADVICE
WOW, I haven't been here in ages ...
Mural I painted, all my friends as "Peanuts" characters.
Monster HOUSE
YESSS... this will be an excellent place to watch the SEXYNESS.

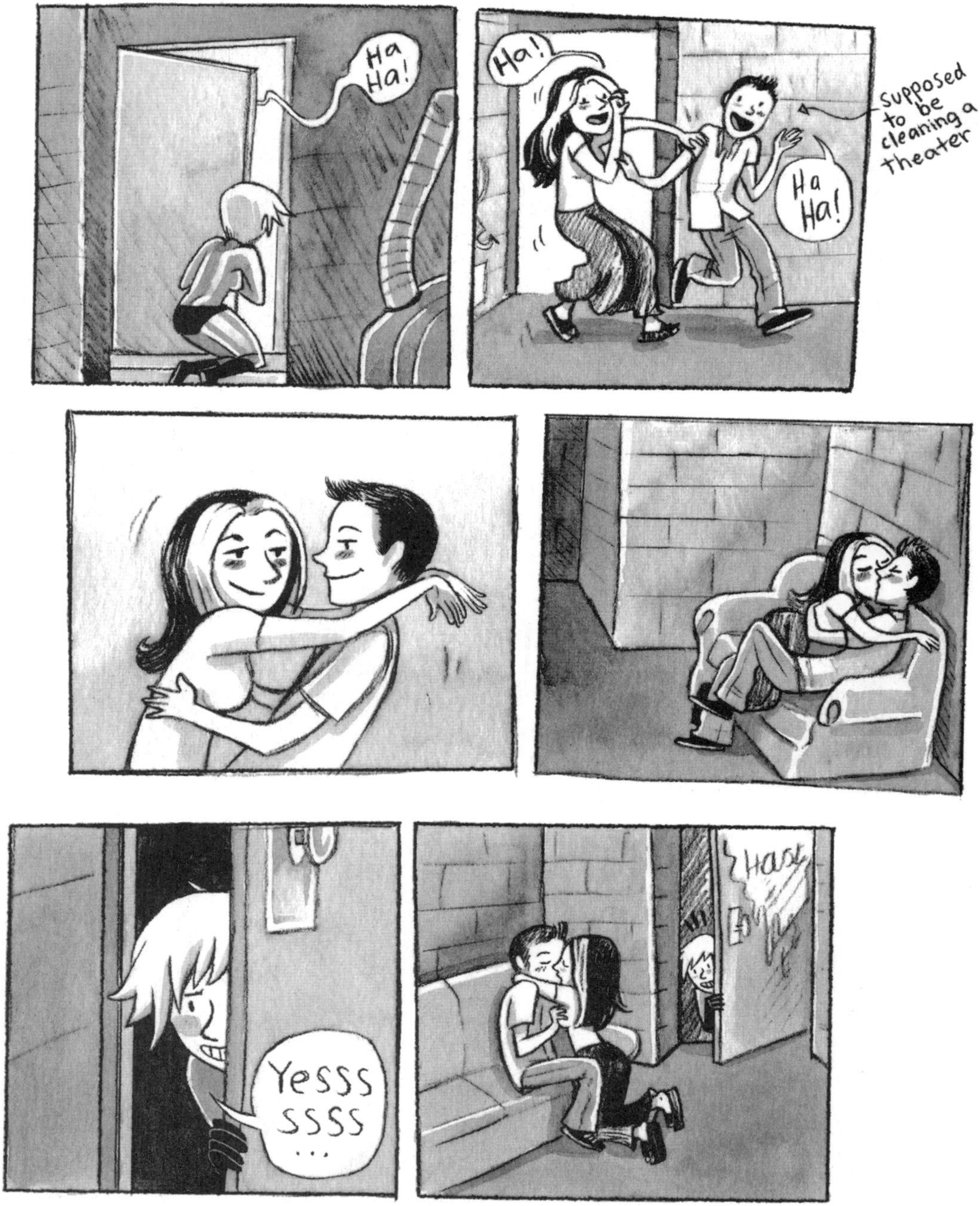
Ha Ha!
Ha!
Supposed to be cleaning a theater
Ha Ha!
Yesss ssss ...

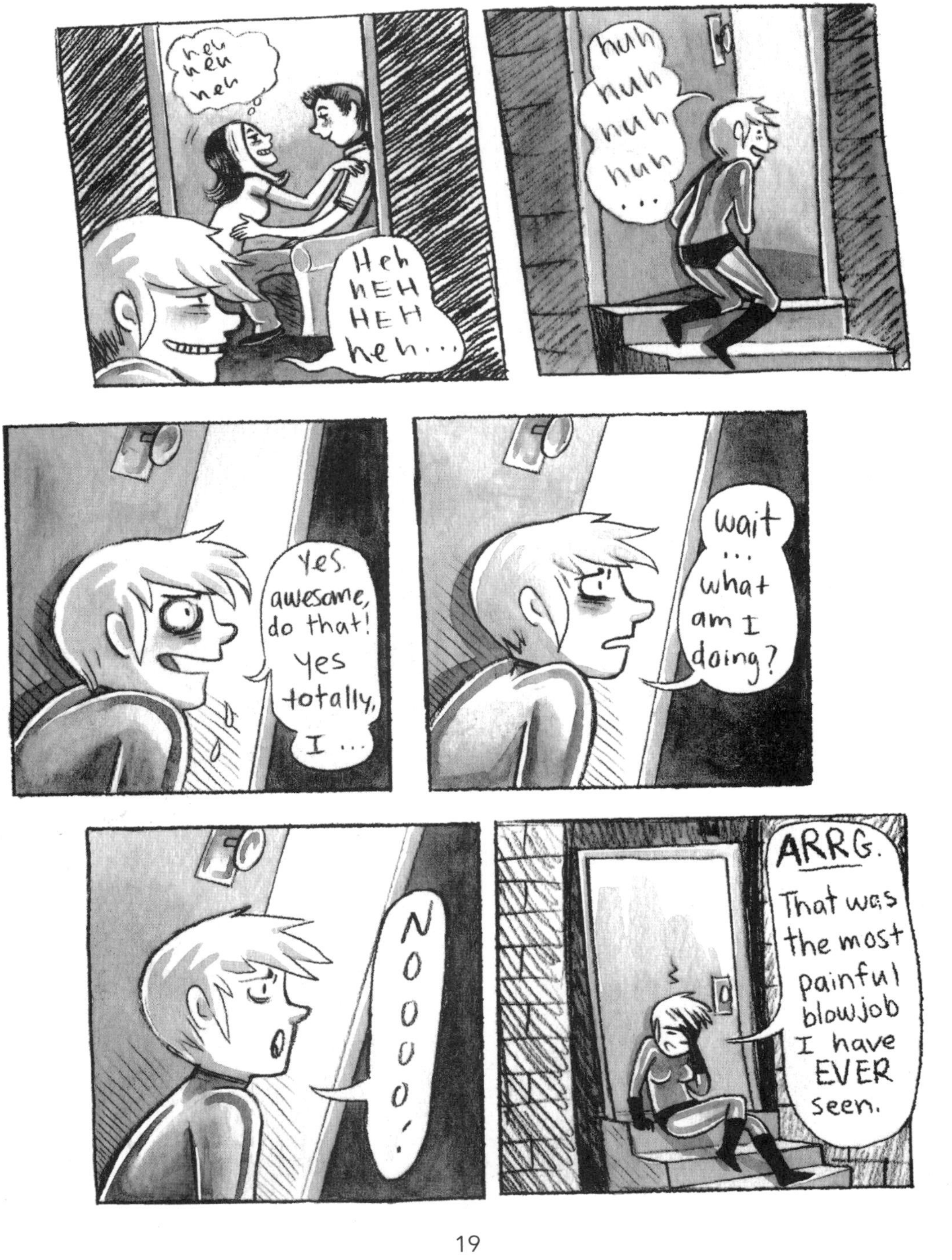
heh heh heh
Heh HEH HEH heh...
huh huh huh huh ...
Yes. awesome, do that! Yes totally, I...
wait ... what am I doing?
NOOOOO!
ARRG. That was the most painful blowjob I have EVER seen.

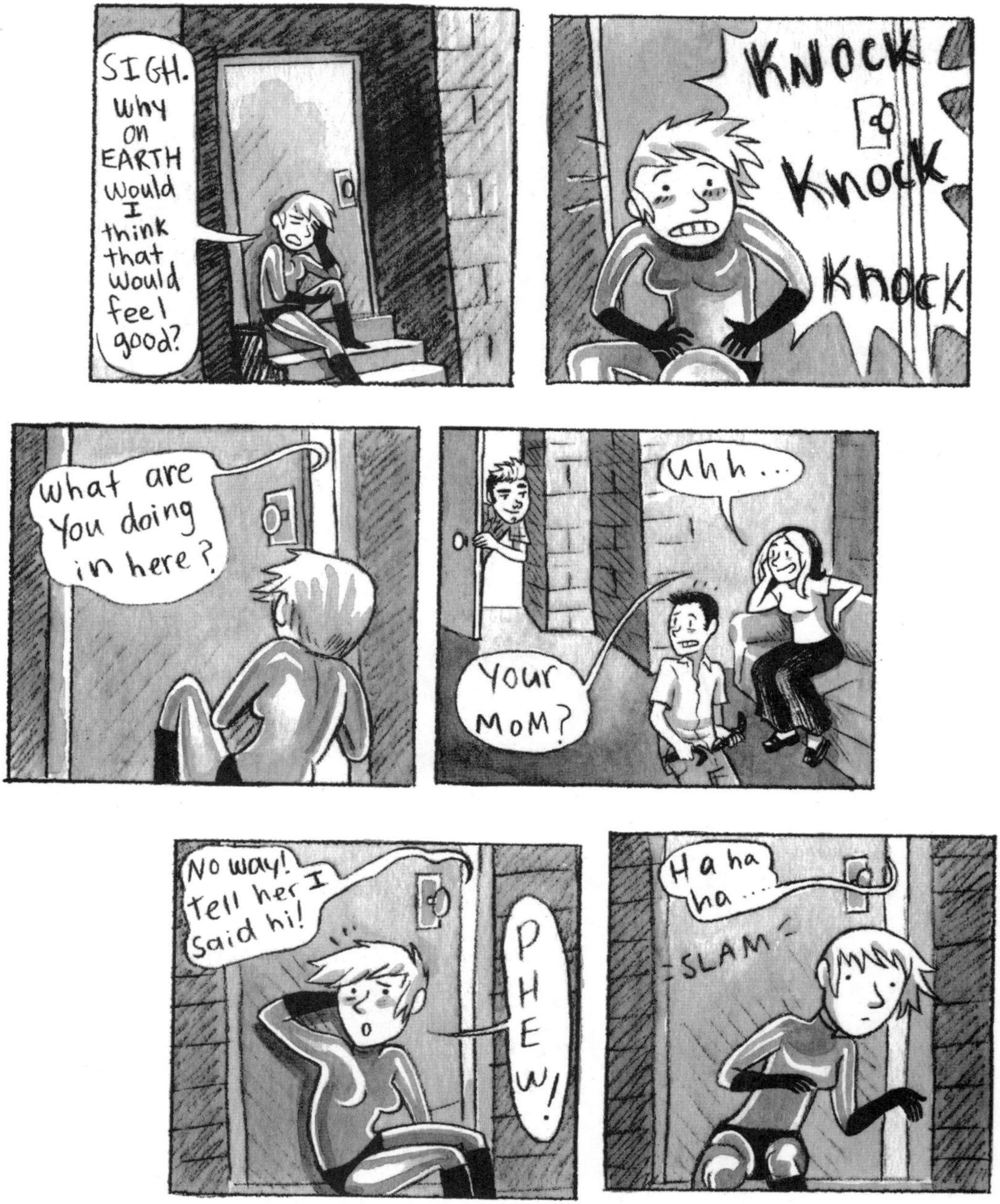
SIGH. Why on EARTH would I think that would feel good?
KNOCK
Knock
Knock
what are You doing in here?
Uhh...
Your MoM?
No way! Tell her I said hi!
PHEW!
Ha ha ha....
SLAM

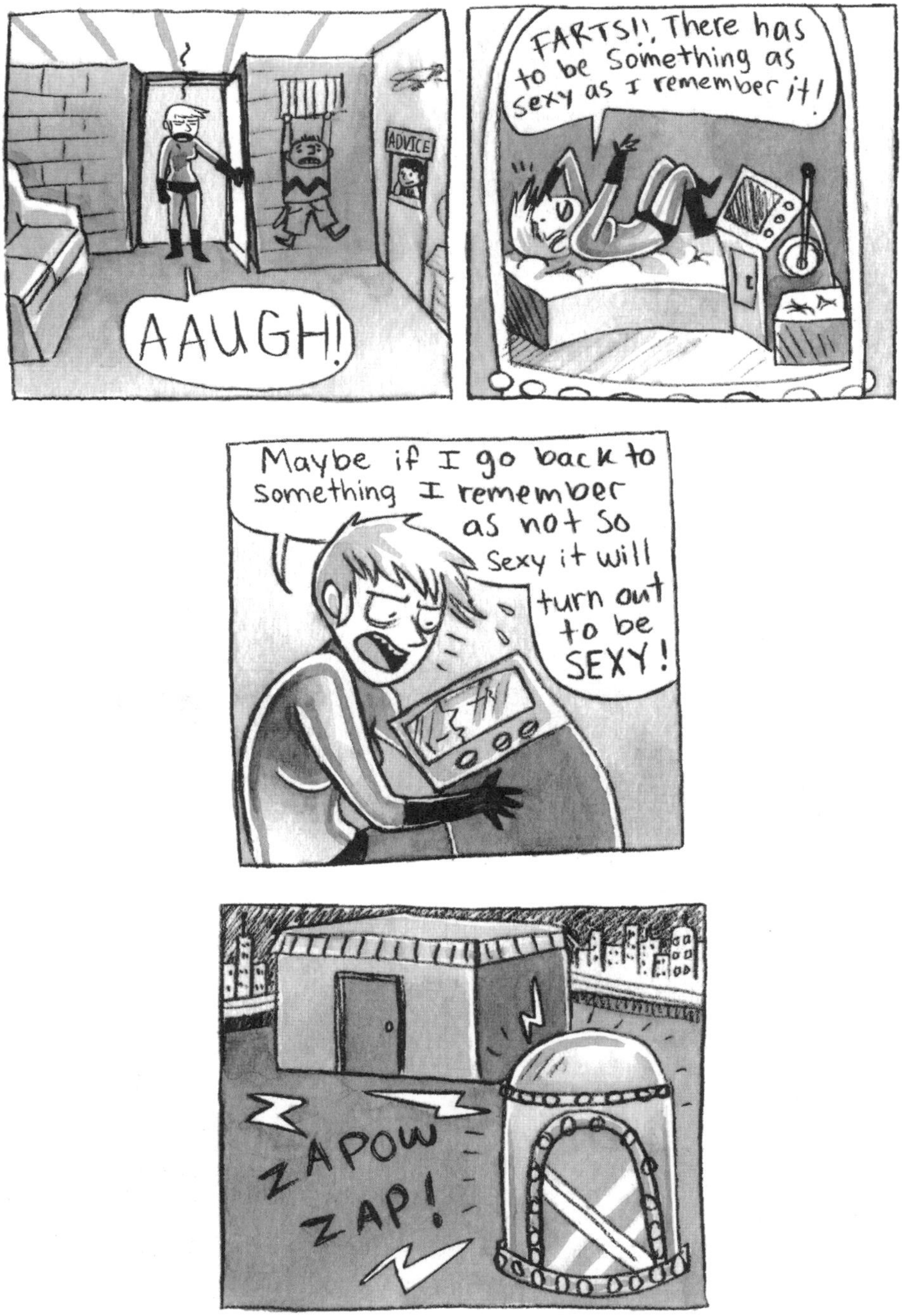
ADVICE
AAUGH!
FARTS!! There has to be Something as sexy as I remember it!
Maybe if I go back to something I remember as not so sexy it will turn out to be SEXY!
ZAPOW
ZAP!

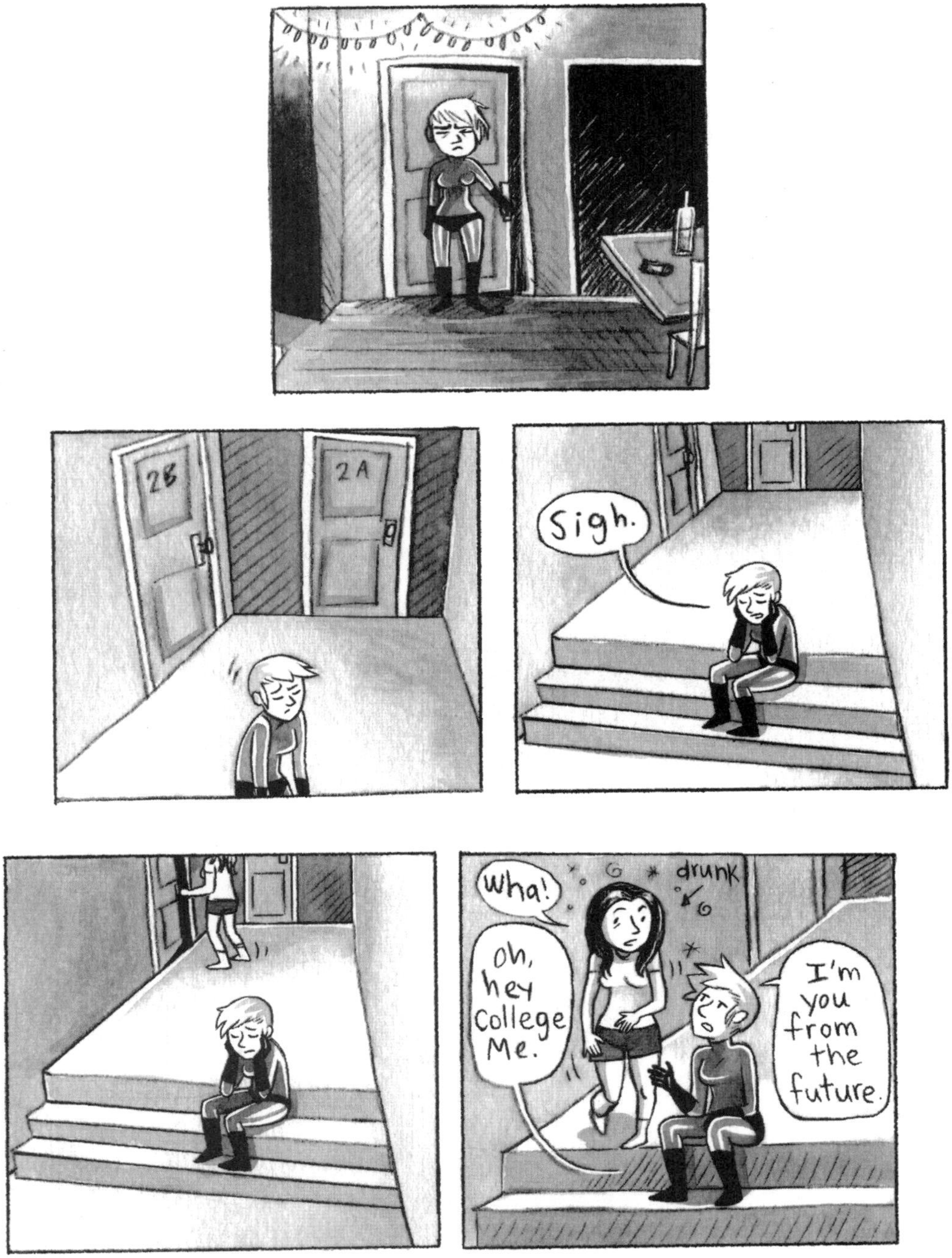
2B
2A
Sigh.
Wha!
drunk
Oh, hey College Me.
I'm you from the future.

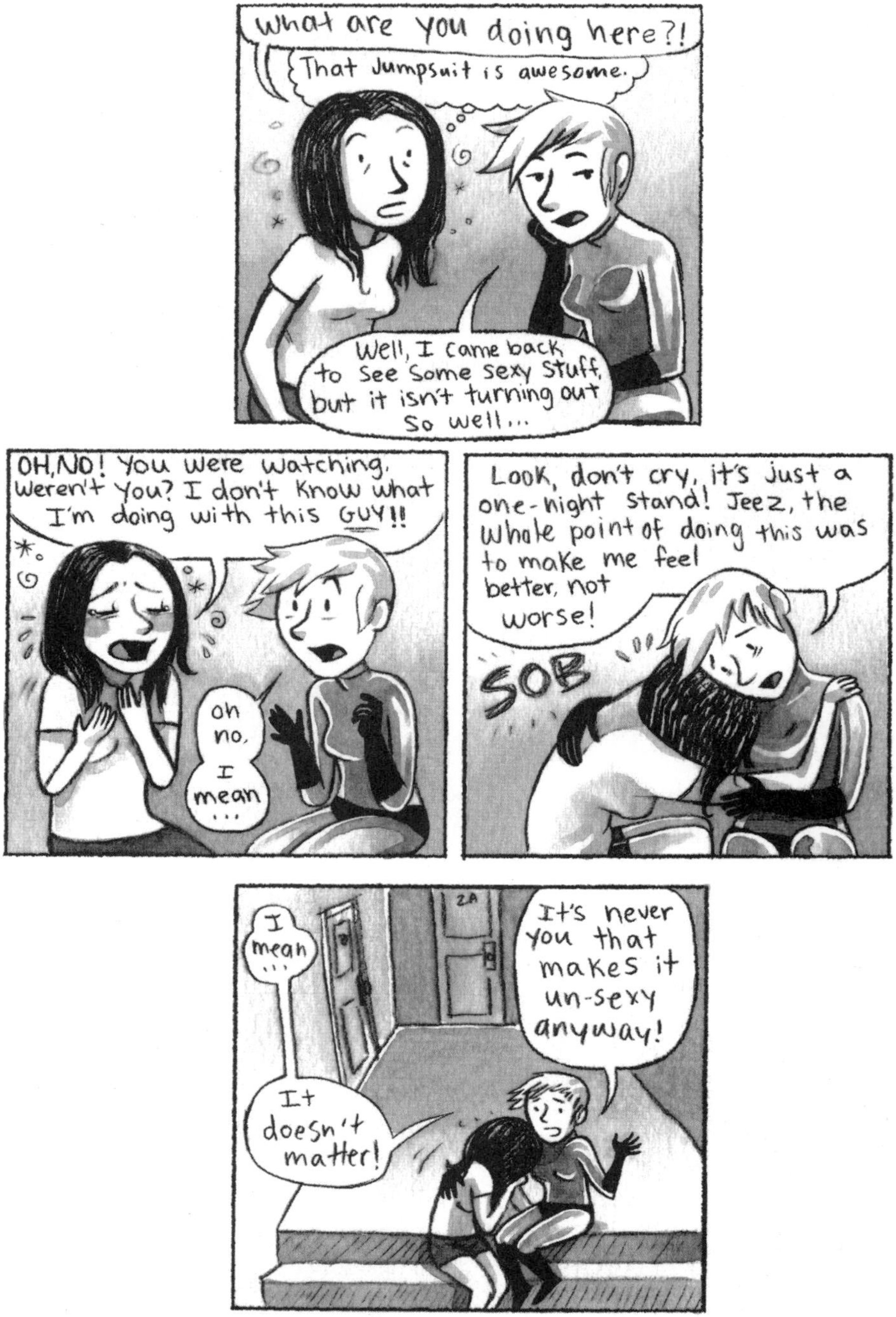
What are you doing here?!
That Jumpsuit is awesome.
Well, I came back to see some sexy stuff, but it isn't turning out so well...
OH, NO! You were watching, weren't you? I don't know what I'm doing with this GUY!!
oh no, I mean...
Look, don't cry, it's just a one-night stand! Jeez, the whole point of doing this was to make me feel better, not worse!
SOB
2A
I mean...
It's never you that makes it un-sexy anyway!
It doesn't matter!

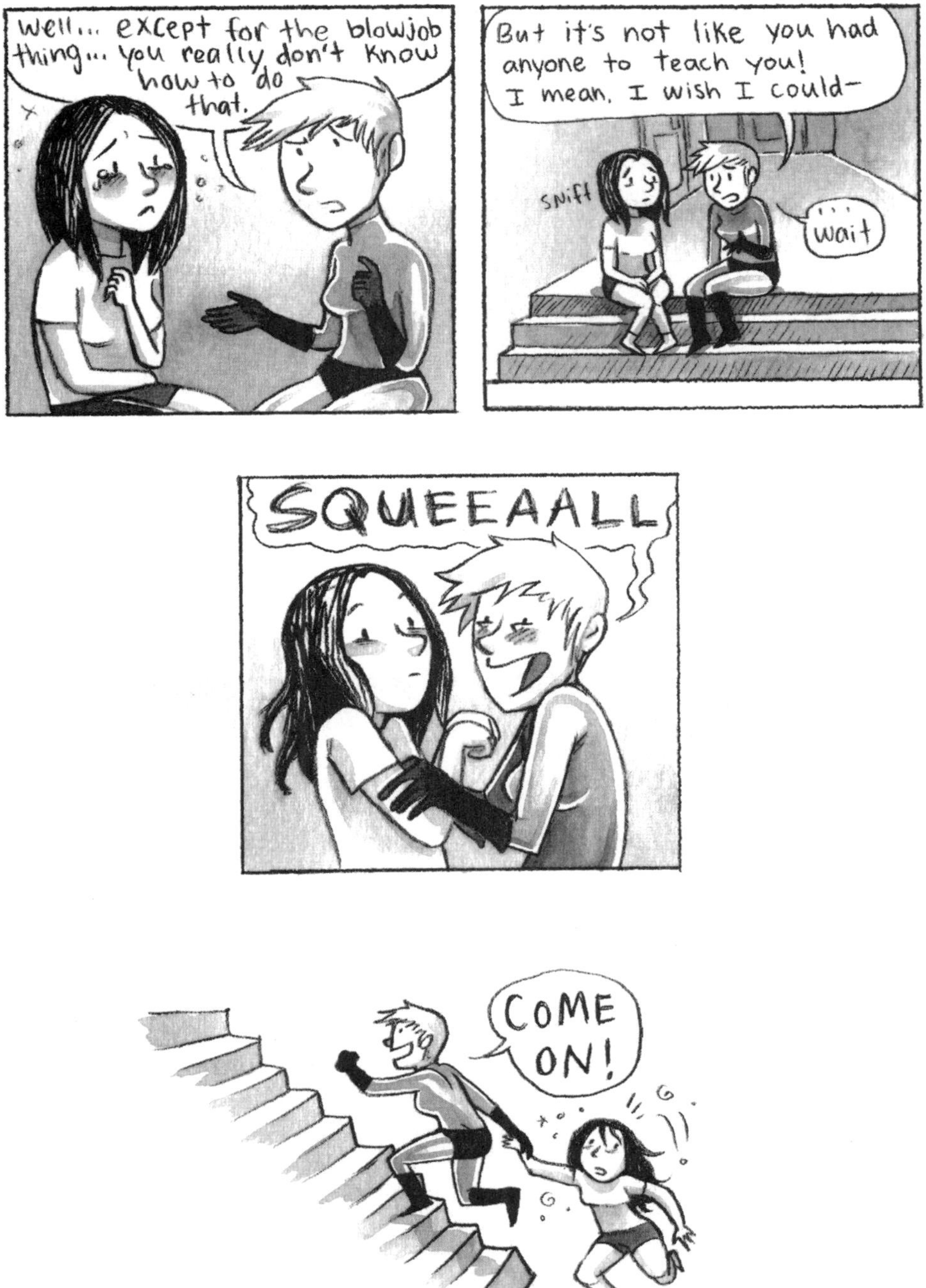
well... except for the blowjob thing... you really don't know how to do that.
But it's not like you had anyone to teach you! I mean, I wish I could-
SNIFF
... wait
SQUEEAALL
COME ON!

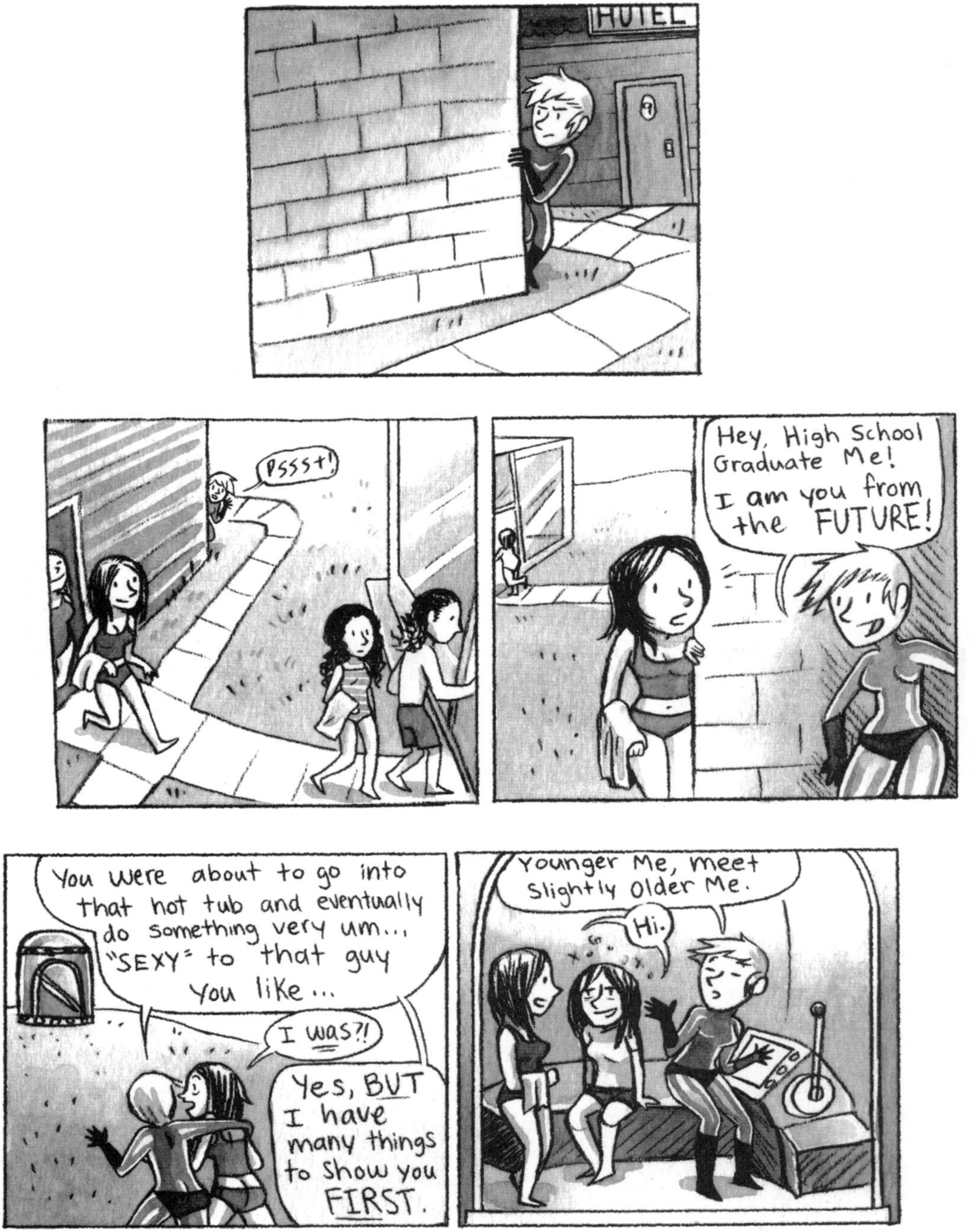
HOTEL
Pssst!
Hey, High School Graduate Me! I am you from the FUTURE!
You were about to go into that hot tub and eventually do something very um... "SEXY" to that guy you like...
I was?!
Yes, BUT I have many things to show you FIRST.
Younger Me, meet Slightly Older Me.
Hi.

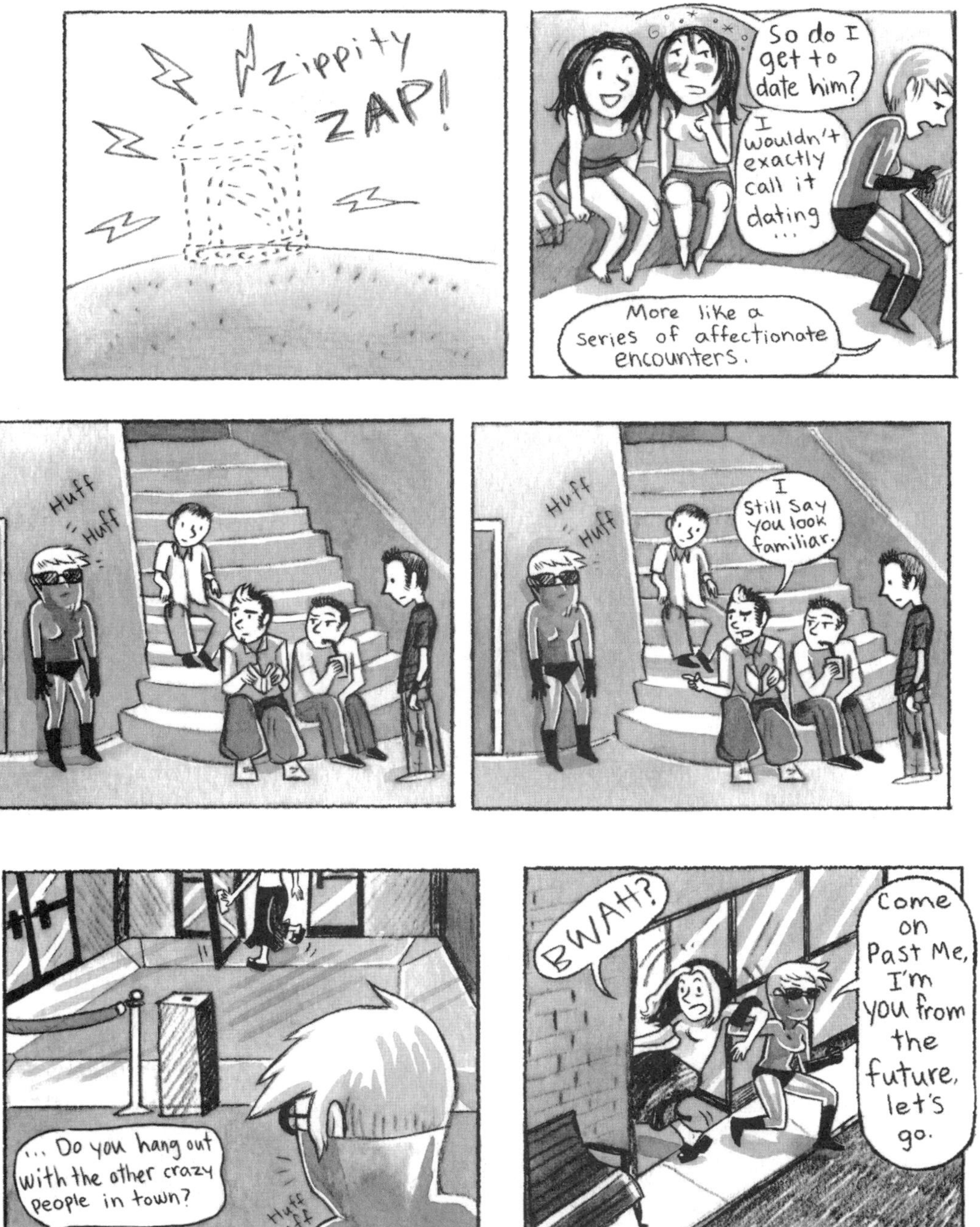
zippity
ZAP!
So do I get to date him?
I wouldn't exactly call it dating ...
More like a series of affectionate encounters.
Huff Huff
Huff Huff
I still say you look familiar.
... Do you hang out with the other crazy people in town?
Huff Huff
BWAH?
Come on Past Me, I'm you from the future, let's go.

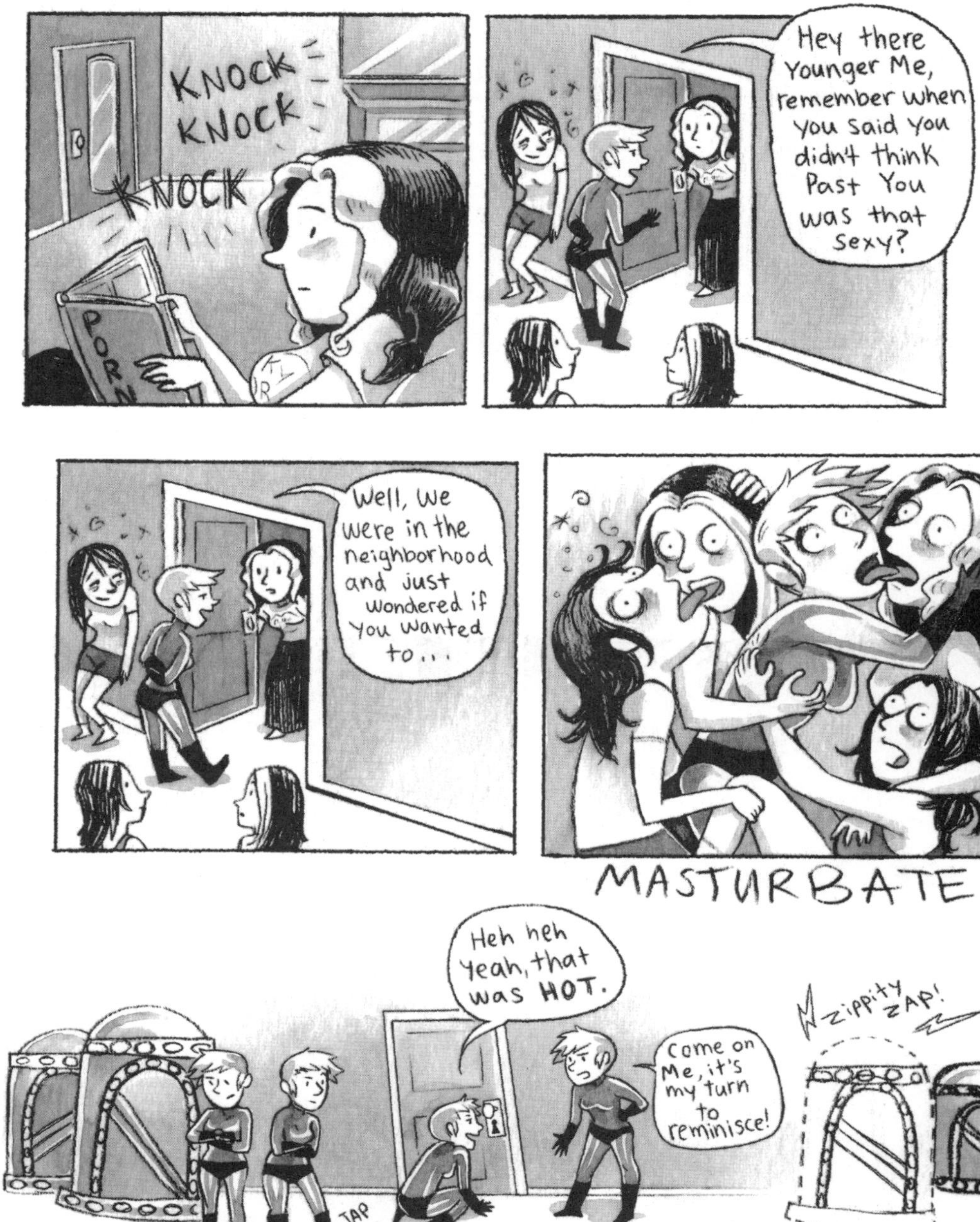
KNOCK
KNOCK
KNOCK
PORN
Hey there Younger Me, remember when you said you didn't think Past You was that sexy?
Well, we were in the neighborhood and just wondered if you wanted to...
MASTURBATE
Heh heh Yeah, that was HOT.
TAP TAP
Come on Me, it's my turn to reminisce!
zippity ZAP!

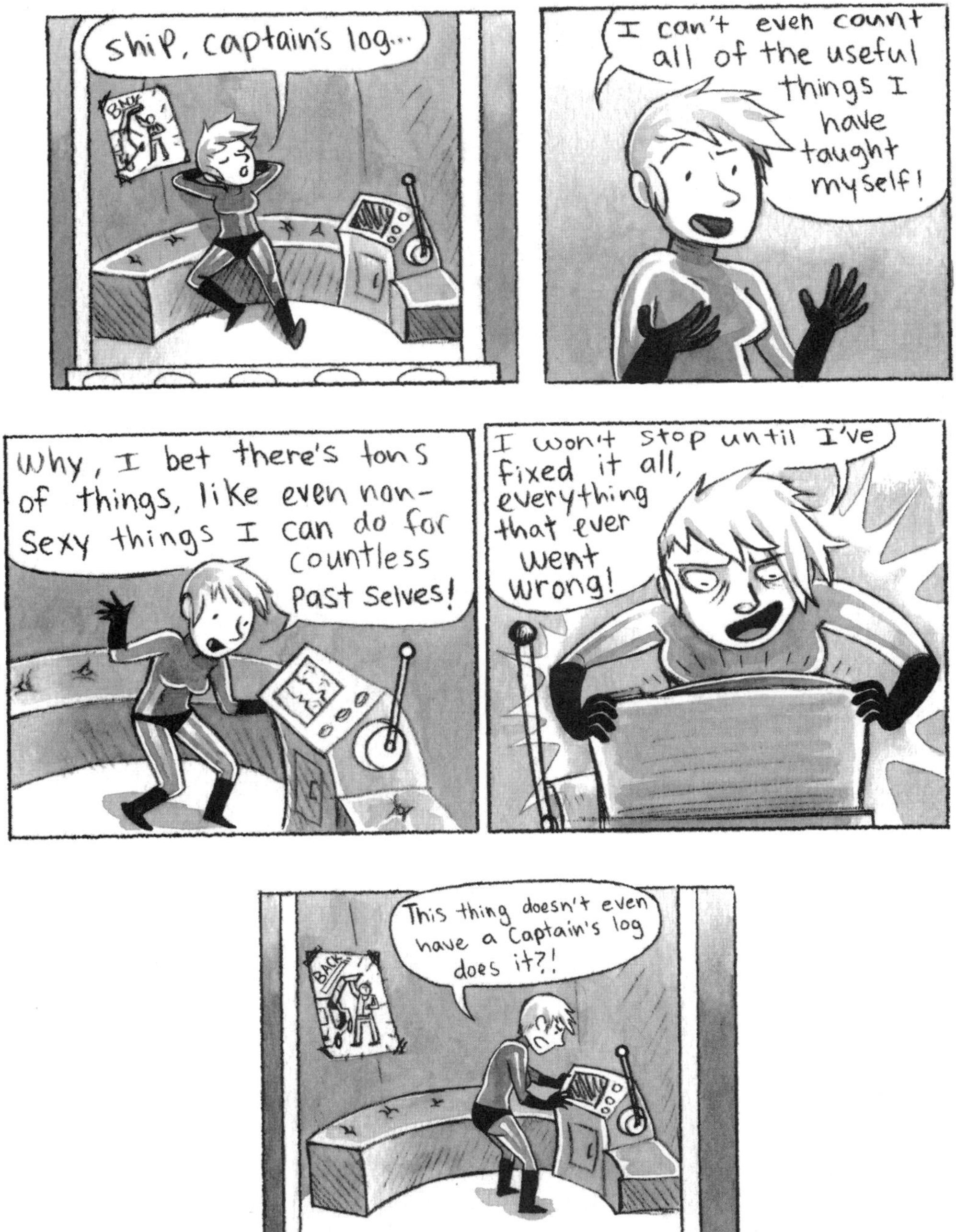

ship, captain's log...
I can't even count all of the useful things I have taught myself!
Why, I bet there's tons of things, like even non-sexy things I can do for countless past selves!
I won't stop until I've fixed it all, everything that ever went wrong!
This thing doesn't even have a Captain's log does it?!

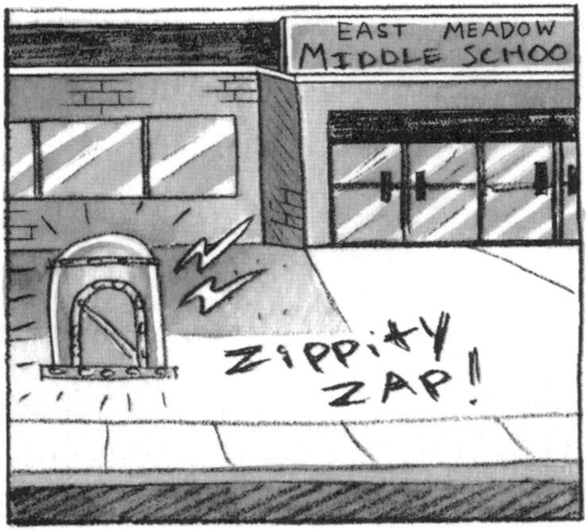
EAST MEADOW
MIDDLE SCHOO
Zippity
ZAP!

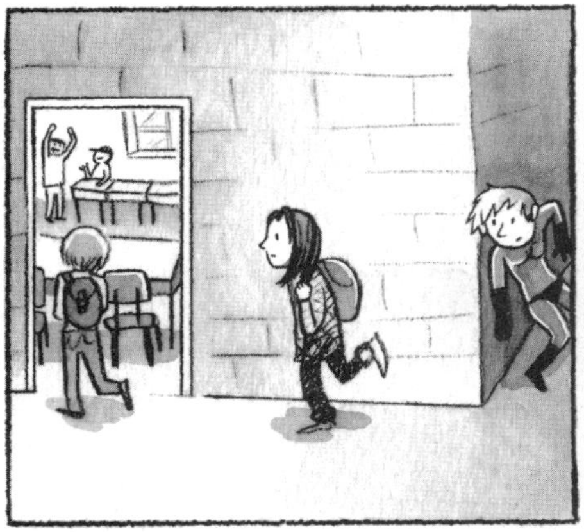

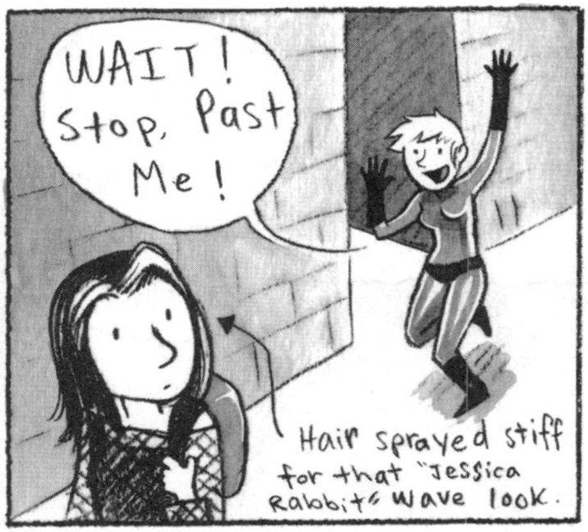
WAIT! Stop, Past Me!
Hair sprayed stiff for that "Jessica Rabbit" wave look.

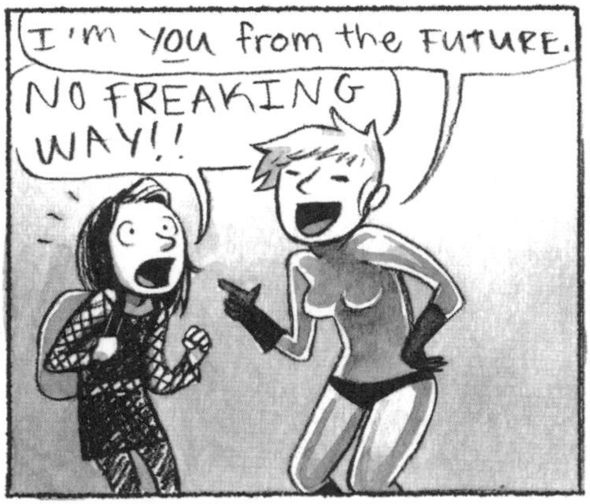
I'm YOU from the FUTURE.
NO FREAKING WAY!!

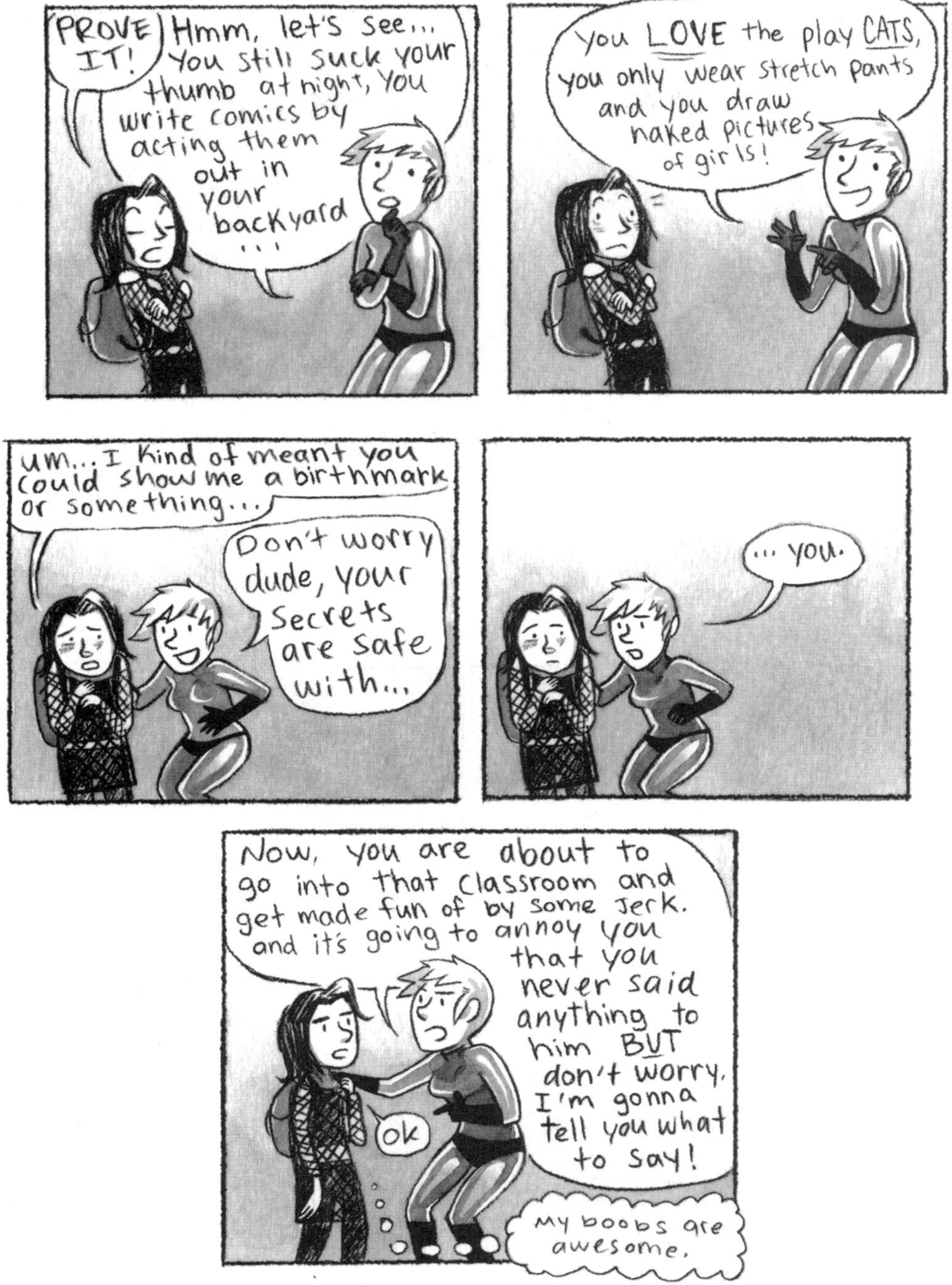

PROVE IT!
Hmm, let's see... You still suck your thumb at night, You write comics by acting them out in your backyard ...
You LOVE the play CATS, you only wear stretch pants and you draw naked pictures of girls!
um... I kind of meant you could show me a birthmark or something...
Don't worry dude, your secrets are safe with...
... you.
Now, you are about to go into that classroom and get made fun of by some jerk. and it's going to annoy you that you never said anything to him BUT don't worry. I'm gonna tell you what to say!
ok
My boobs are awesome.

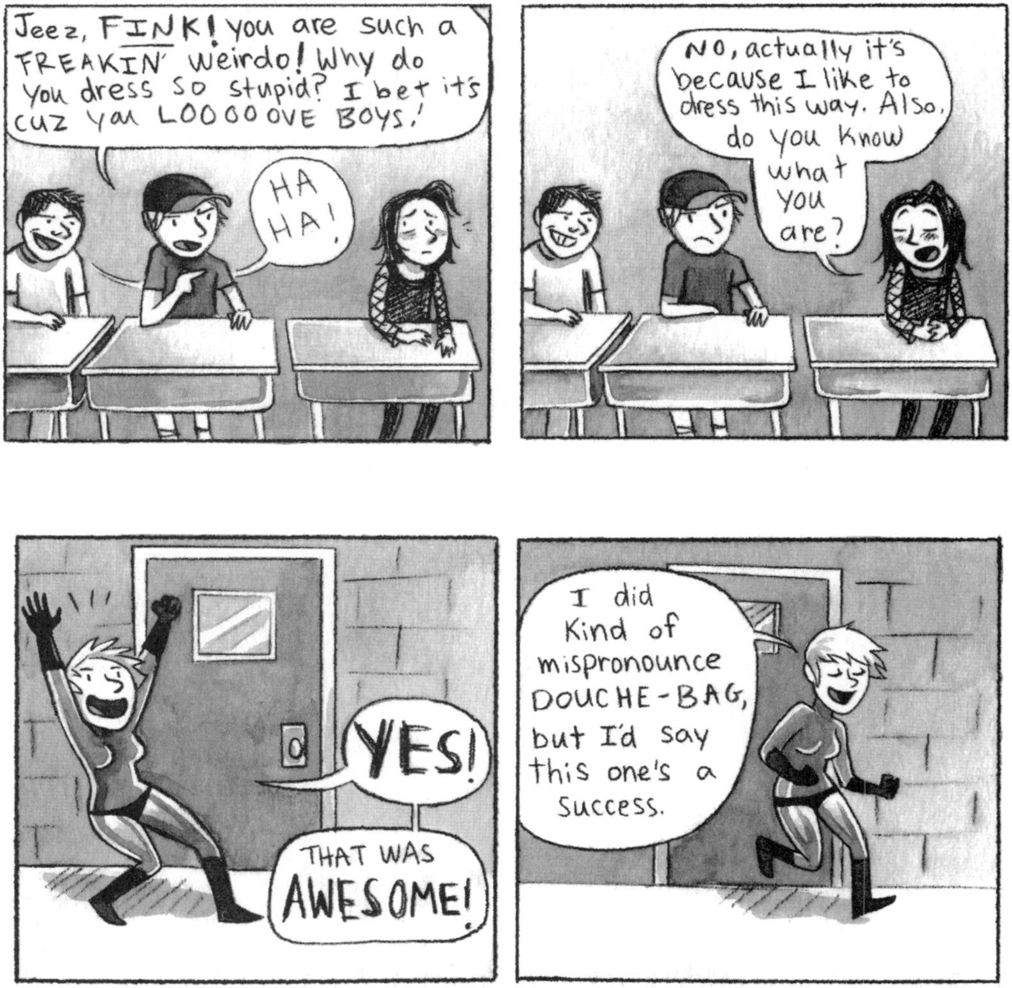
Jeez, FINK! you are such a FREAKIN' weirdo! Why do you dress so stupid? I bet it's cuz you LOOOOOVE BOYS!
HA HA!
NO, actually it's because I like to dress this way. Also, do you know what you are?
YES!
THAT WAS AWESOME!
I did Kind of mispronounce DOUCHE-BAG, but I'd say this one's a success.

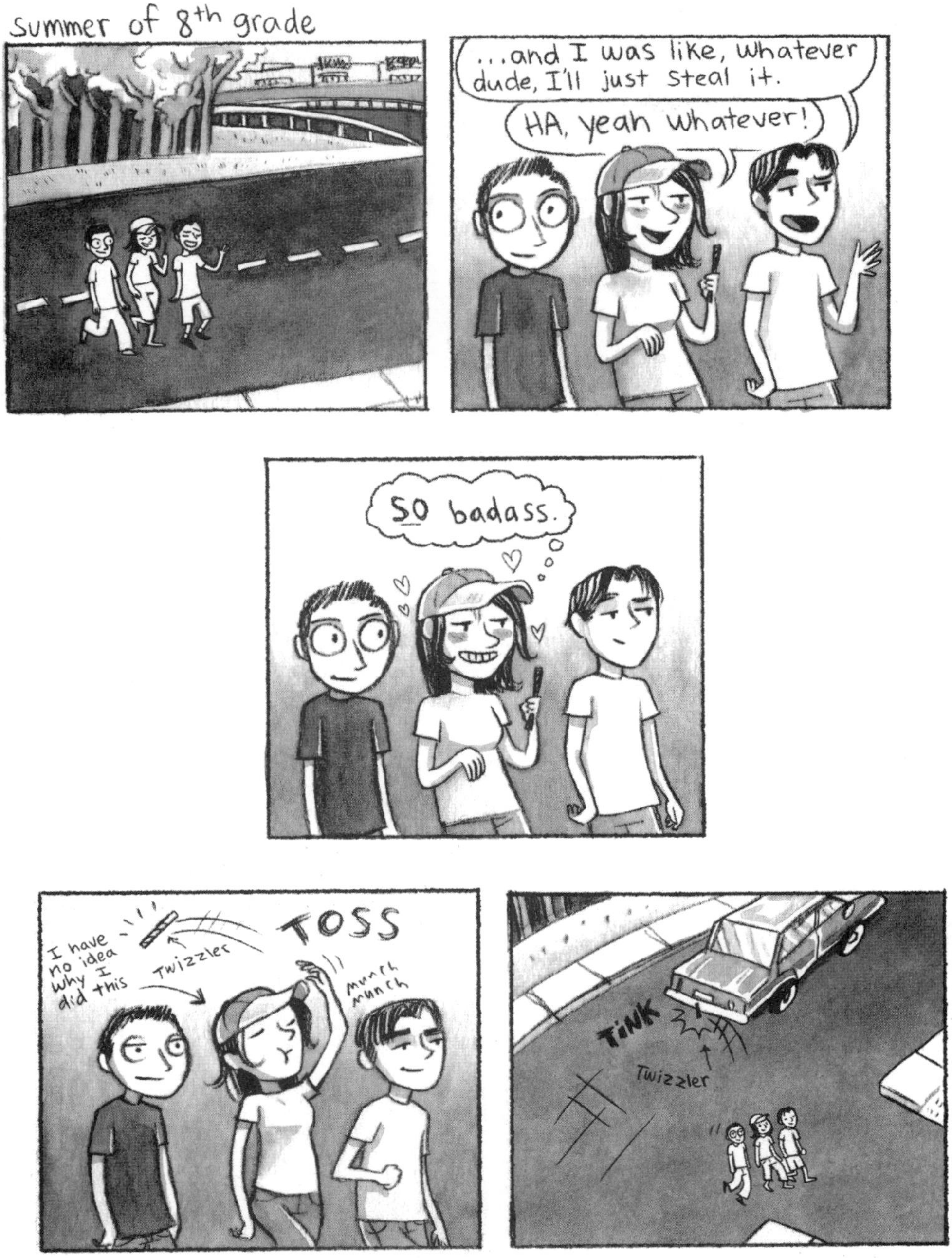
summer of 8th grade
...and I was like, whatever dude, I'll just steal it.
HA, yeah whatever!
SO badass.
I have no idea why I did this
Twizzler
TOSS
munch munch
TINK
Twizzler

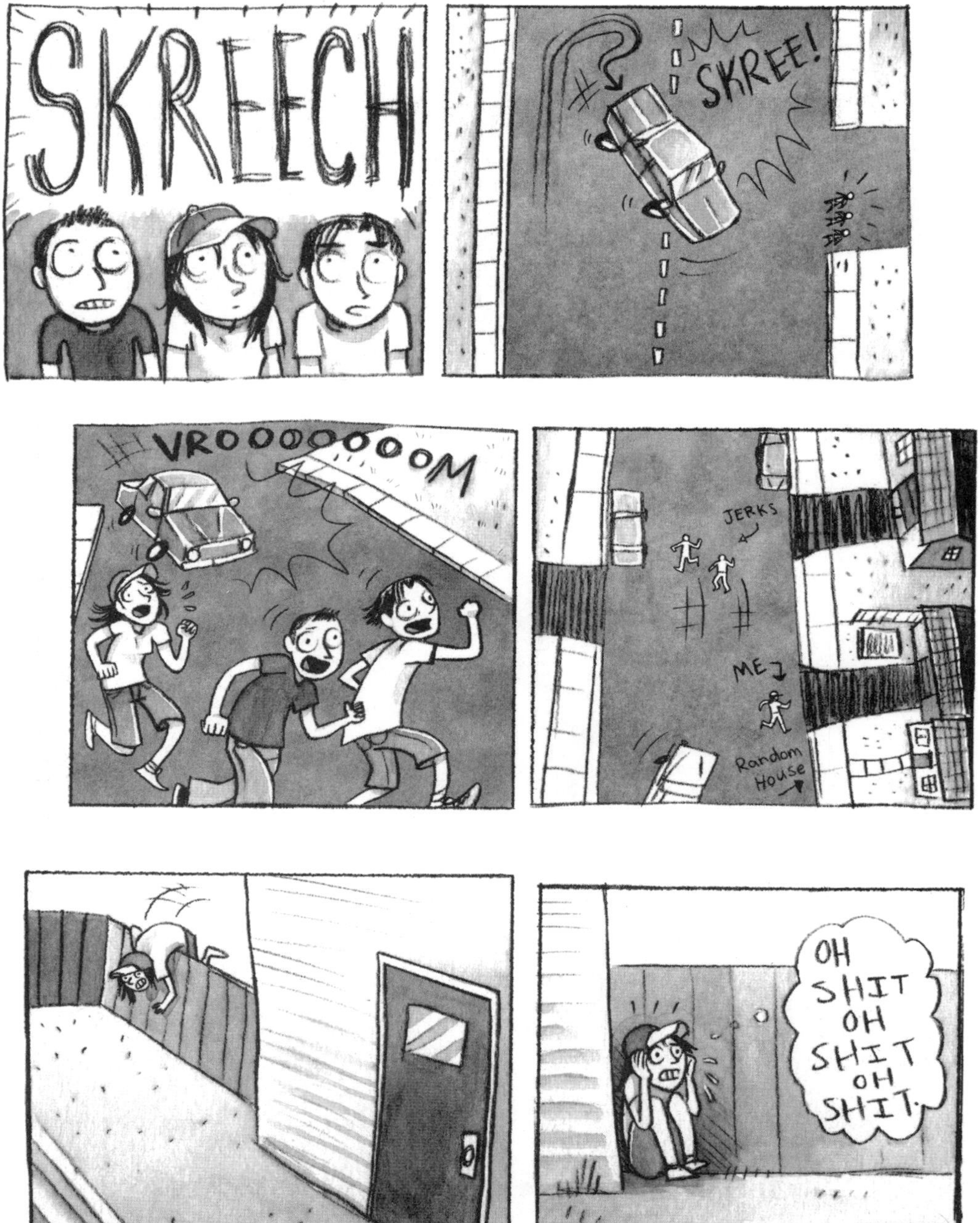
SKREECH
SKREE!
VROOOOOOOM
JERKS
ME
Random House
OH SHIT OH SHIT OH SHIT.

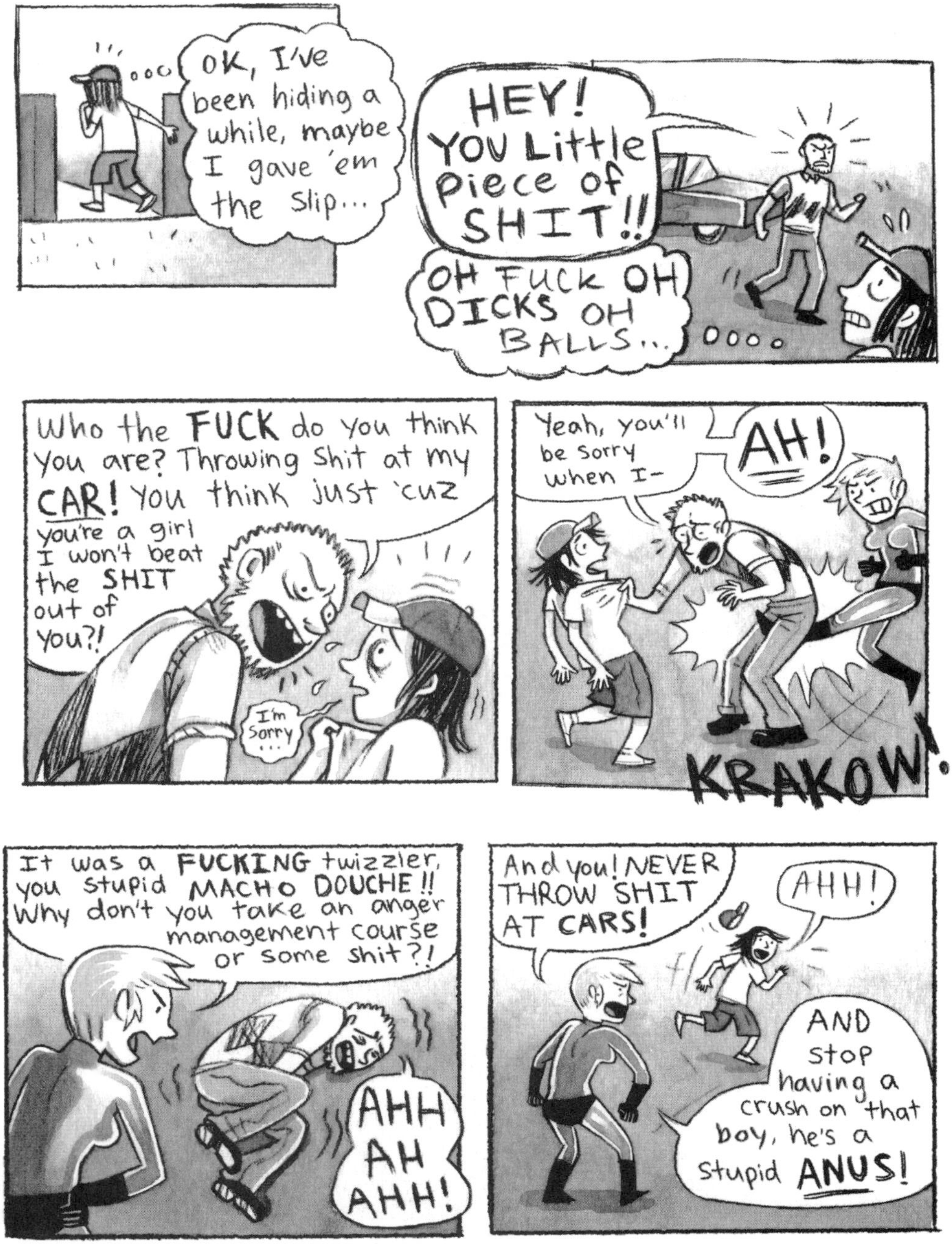
OK, I've been hiding a while, maybe I gave 'em the slip...
HEY! YOU Little piece of SHIT!!
OH FUCK OH DICKS OH BALLS...
Who the FUCK do you think you are? Throwing Shit at my CAR! You think just 'cuz you're a girl I won't beat the SHIT out of you?!
I'm Sorry...
Yeah, you'll be sorry when I-
AH!
KRAKOW!
It was a FUCKING twizzler, you stupid MACHO DOUCHE!! Why don't you take an anger management course or some shit?!
AHH AH AHH!
And you! NEVER THROW SHIT AT CARS!
AHH!
AND stop having a crush on that boy, he's a stupid ANUS!

High School - 9th Grade

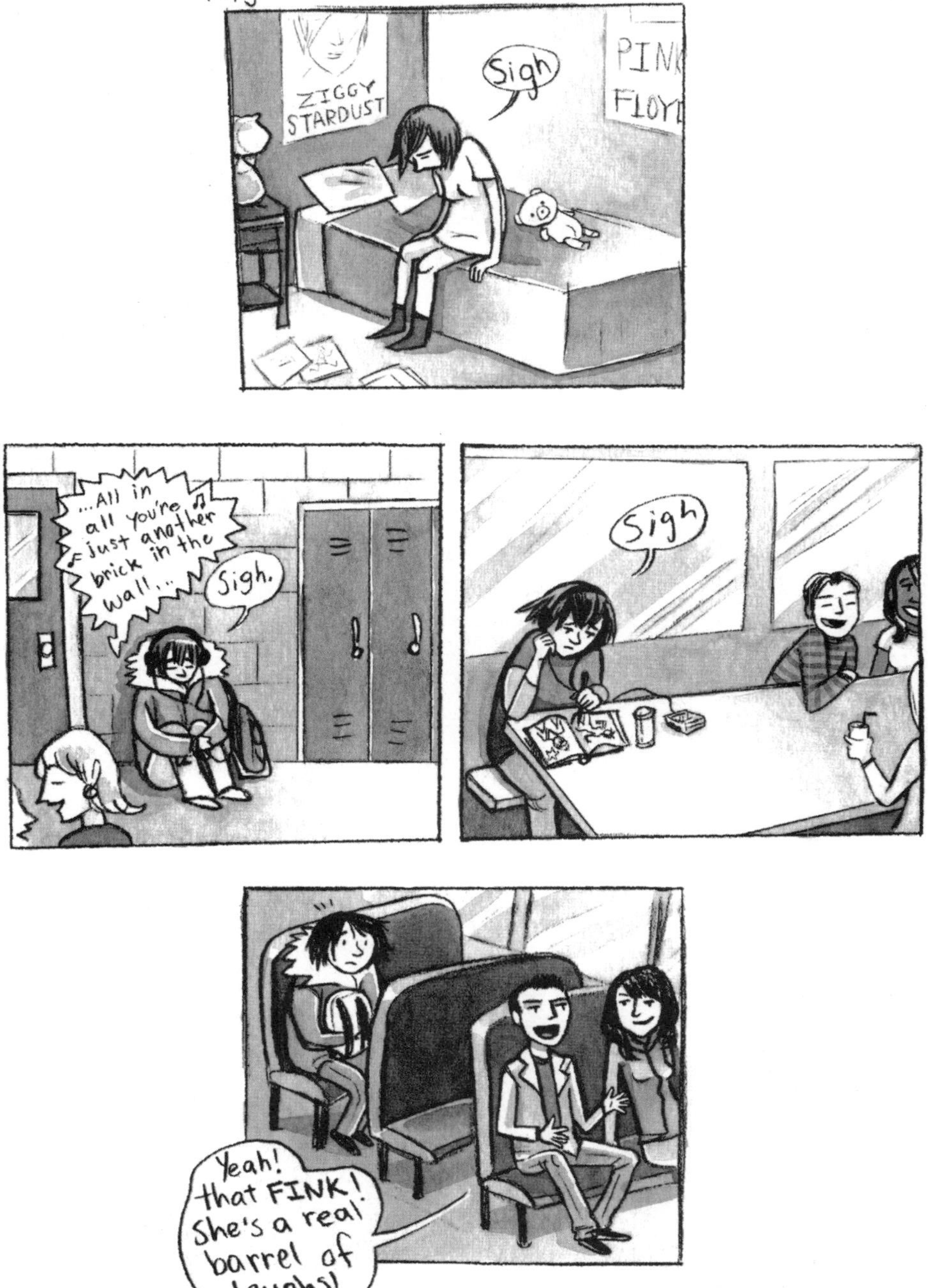
ZIGGY STARDUST
PINK FLOY
Sigh
...All in all you're just another brick in the wall...
Sigh.
Sigh
Yeah! that FINK! She's a real barrel of laughs!

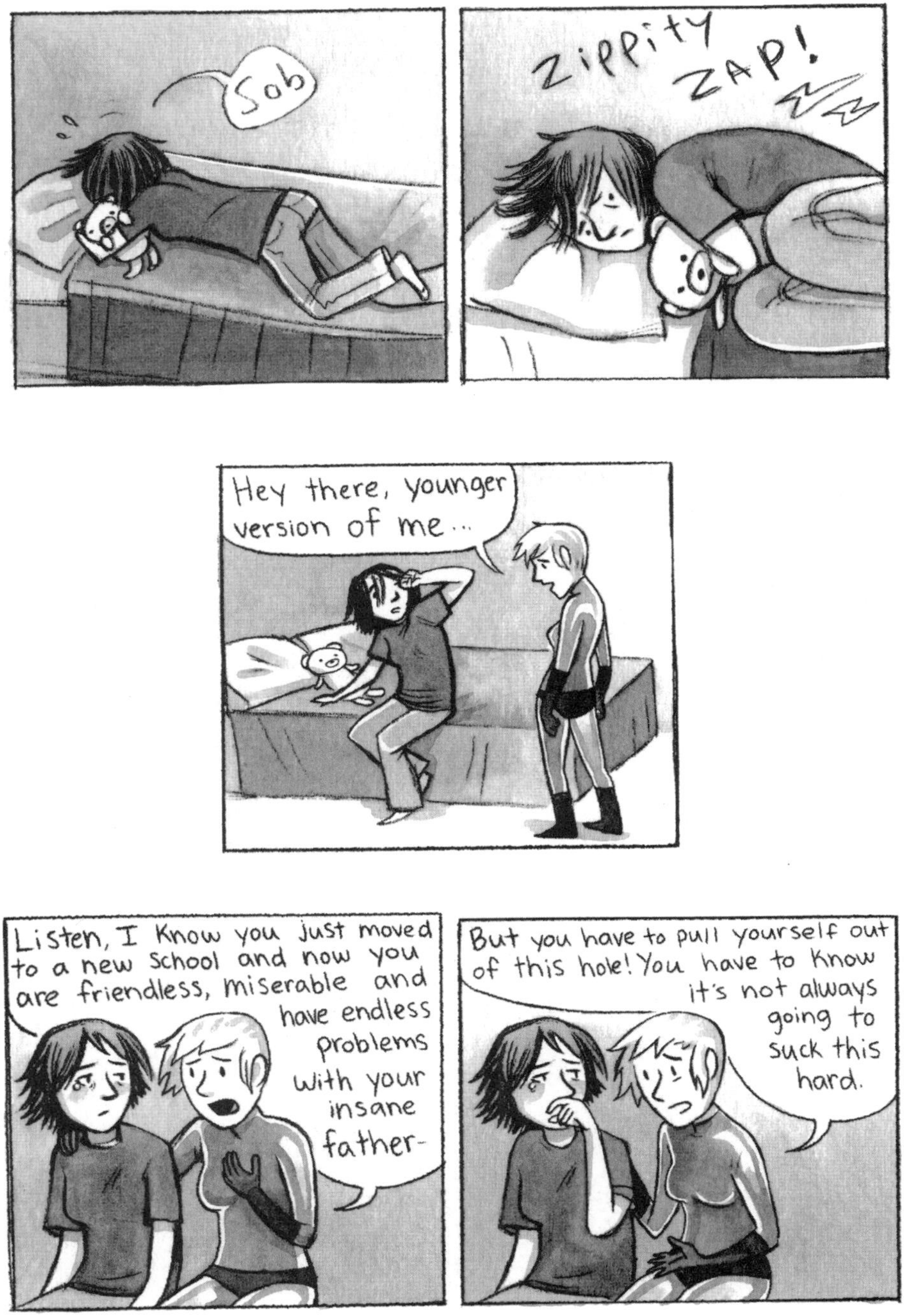
Sob
ZiPPity ZAP!
Hey there, younger version of me...
Listen, I Know you just moved to a new School and now you are friendless, miserable and have endless problems with your insane father-
But you have to pull yourself out of this hole! You have to Know it's not always going to suck this hard.

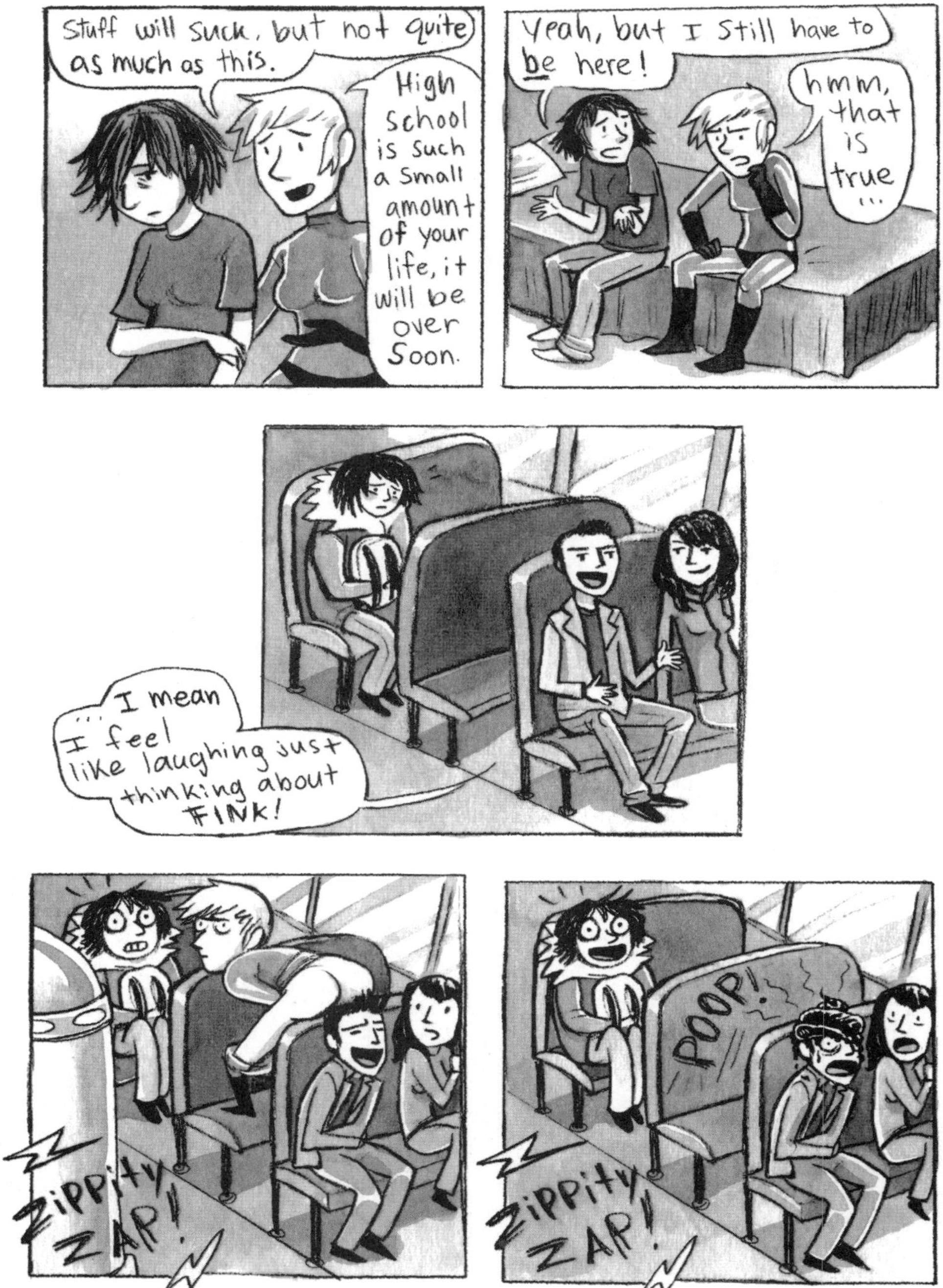
Stuff will suck, but not quite as much as this.
High school is such a small amount of your life, it will be over soon.
Yeah, but I still have to be here!
hmm, that is true ...
... I mean I feel like laughing just thinking about FINK!
ZIPPITY ZAP!
POOP!
ZIPPITY ZAP!

High School-10th Grade

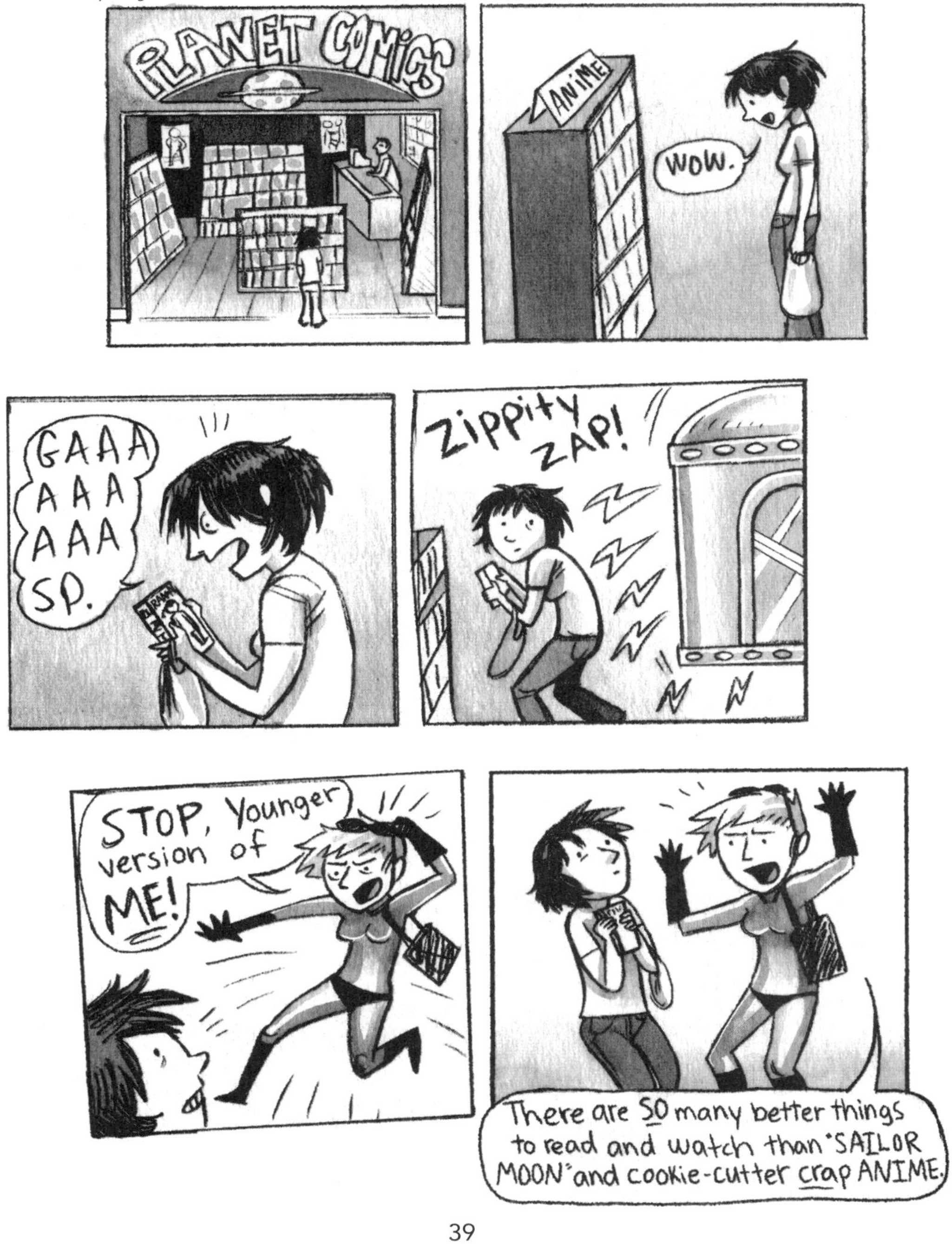
PLANET COMICS
ANIME
WOW.
GAAA AAA AAA SP.
Zippity ZAP!
STOP, Younger version of ME!
There are SO many better things to read and watch than "SAILOR MOON" and cookie-cutter crap ANIME.

Here, This is a comic by OSAMU TEZUKA called "PHOENIX", and I am also giving you some Lynda Barry...

There's good manga you gotta read like Nausicaä and... what's this you were looking at any-way?

OOOOOOOOOH, RANMA ½

obsessed with Drag Queens

It's about a BOY who turns into a GIRL when he gets WET.

And so then LATER:

SPLASH
AKANE!!

That's Pretty hot.

40

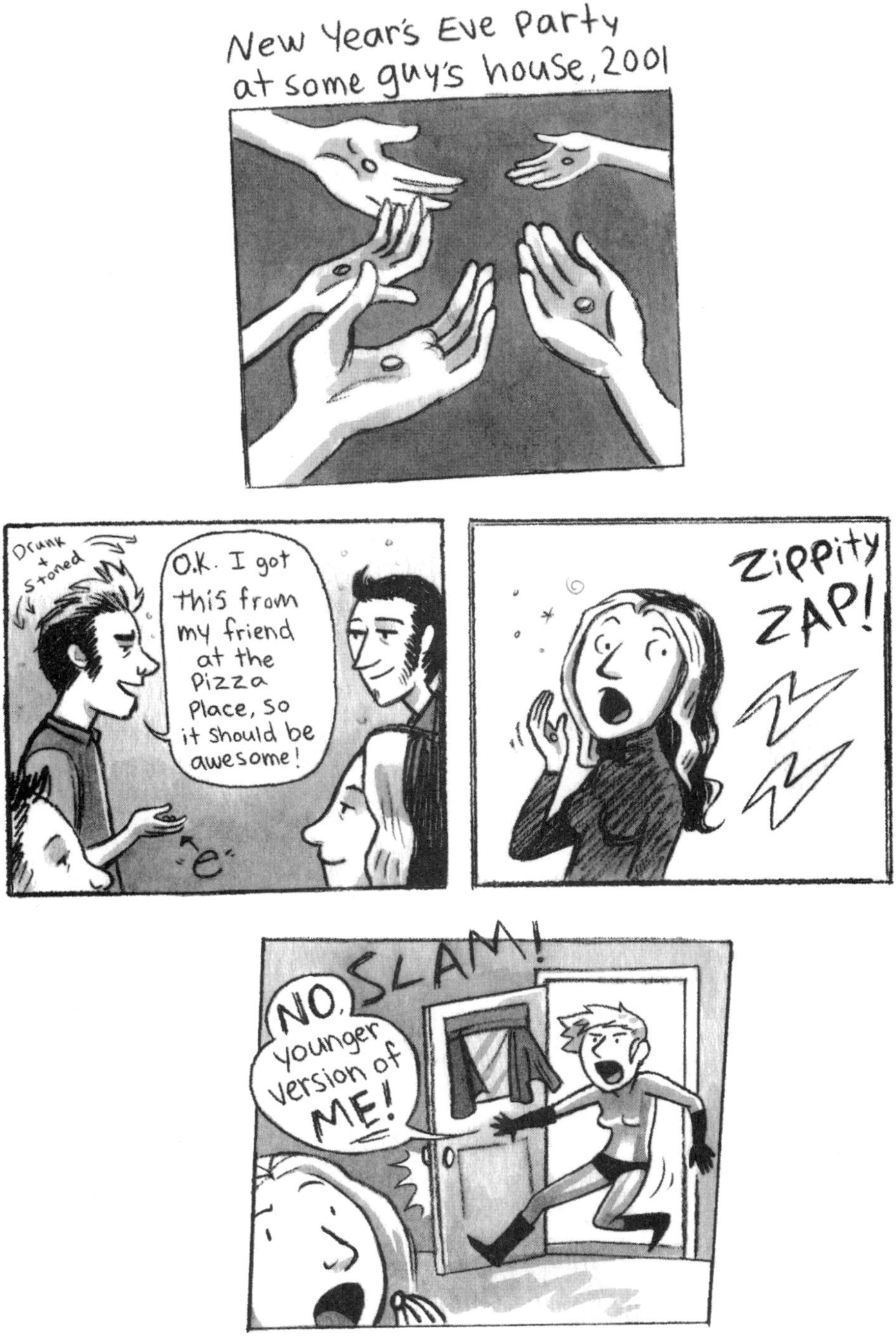
New Year's Eve Party at some guy's house, 2001
Drunk + stoned
O.K. I got this from my friend at the pizza place, so it should be awesome!
e
Zippity ZAP!
SLAM!
NO, younger version of ME!

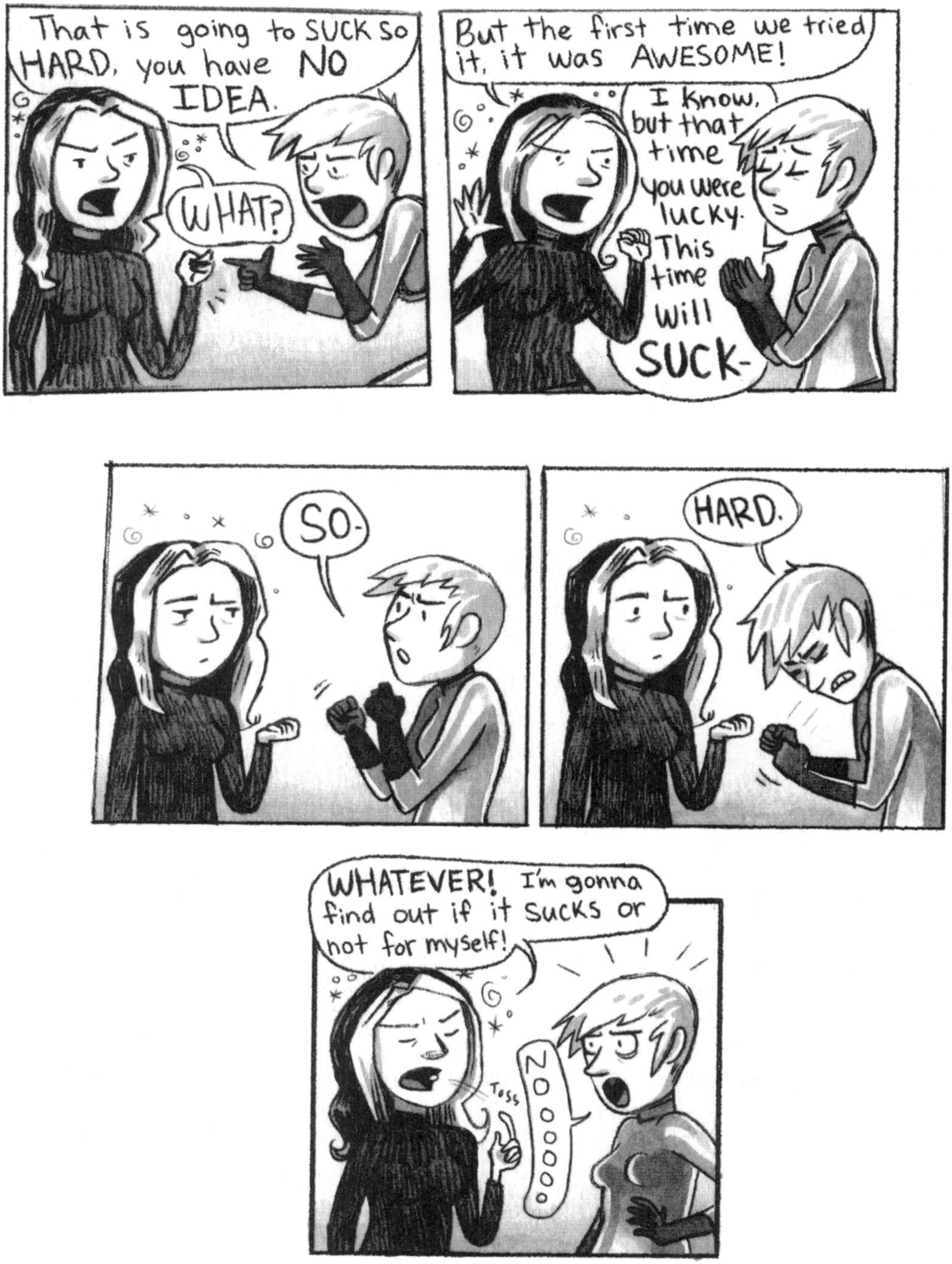
That is going to SUCK so HARD, you have NO IDEA.
WHAT?
But the first time we tried it, it was AWESOME!
I know, but that time you were lucky. This time will SUCK-
SO-
HARD.
WHATEVER! I'm gonna find out if it SUCKS or not for myself!
Toss
NOOOOOOO

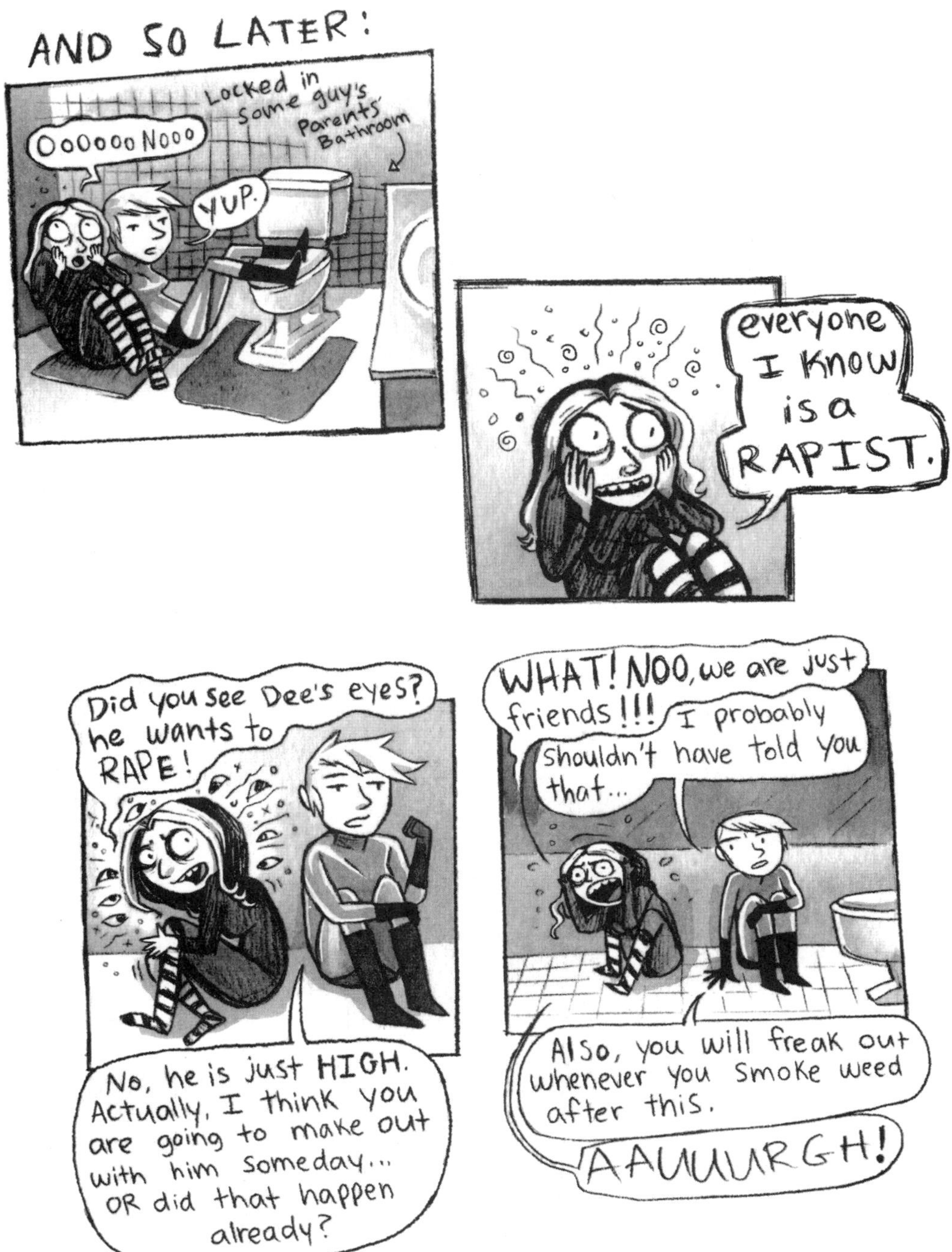
AND SO LATER:
Locked in Some guy's Parents' Bathroom
OOoooo Nooo
YUP.
everyone I Know is a RAPIST.
Did you see Dee's eyes? he wants to RAPE!
No, he is just HIGH. Actually, I think you are going to make out with him someday... OR did that happen already?
WHAT! NOO, we are just friends!!!
I probably shouldn't have told you that...
Also, you will freak out whenever you smoke weed after this.
AAUUURGH!

Zippity
ZAP!

WAIt! younger version of ME!

I'm you from the future, and trust me, you don't want to work here!

...But I loved this Place in High School! Me and MS. B are Buddies!

CATWOMAN

Yeah, that's why it'll feel 10 times worse when she fires you and you can't figure out why.

What?!

MS. B wouldn't do that to me!

Sorry, it's just not going to turn out the way you want!

Zippity
ZAP!

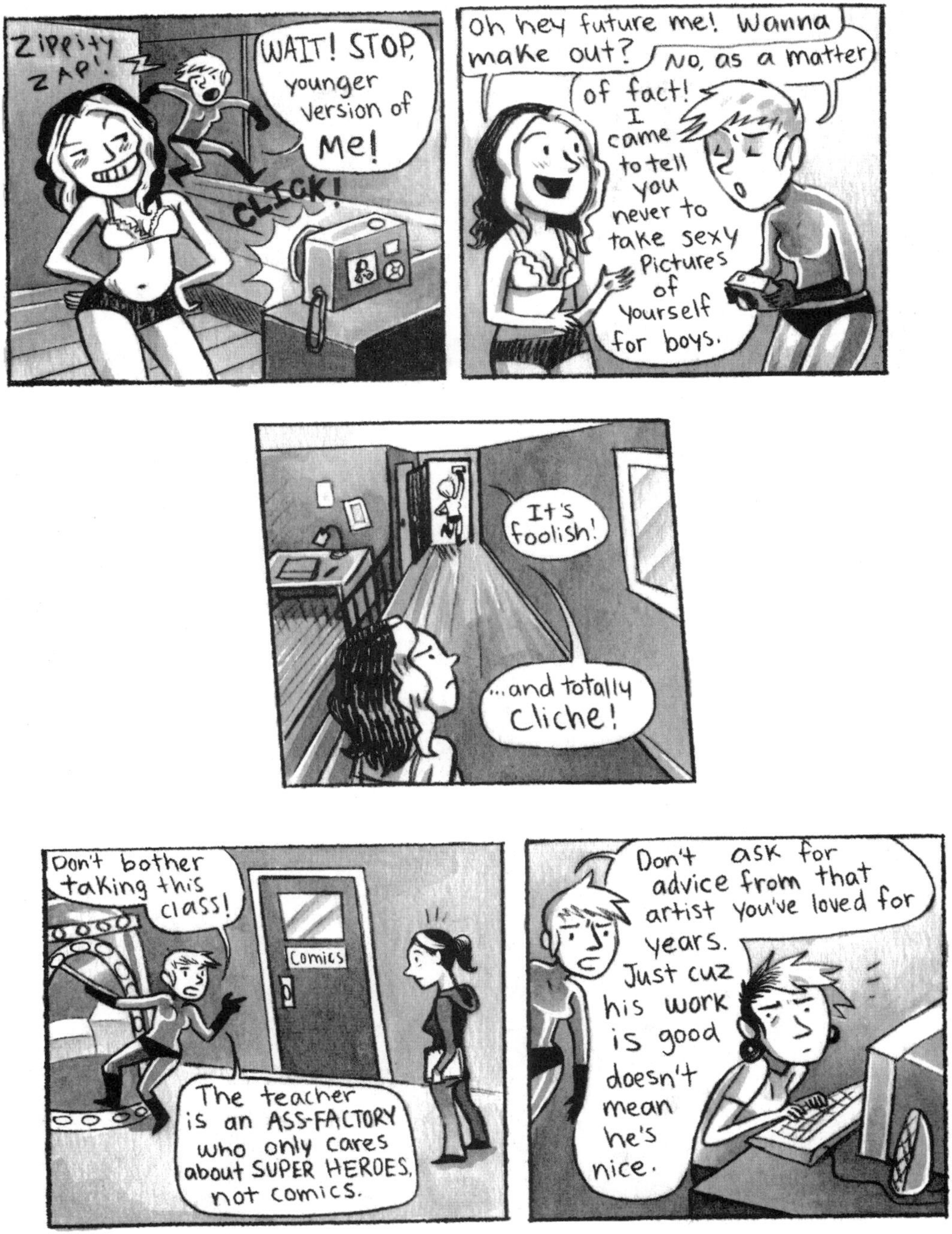

ZIPPITY ZAP!
WAIT! STOP, younger version of Me!
CLICK!
Oh hey future me! Wanna make out?
No, as a matter of fact! I came to tell you never to take sexy pictures of yourself for boys.
It's foolish!
...and totally Cliche!
Don't bother taking this class!
Comics
The teacher is an ASS-FACTORY who only cares about SUPER HEROES, not comics.
Don't ask for advice from that artist you've loved for years. Just cuz his work is good doesn't mean he's nice.

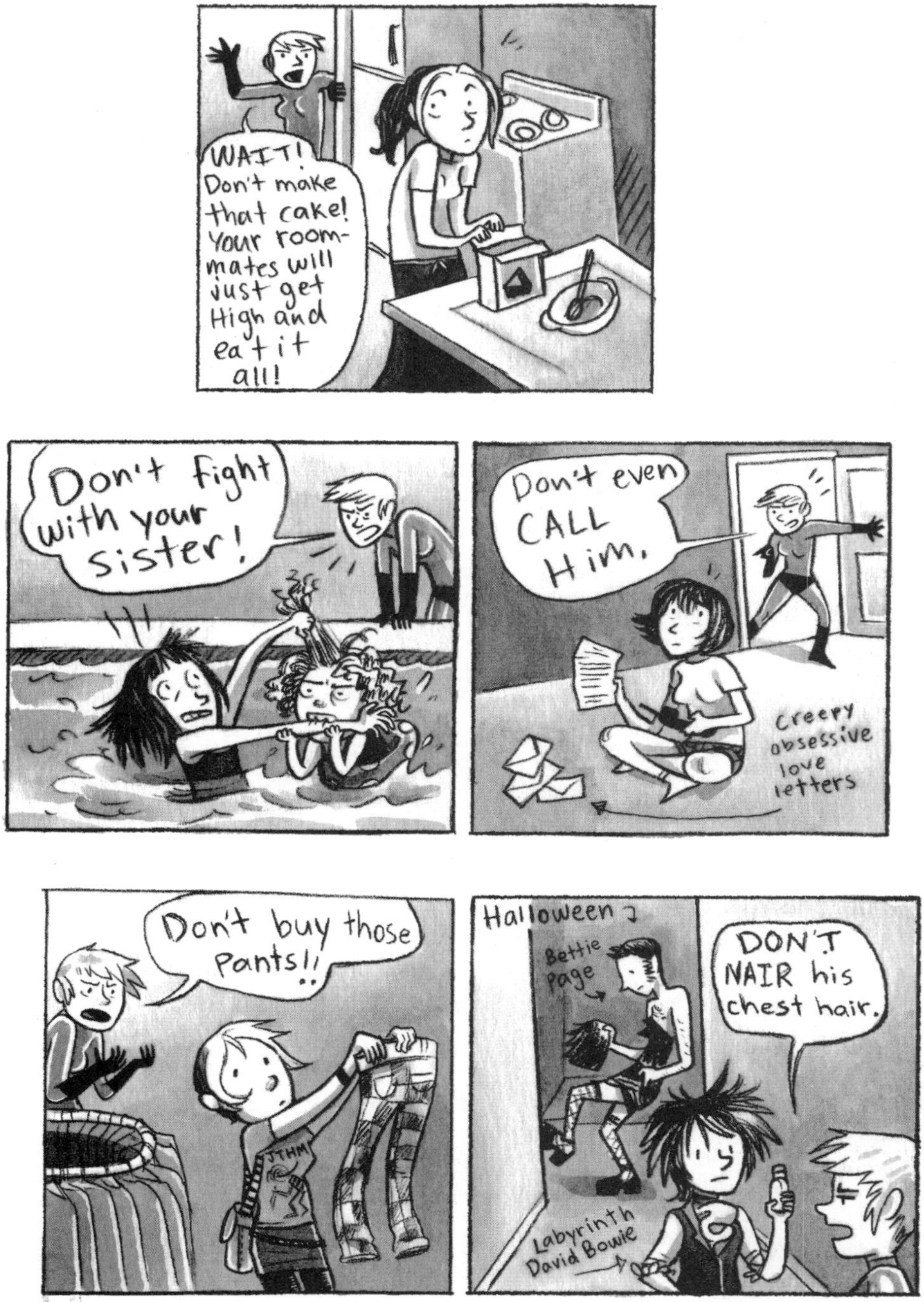
WAIT! Don't make that cake! Your room-mates will just get High and eat it all!
Don't fight with your sister!
Don't even CALL Him.
Creepy obsessive love letters
Don't buy those pants!!
Halloween
Bettie Page
DON'T NAIR his chest hair.
JTHM
Labyrinth David Bowie

DON'T start smoking just because your roomates do and don't let people boss you around and don't be Jessica Rabbit for Halloween and don't...

SHUT THE FUCK UP!!

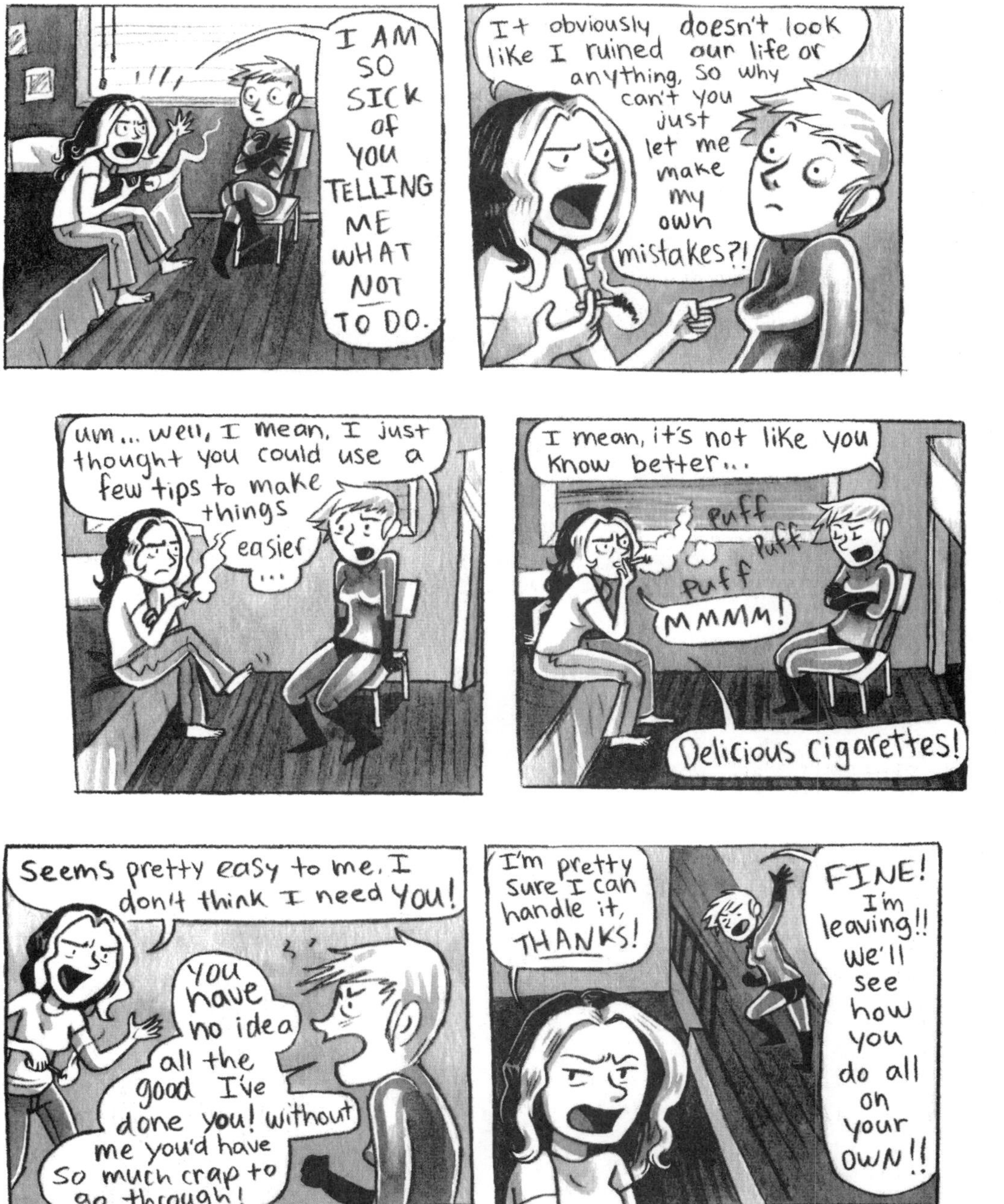
I AM SO SICK of YOU TELLING ME WHAT NOT TO DO.
It obviously doesn't look like I ruined our life or anything, so why can't you just let me make my own mistakes?!
um... well, I mean, I just thought you could use a few tips to make things
easier ...
I mean, it's not like you know better...
puff
puff
puff
MMMM!
Delicious cigarettes!
Seems pretty easy to me. I don't think I need YOU!
You have no idea all the good I've done you! without me you'd have so much crap to go through!
I'm pretty sure I can handle it, THANKS!
FINE! I'm leaving!! We'll see how you do all on your OWN!!

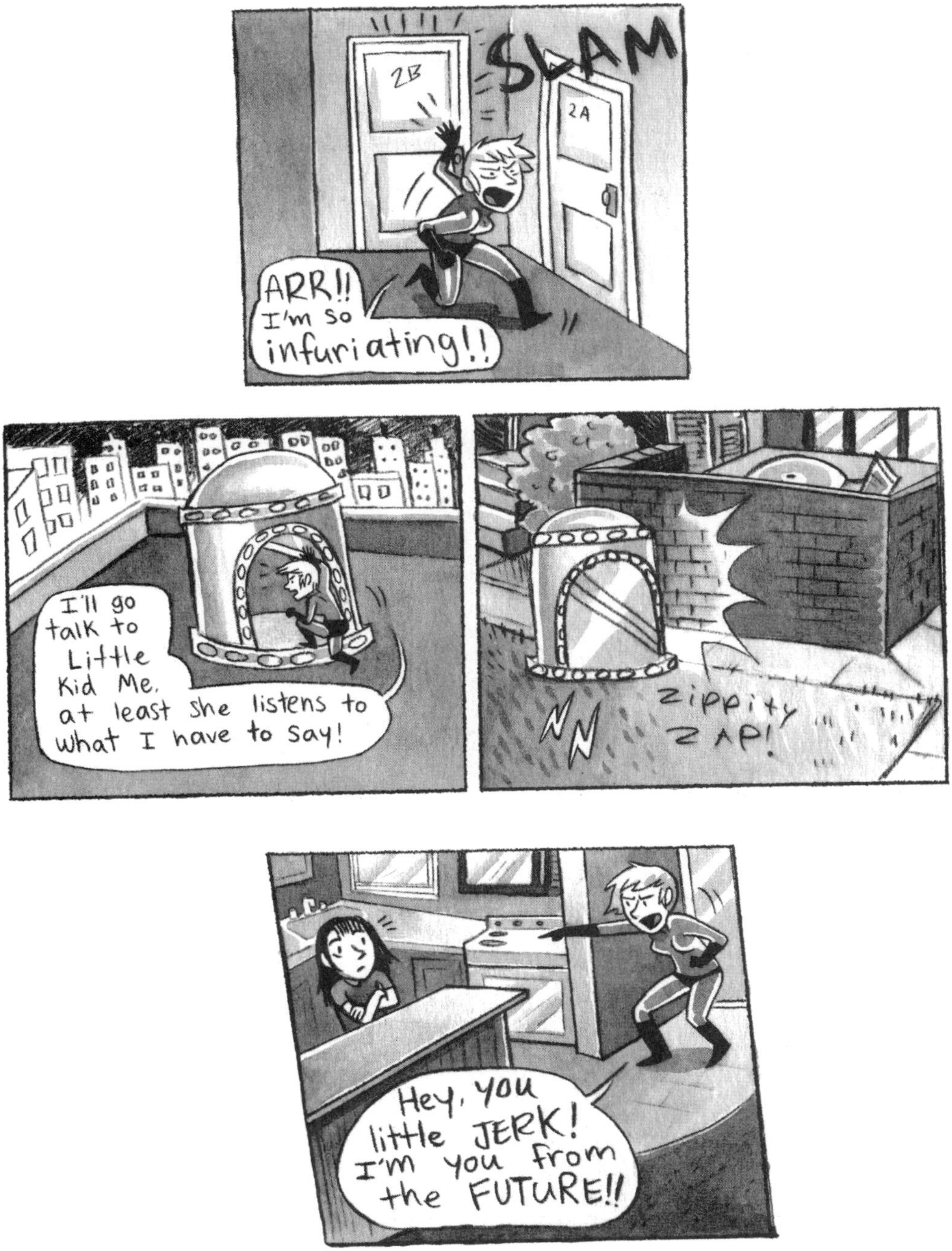
2B
2A
SLAM
ARR!! I'm so infuriating!!
I'll go talk to Little Kid Me. at least she listens to what I have to say!
zippity ZAP!
Hey, you little JERK! I'm you from the FUTURE!!

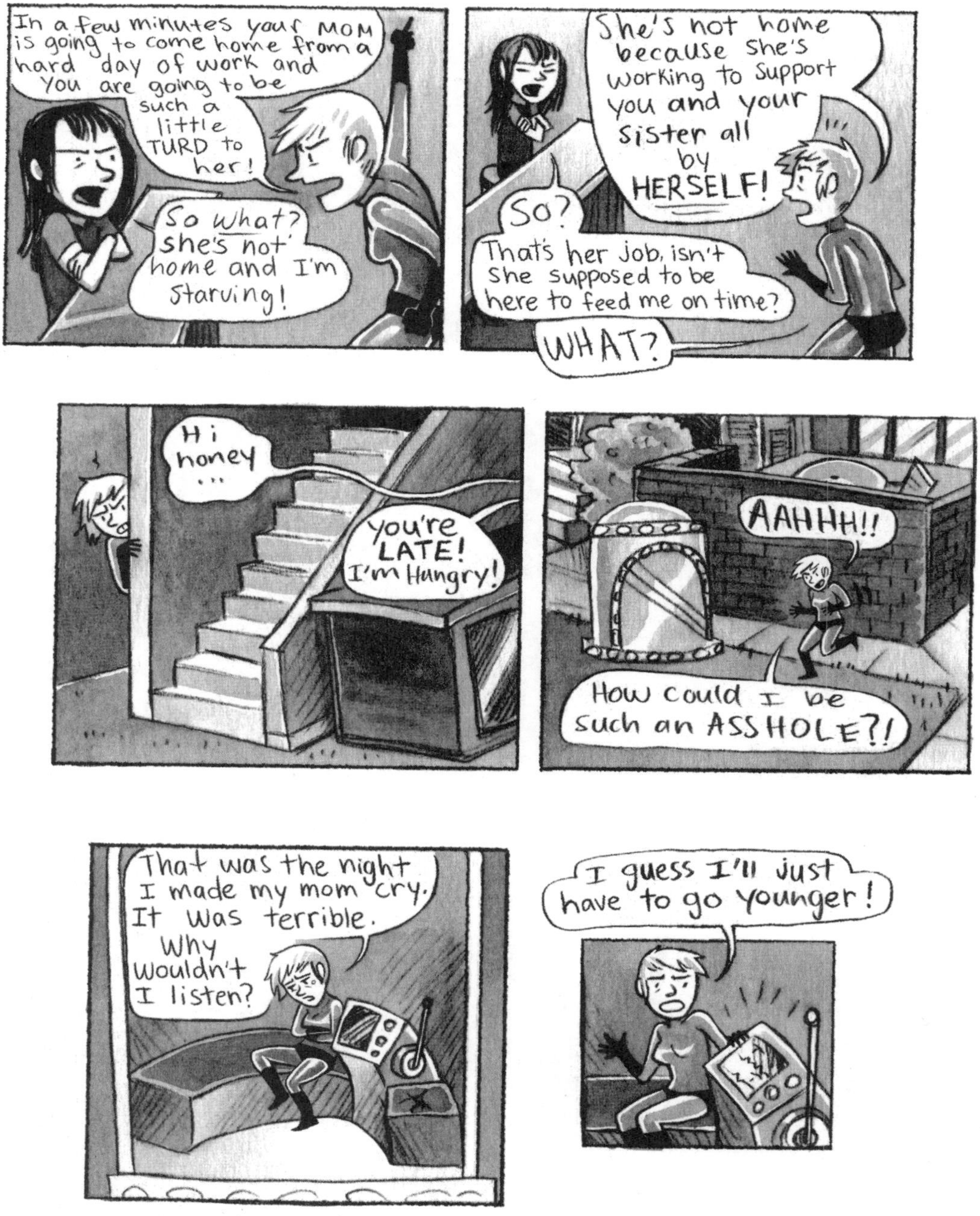
In a few minutes your MOM is going to come home from a hard day of work and You are going to be such a little TURD to her!
So what? she's not home and I'm starving!
She's not home because she's working to support you and your sister all by HERSELF!
So?
That's her job, isn't she supposed to be here to feed me on time?
WHAT?
Hi honey ...
You're LATE! I'm Hungry!
AAHHH!!
How could I be such an ASSHOLE?!
That was the night I made my mom cry. It was terrible. Why wouldn't I listen?
I guess I'll just have to go younger!

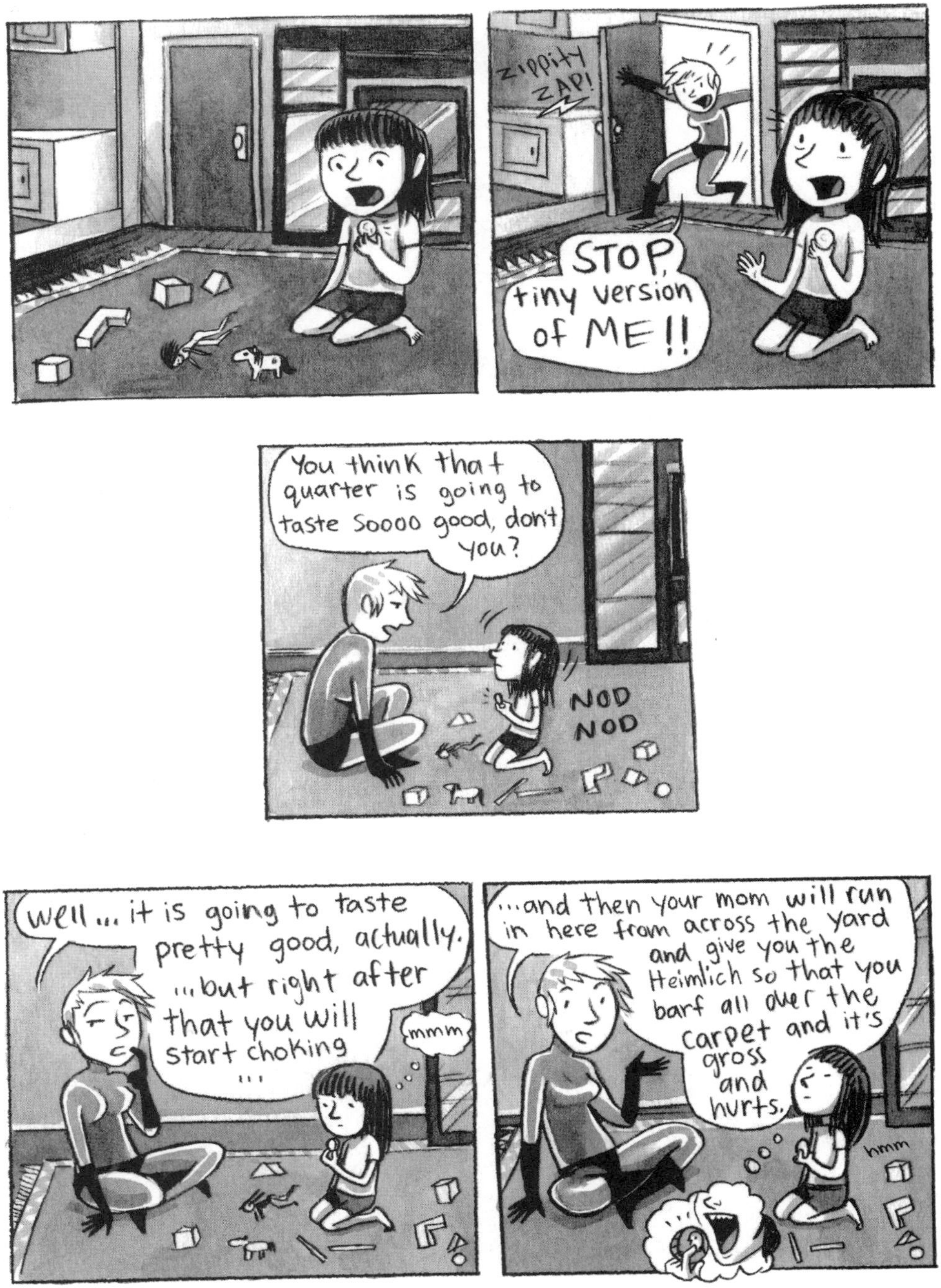
zippity ZAP!
STOP, tiny version of ME!!
You think that quarter is going to taste Soooo good, don't you?
NOD NOD
well... it is going to taste pretty good, actually. ...but right after that you will start choking ...
mmm
...and then your mom will run in here from across the yard and give you the Heimlich so that you barf all over the carpet and it's gross and hurts.
hmm

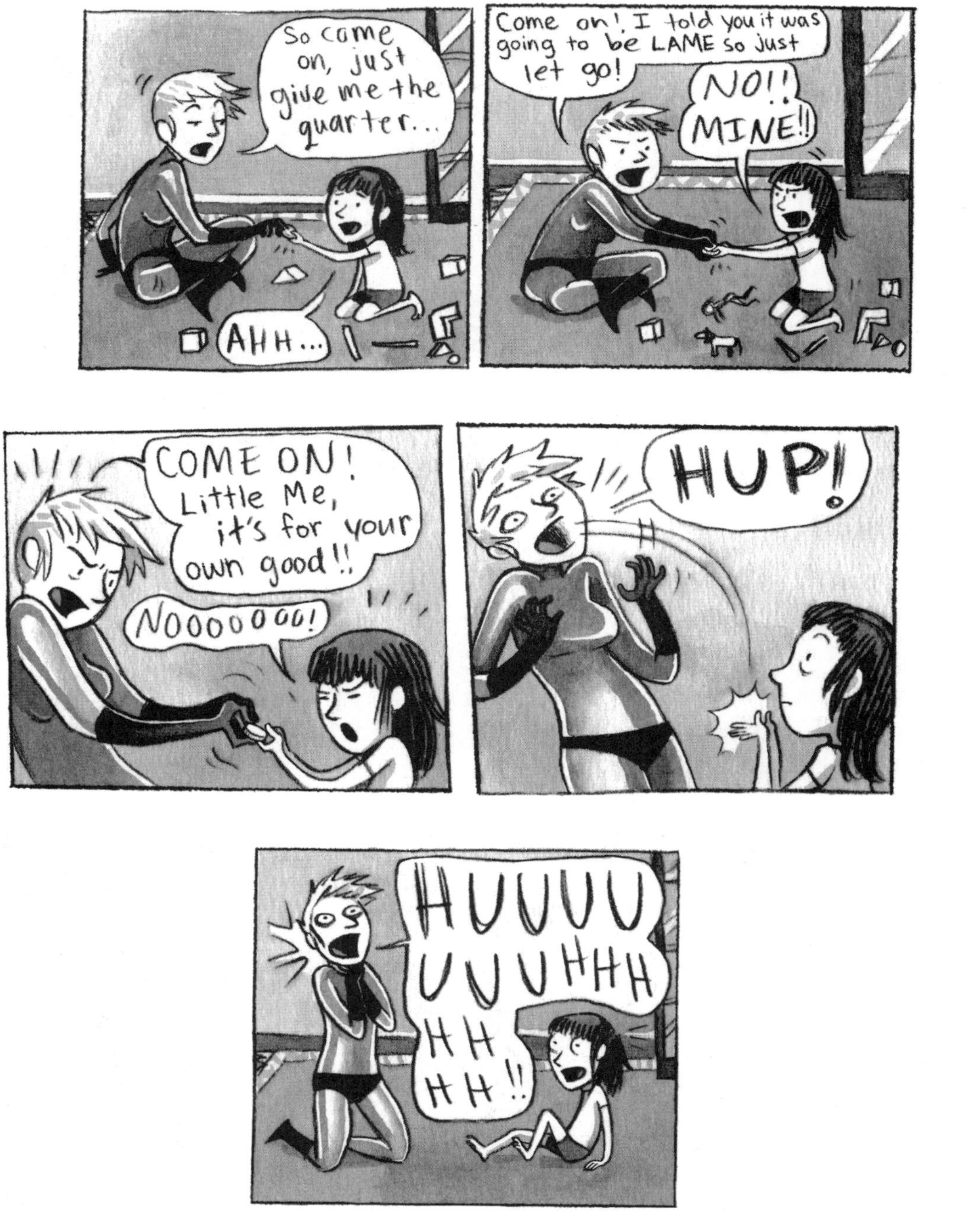
So come on, just give me the quarter...
AHH...
Come on! I told you it was going to be LAME so just let go!
NO!! MINE!!
COME ON! Little Me, it's for your own good!!
NOOOOOOO!
HUP!
HUUUUUUUUHHHHHHH!!

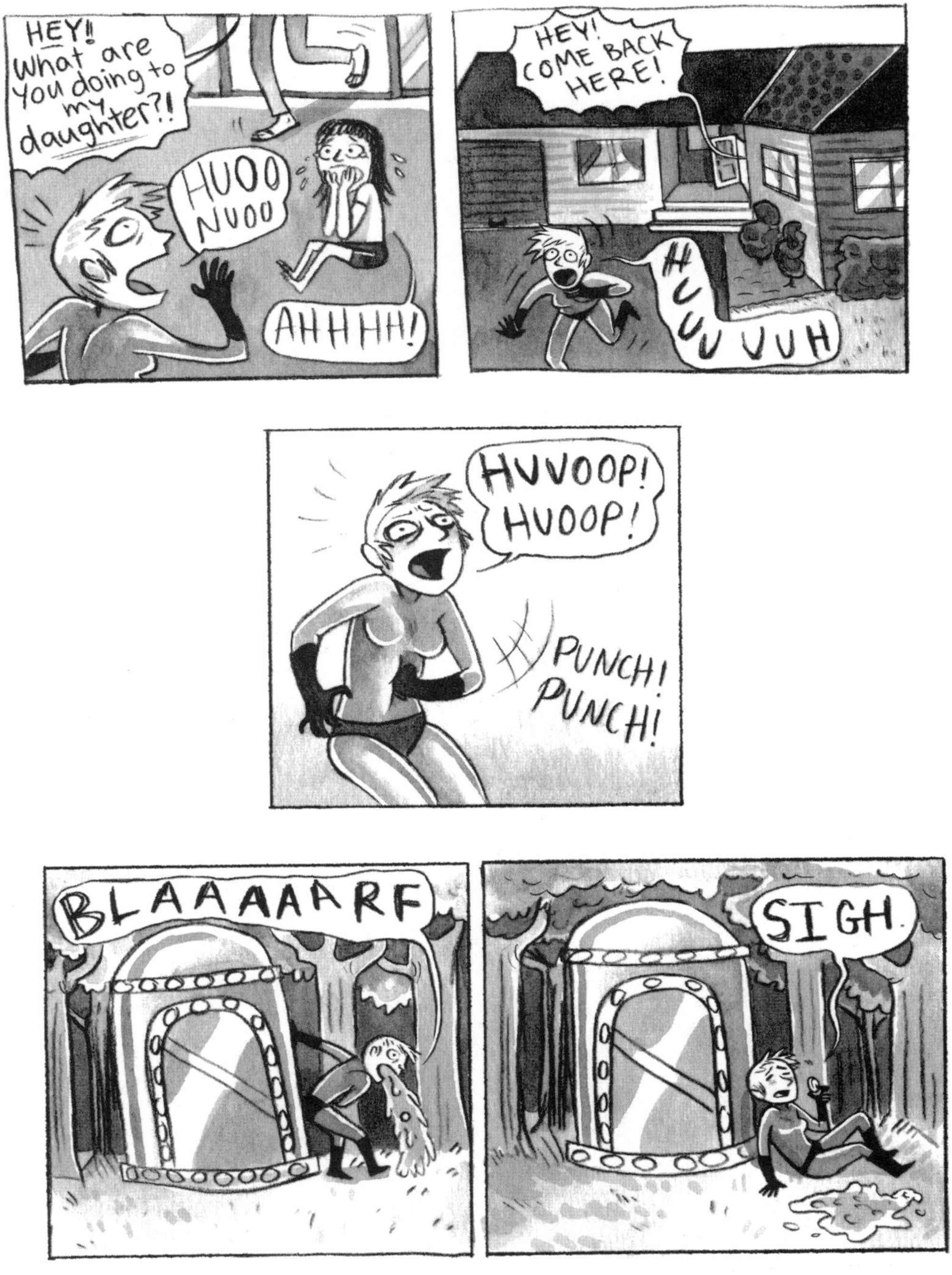
HEY!! What are You doing to my daughter?!!
HUOO NUOO
AHHHH!
HEY! COME BACK HERE!
HUUU VUH
HUVOOP! HUOOP!
PUNCH! PUNCH!
BLAAAAARF
SIGH.

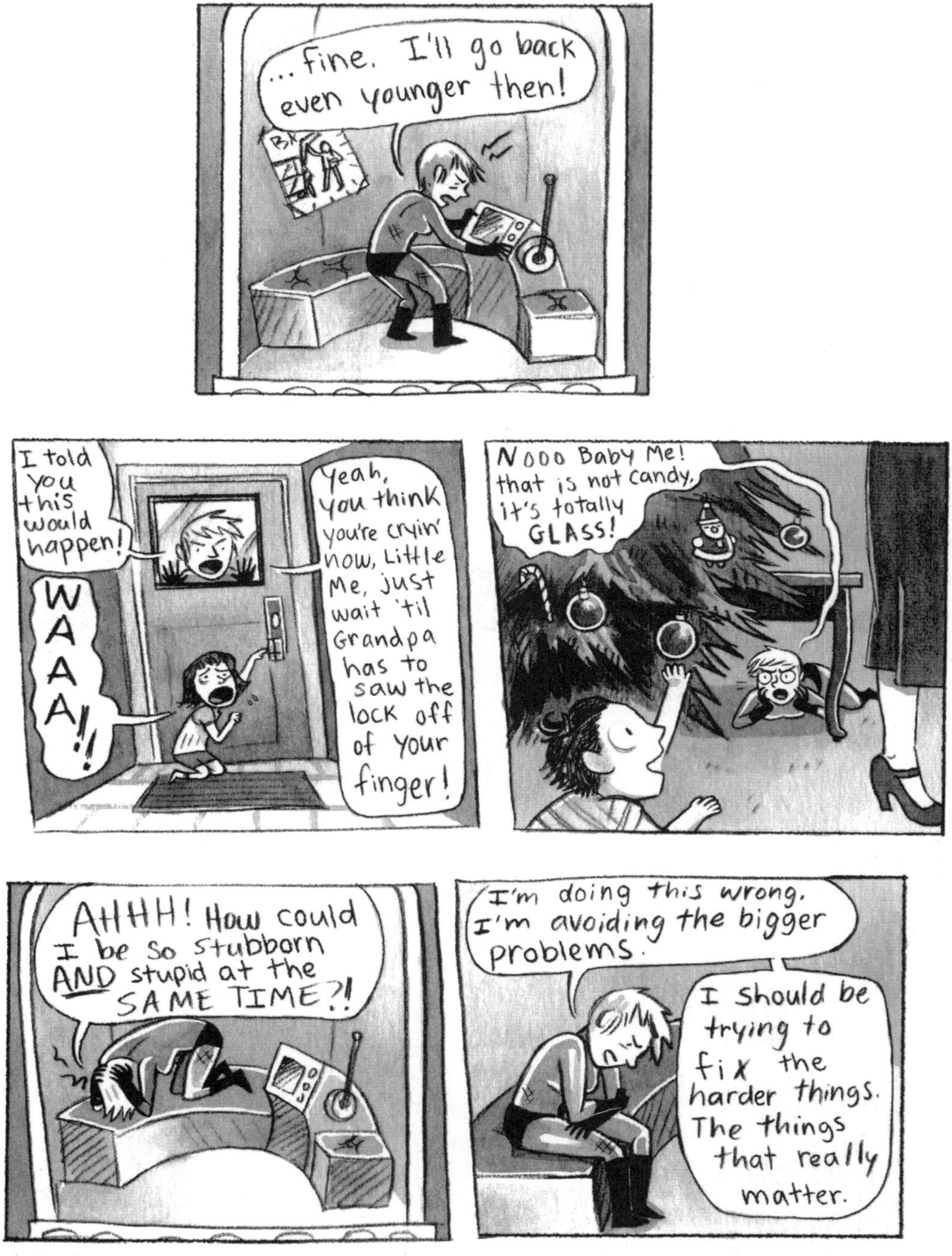
...fine. I'll go back even younger then!
I told you this would happen!
WAAAA!!
Yeah, you think you're cryin' now, Little Me, just wait 'til Grandpa has to saw the lock off of your finger!
Nooo Baby Me! that is not candy, it's totally GLASS!
AHHH! How could I be so stubborn AND stupid at the SAME TIME?!
I'm doing this wrong. I'm avoiding the bigger problems.
I should be trying to fix the harder things. The things that really matter.

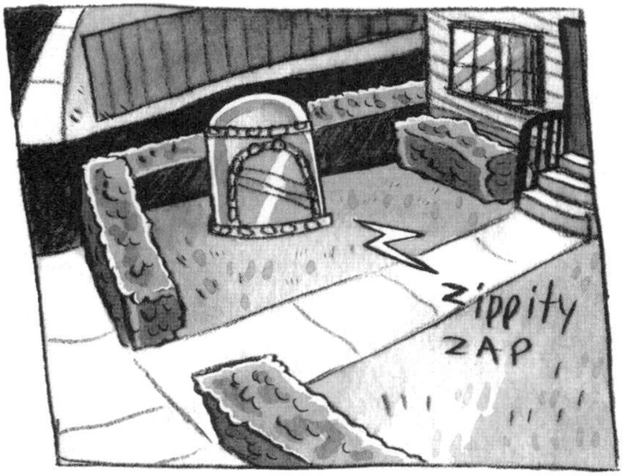
zippity
ZAP

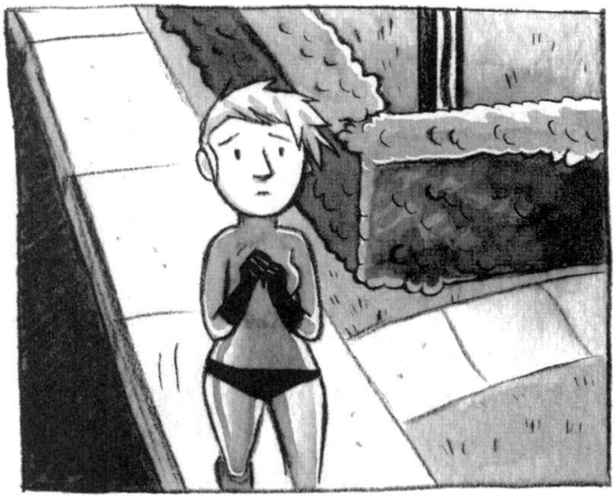

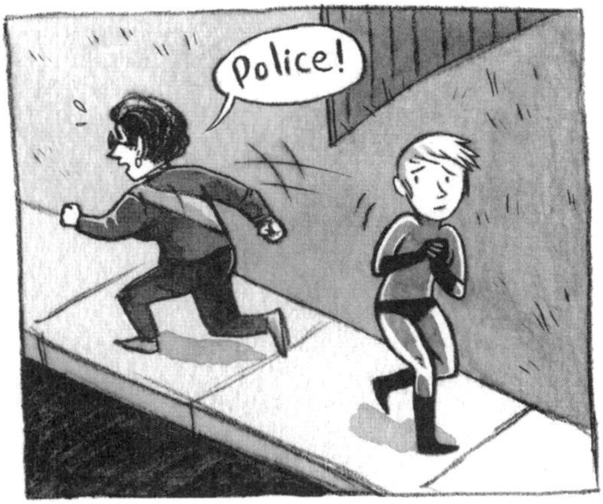
Police!

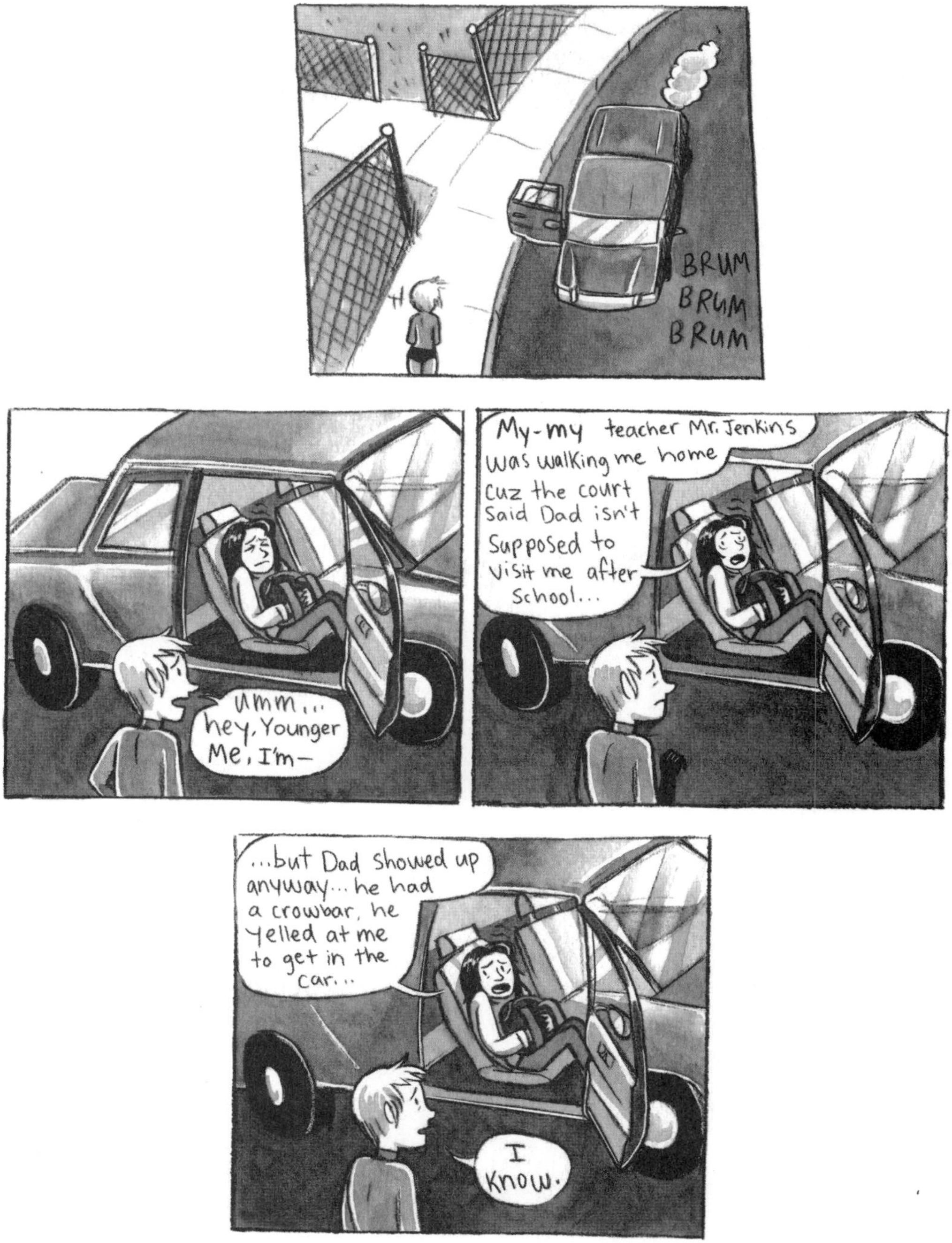
BRUM
BRUM
BRUM
umm... hey, Younger Me, I'm—
My-my teacher Mr. Jenkins was walking me home cuz the court said Dad isn't supposed to visit me after school...
...but Dad showed up anyway... he had a crowbar, he yelled at me to get in the car...
I know.

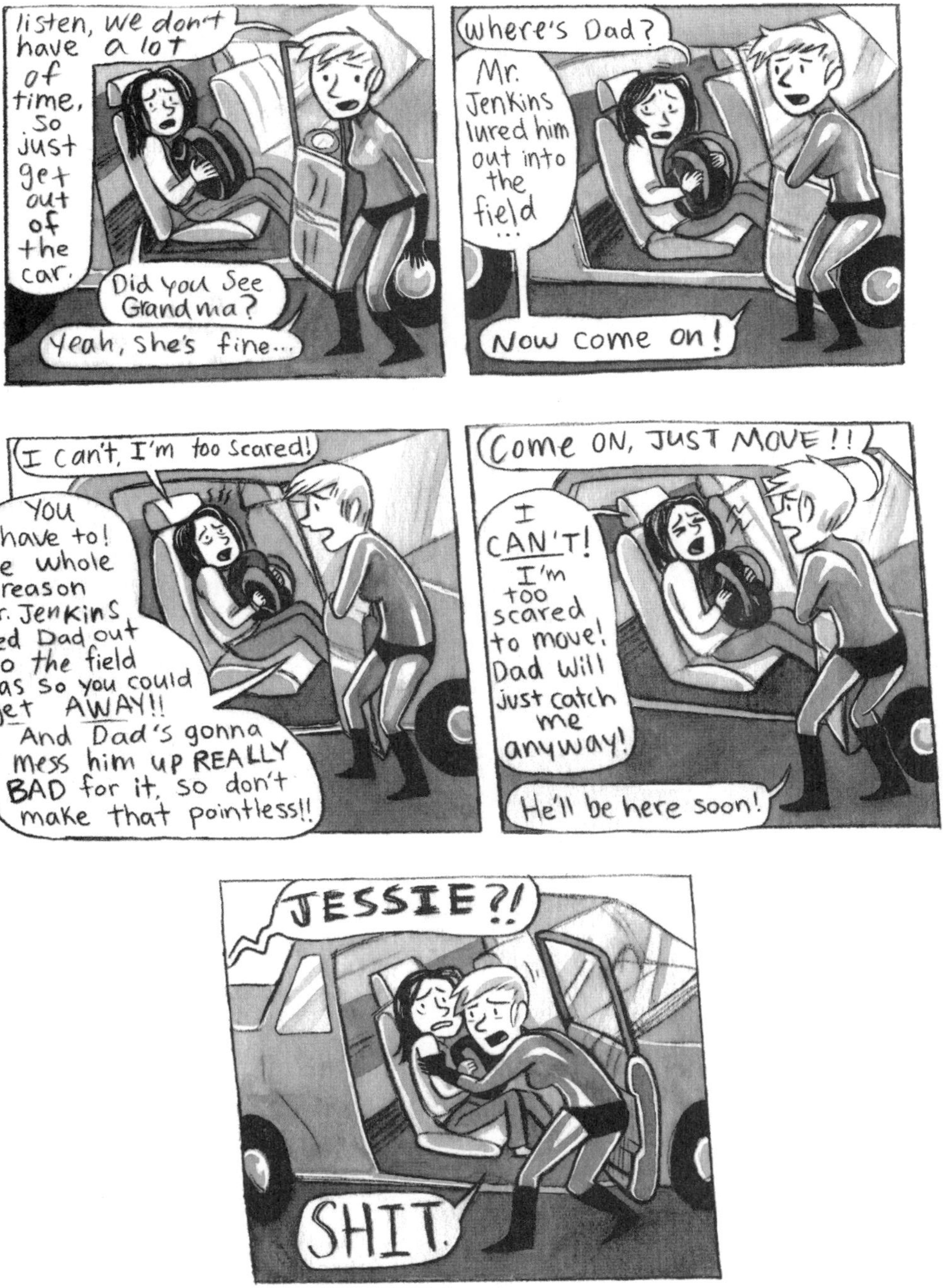
listen, we don't have a lot of time, so just get out of the car.
Did you See Grandma?
Yeah, she's fine...
where's Dad?
Mr. Jenkins lured him out into the field ...
Now come on!
I can't, I'm too Scared!
You have to! The whole reason Mr. Jenkins called Dad out into the field was so you could get AWAY!! And Dad's gonna mess him up REALLY BAD for it, so don't make that pointless!!
Come ON, JUST MOVE!!
I CAN'T! I'm too scared to move! Dad will just catch me anyway!
He'll be here soon!
JESSIE?!
SHIT.

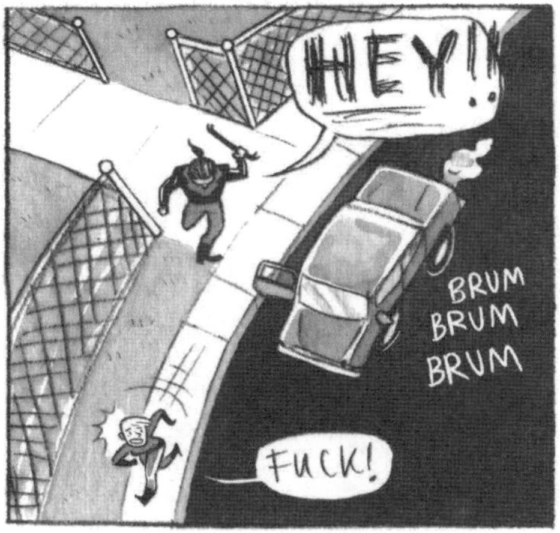
HEY!!
BRUM
BRUM
BRUM
FUCK!

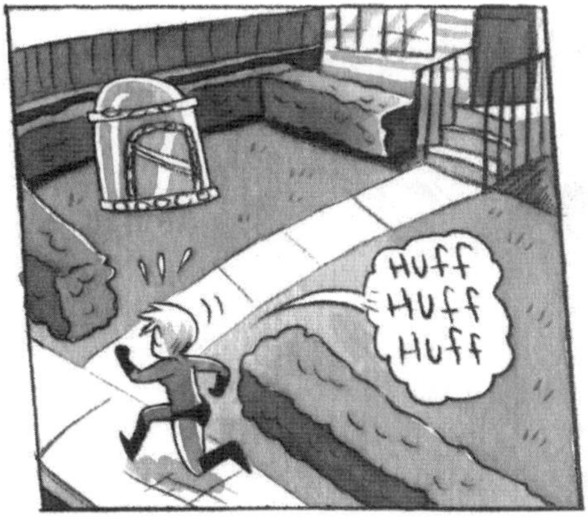
Huff
Huff
Huff

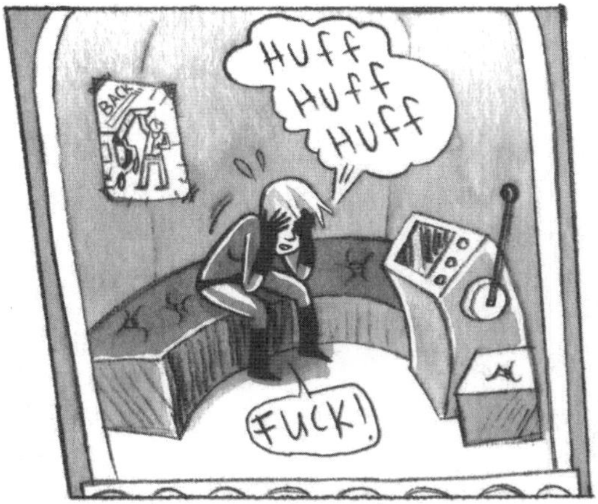
BACK
Huff
Huff
Huff
FUCK!

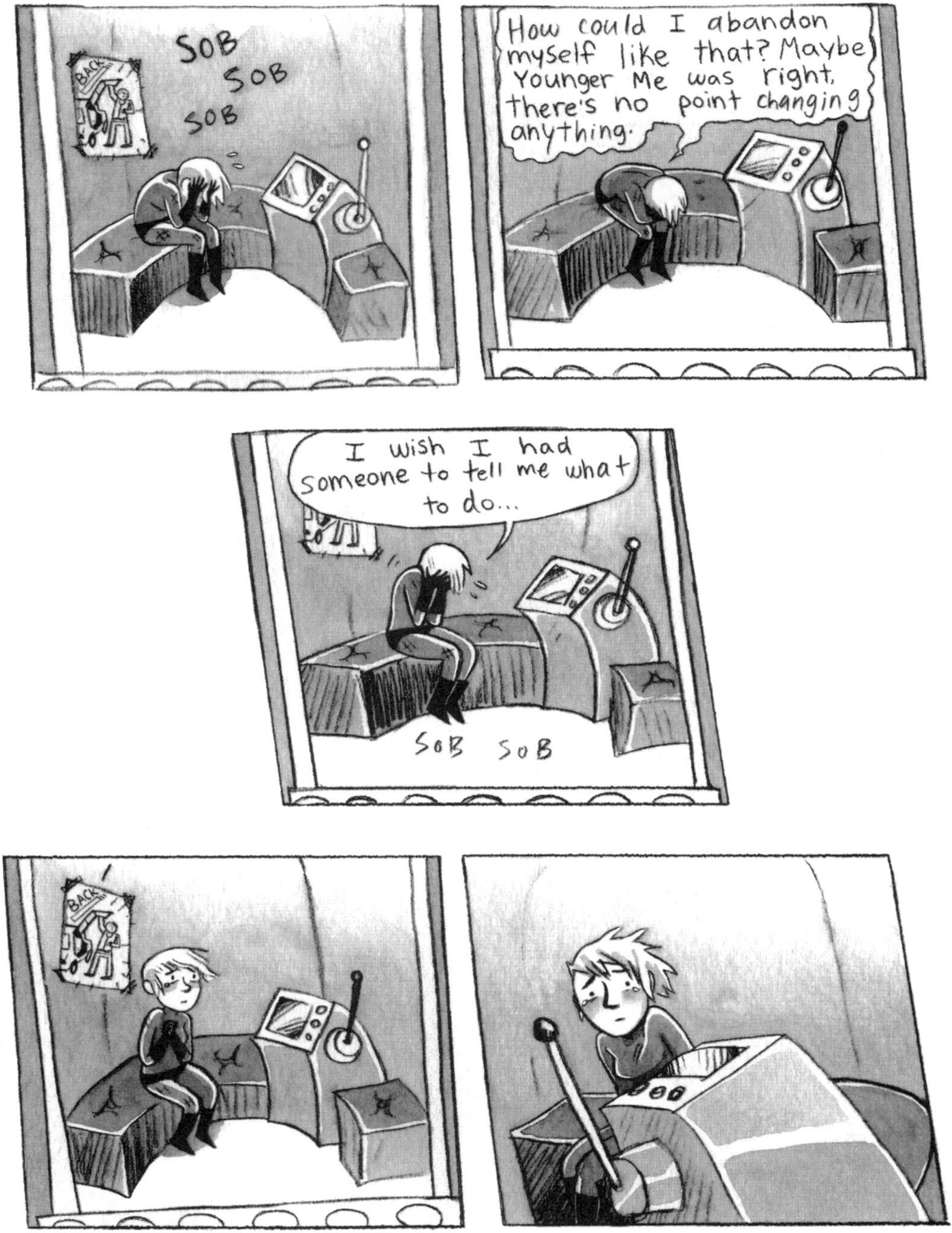
BACK
SOB SOB SOB
How could I abandon myself like that? Maybe Younger Me was right, there's no point changing anything.
I wish I had someone to tell me what to do...
SOB SOB
BACK

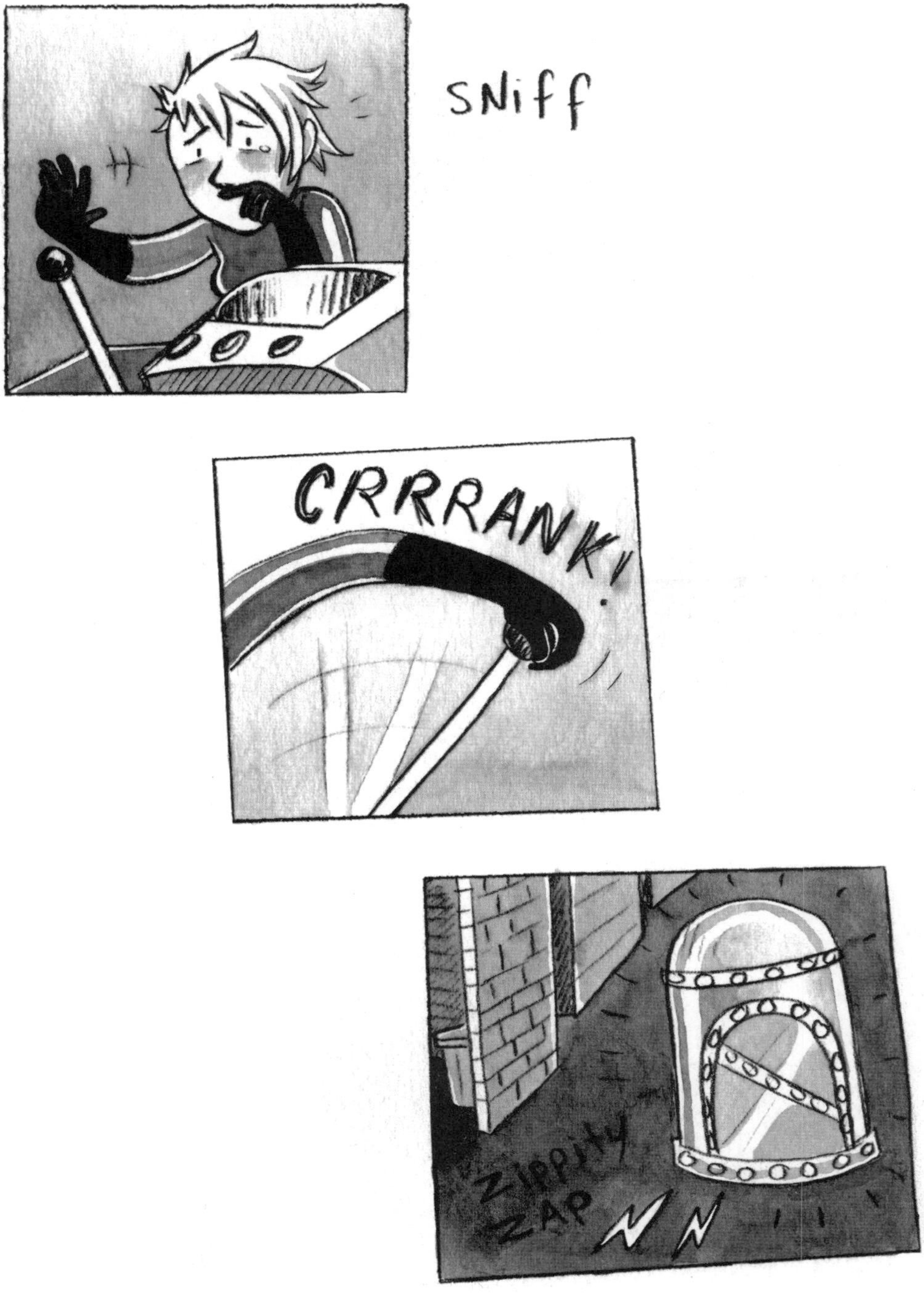
SNiff
CRRRANK!
ZiPPiTY
ZAP

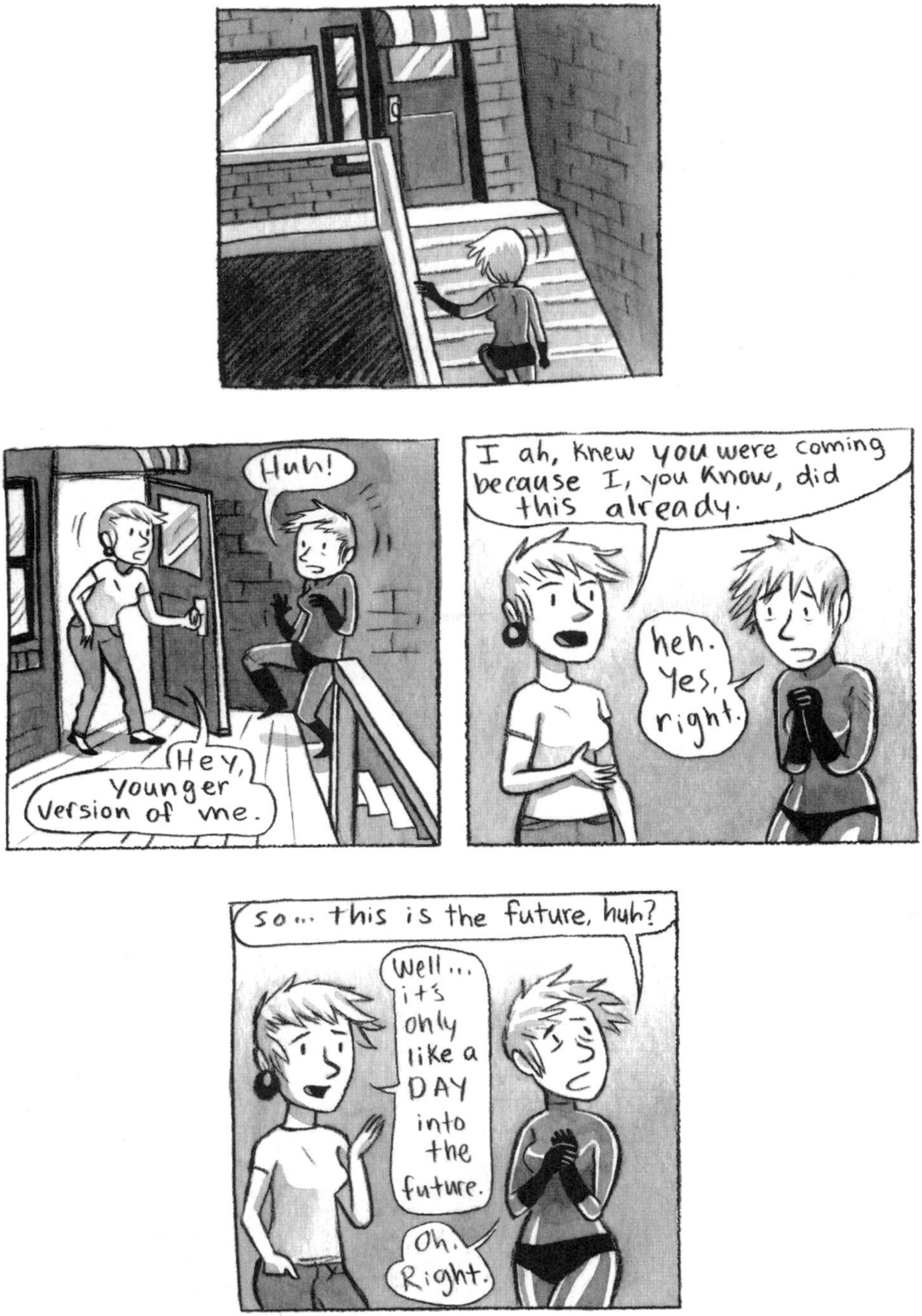
Huh!
Hey, younger version of me.
I ah, knew you were coming because I, you know, did this already.
heh. Yes, right.
so... this is the future, huh?
Well... it's only like a DAY into the future.
Oh. Right.

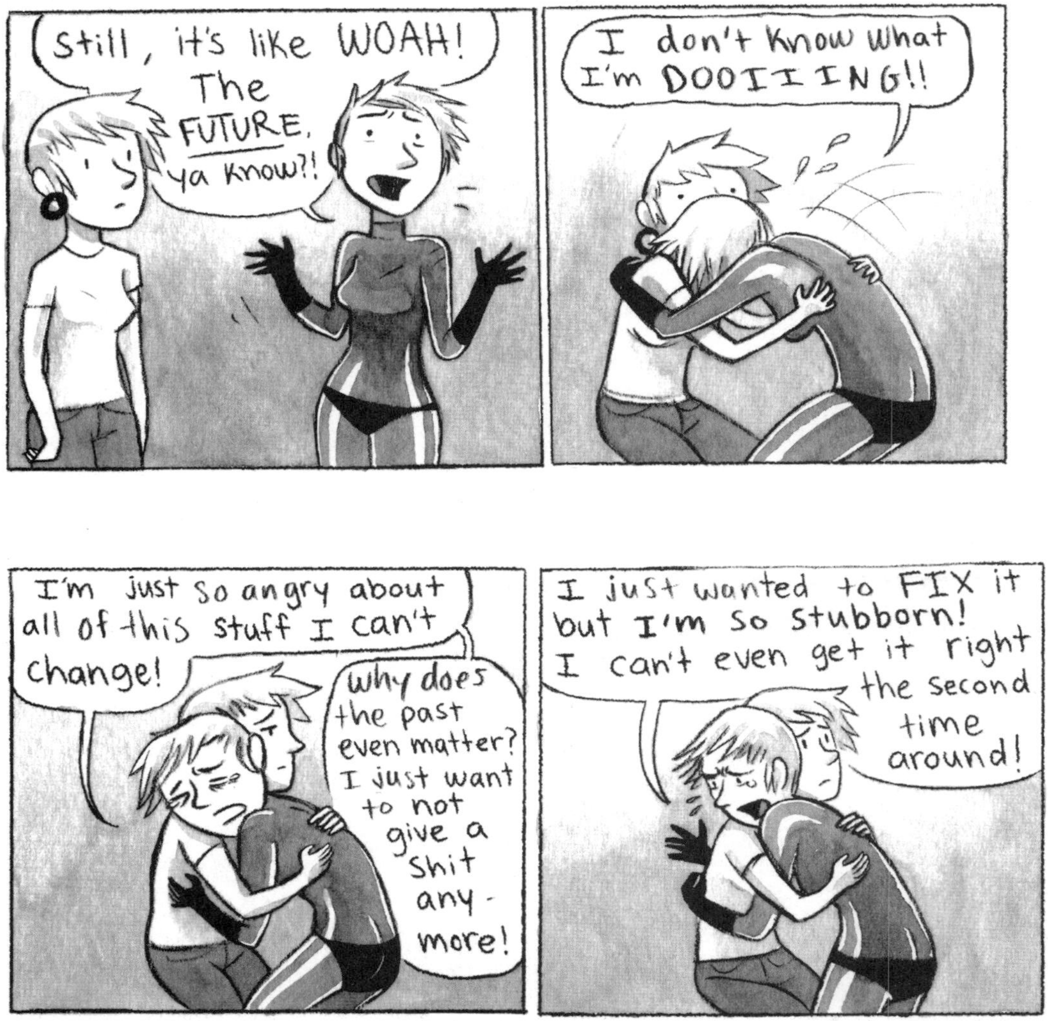
Still, it's like WOAH! The FUTURE, ya know?!
I don't know what I'm DOOIIING!!
I'm just so angry about all of this stuff I can't change!
why does the past even matter? I just want to not give a shit any-more!
I just wanted to FIX it but I'm so stubborn! I can't even get it right the second time around!

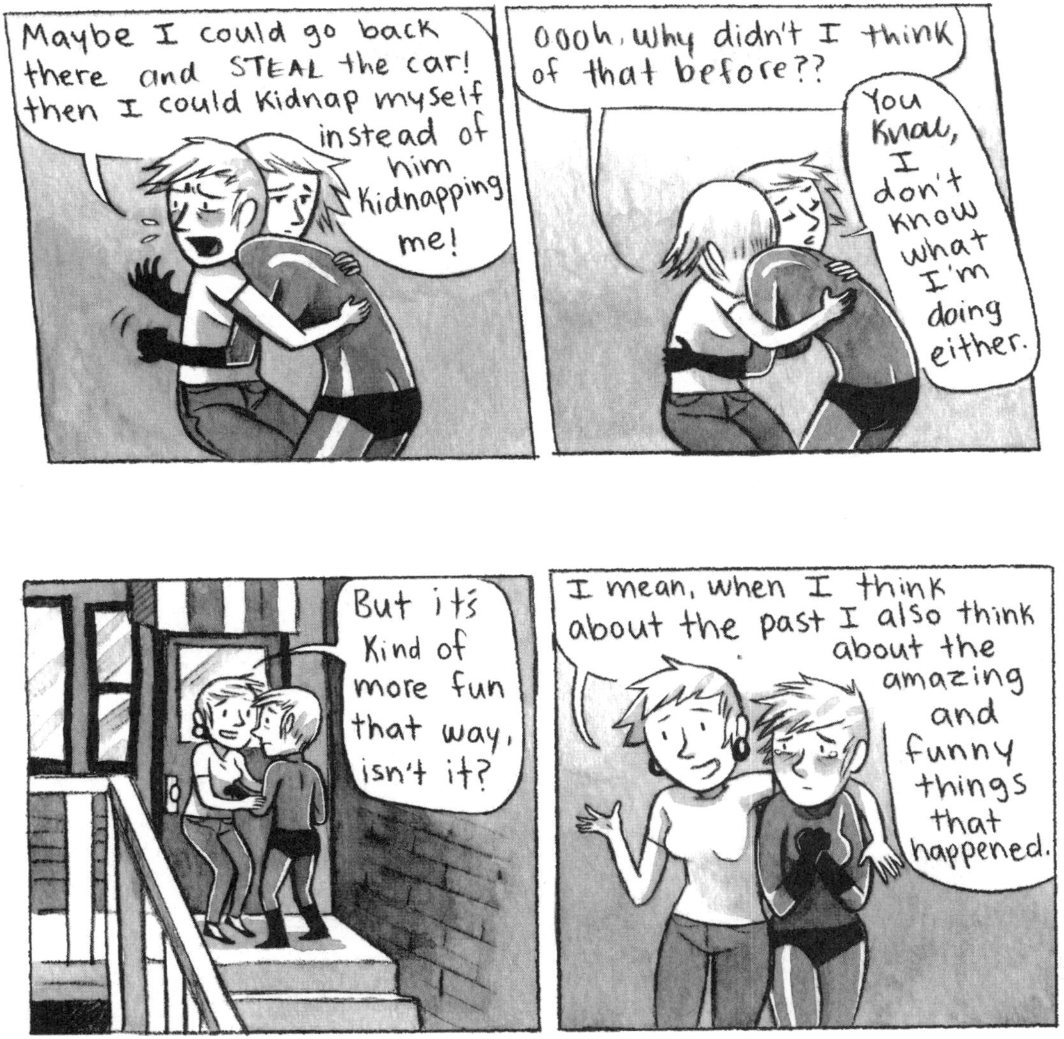
Maybe I could go back there and STEAL the car! then I could Kidnap myself instead of him Kidnapping me!
Oooh, why didn't I think of that before??
You Know, I don't Know what I'm doing either.
But it's Kind of more fun that way, isn't it?
I mean, when I think about the past I also think about the amazing and funny things that happened.

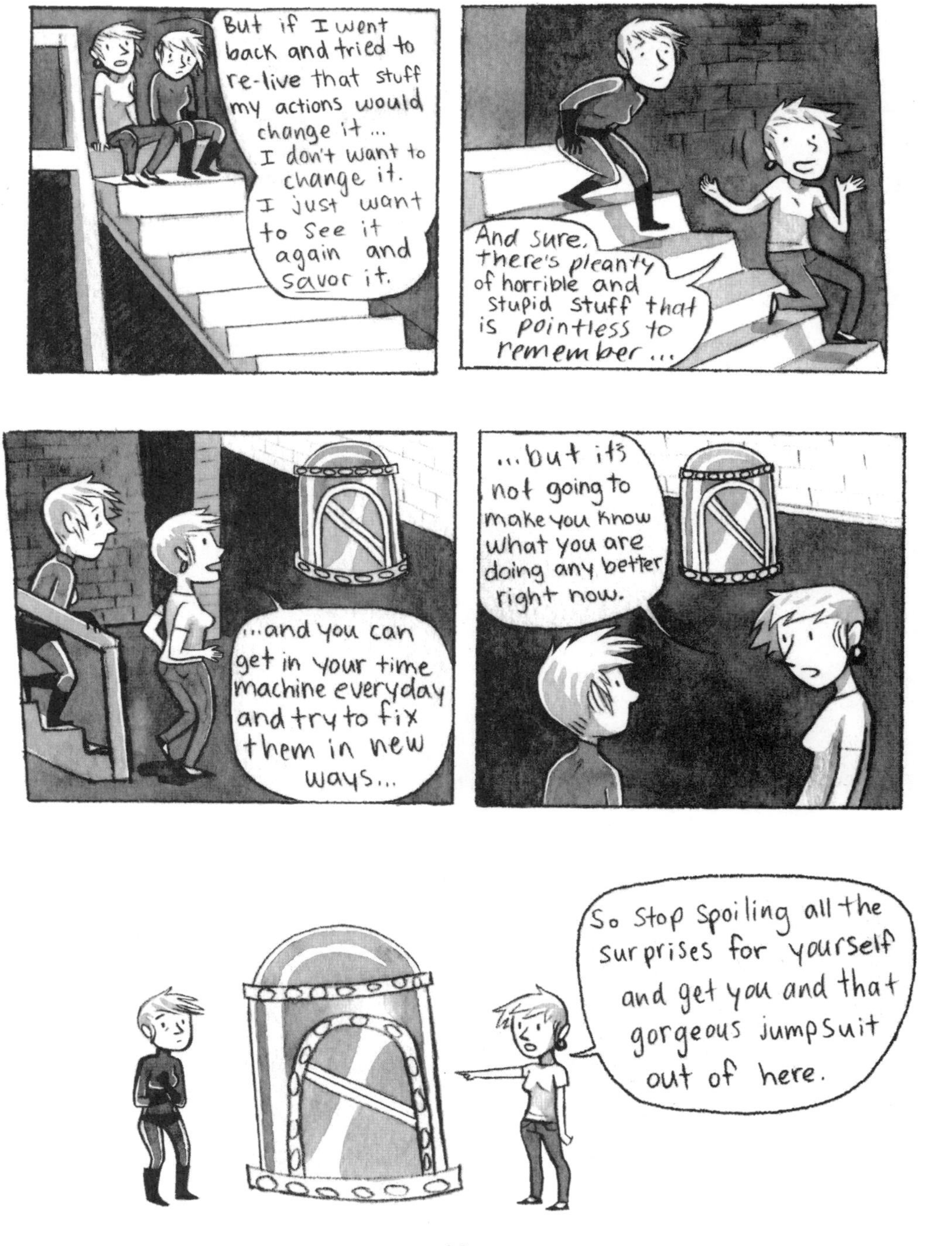
But if I went back and tried to re-live that stuff my actions would change it... I don't want to change it. I just want to see it again and savor it.
And sure, there's pleanty of horrible and stupid stuff that is pointless to remember...
...and you can get in your time machine everyday and try to fix them in new ways...
...but it's not going to make you know what you are doing any better right now.
So stop spoiling all the surprises for yourself and get you and that gorgeous jumpsuit out of here.

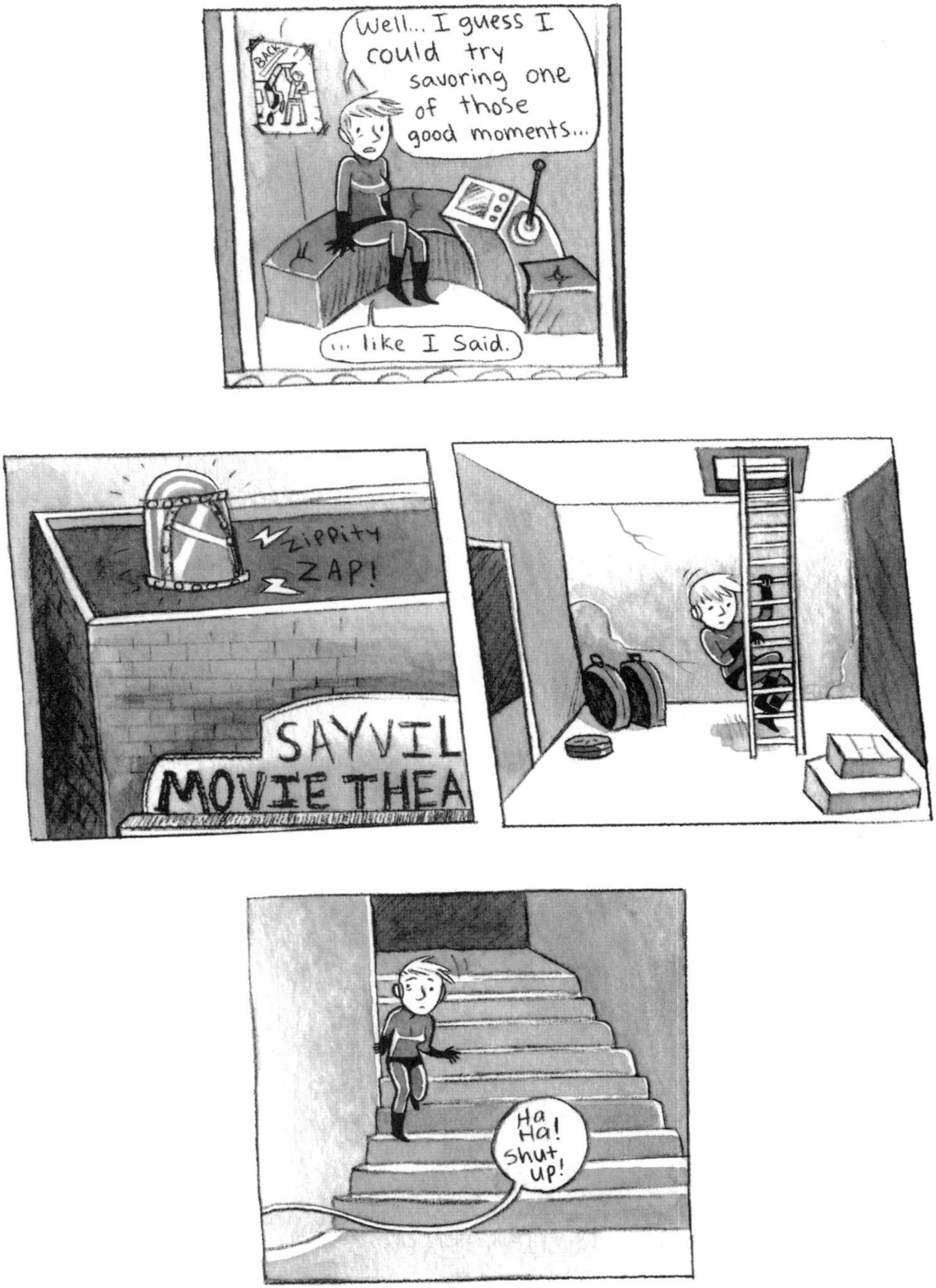
BACK
Well... I guess I could try savoring one of those good moments...
... like I Said.
Zippity ZAP!
SAYVIL
MOVIE THEA
Ha Ha! shut up!

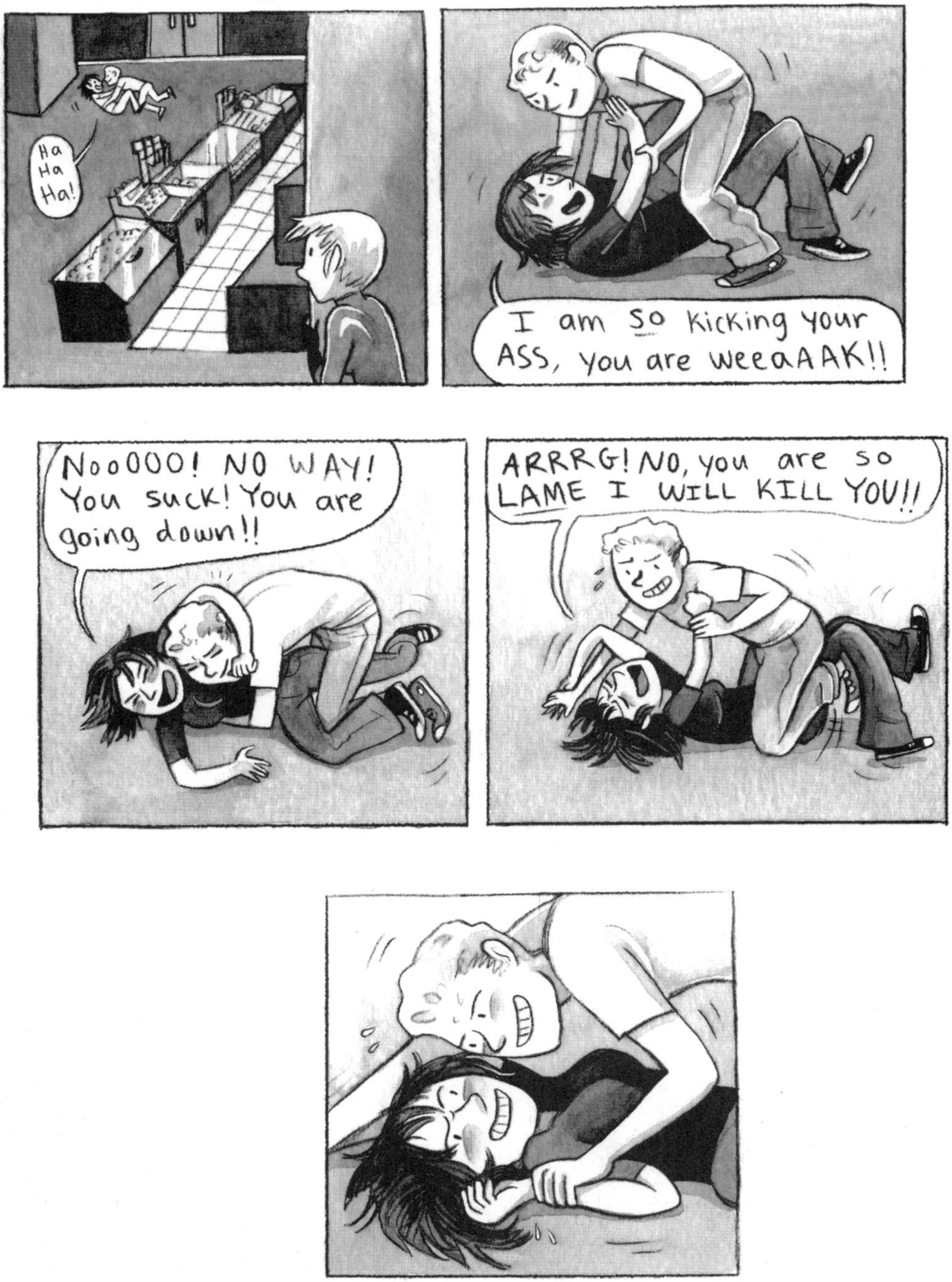
Ha Ha Ha!
I am SO Kicking your ASS, you are weeaAAK!!
NooOOO! NO WAY! You suck! You are going down!!
ARRRG! NO, you are so LAME I WILL KILL YOU!!

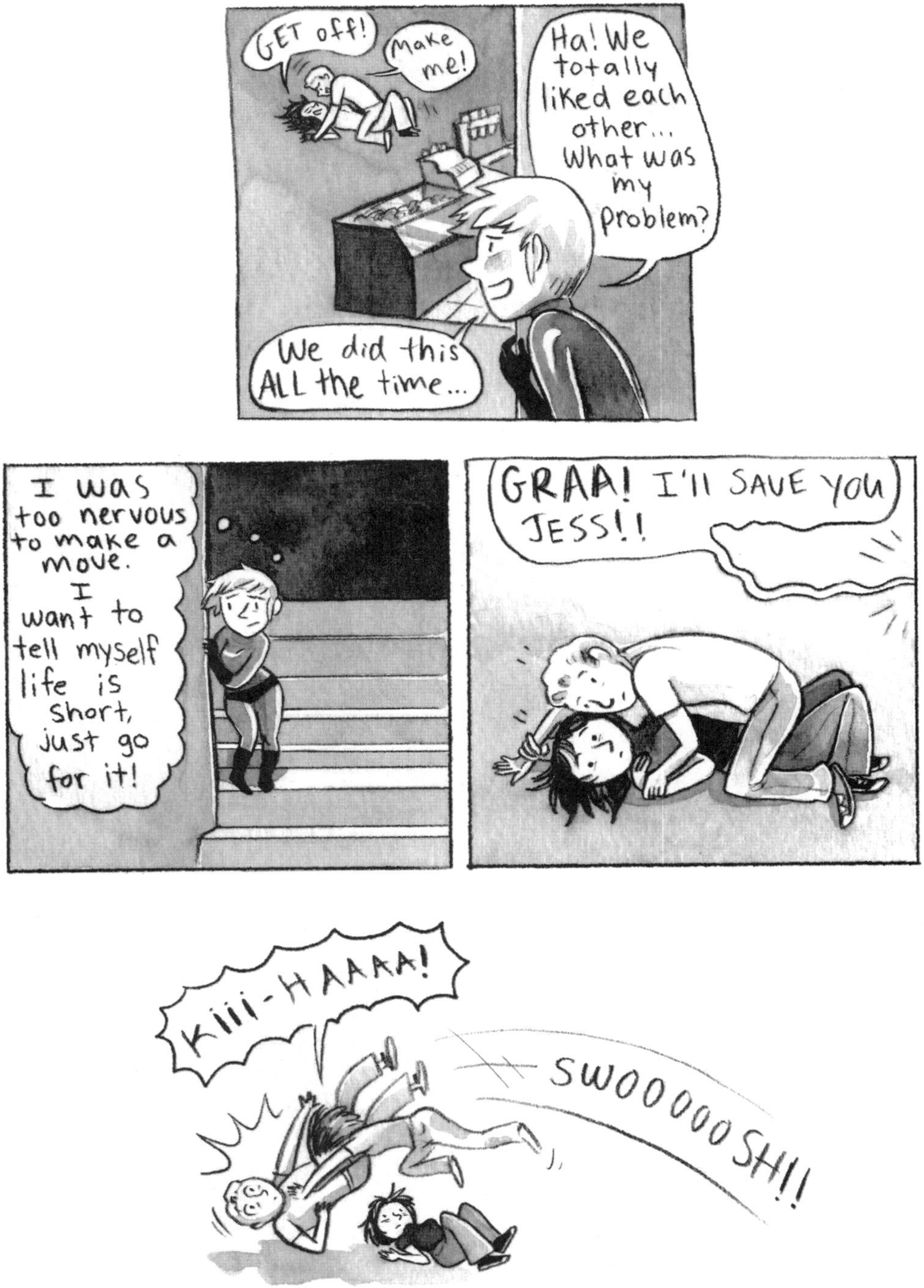
GET off!
Make me!
Ha! We totally liked each other... What was my problem?
We did this ALL the time...
I was too nervous to make a move. I want to tell myself life is short, just go for it!
GRAA! I'll SAVE YOU JESS!!
KIII-HAAAA!
SWOOOOOOSH!!

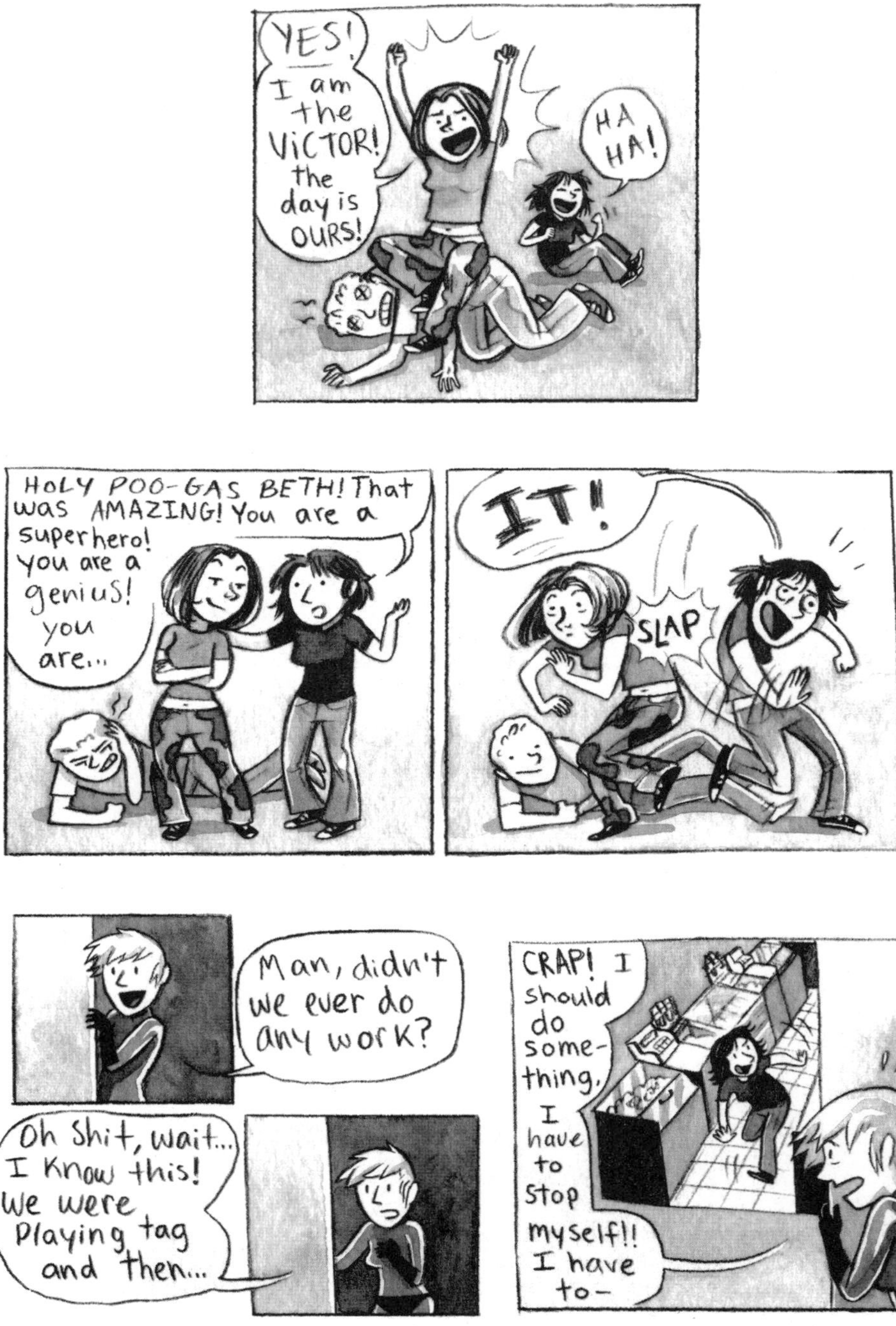
YES!
I am the VICTOR! the day is OURS!
HA HA!
HOLY POO-GAS BETH! That was AMAZING! You are a superhero! You are a genius! you are...
IT!
SLAP
Man, didn't we ever do any work?
Oh Shit, wait... I Know this! We were Playing tag and then...
CRAP! I should do some-thing, I have to stop myself!! I have to—

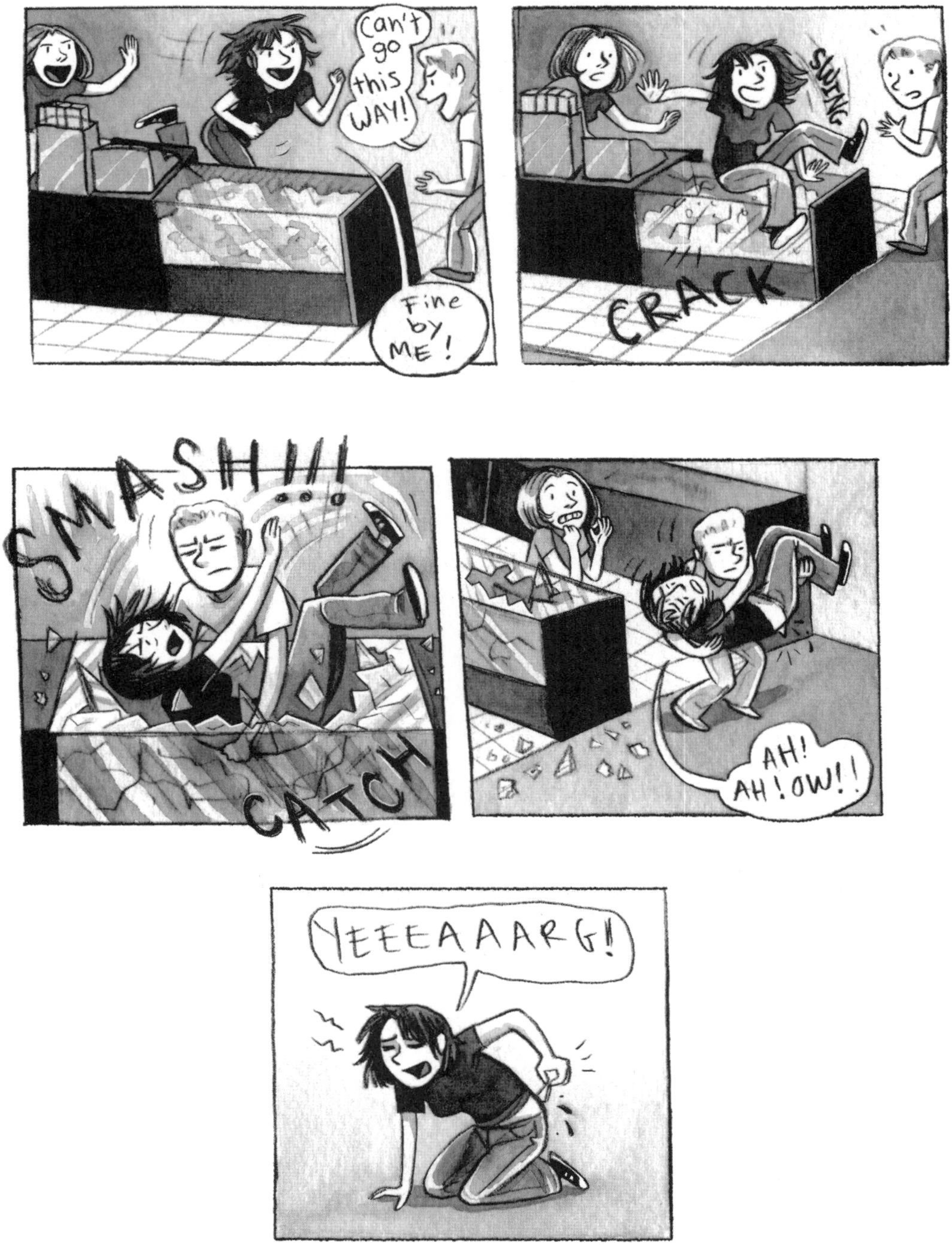
Can't go this WAY!
Fine by ME!
SWING
CRACK
SMASH!!!!
CATCH
AH! AH! OW!!
YEEEAAARG!

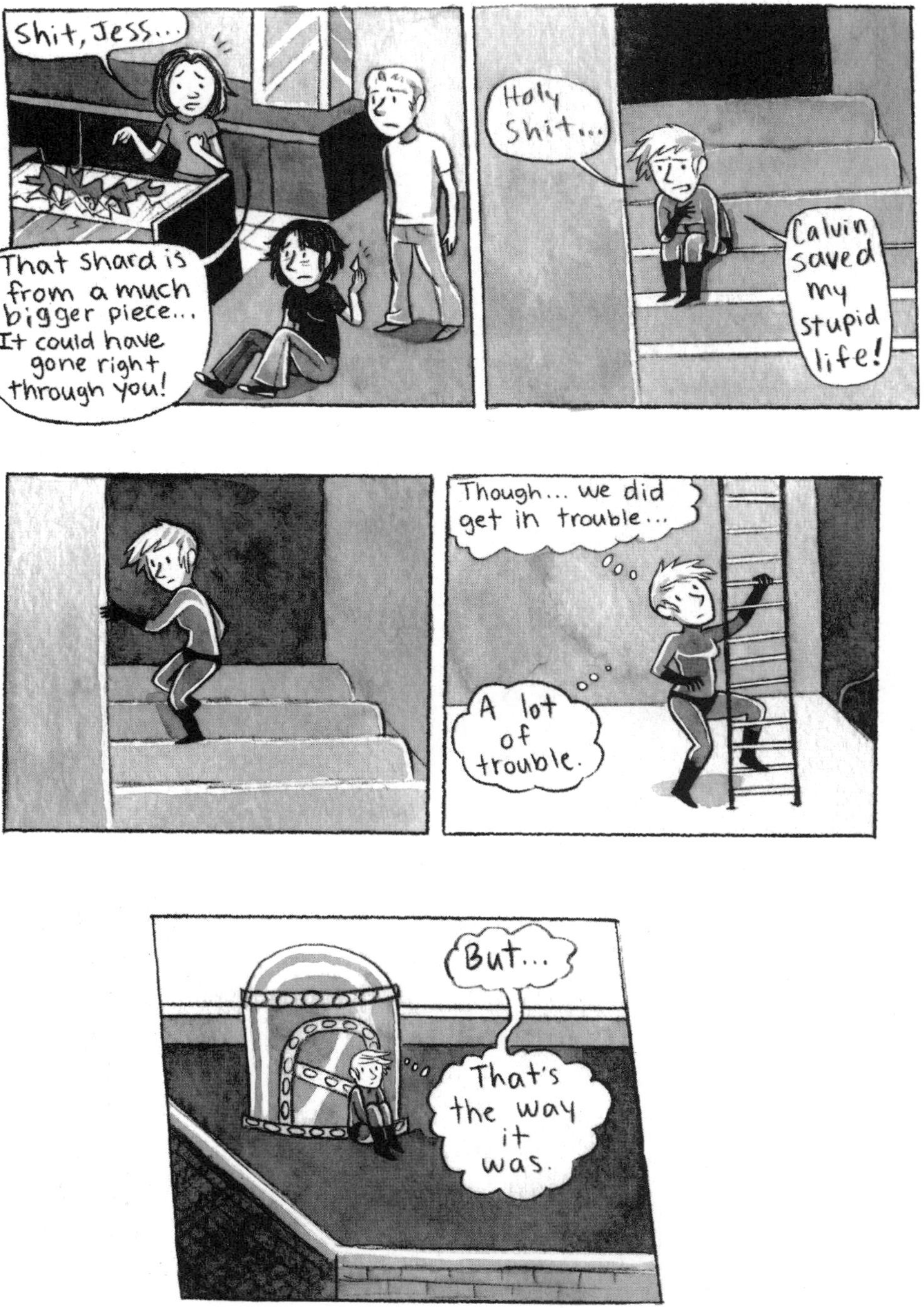

Shit, Jess...
That shard is from a much bigger piece... It could have gone right through you!
Holy Shit...
Calvin saved my stupid life!
Though... we did get in trouble...
A lot of trouble.
But...
That's the way it was.

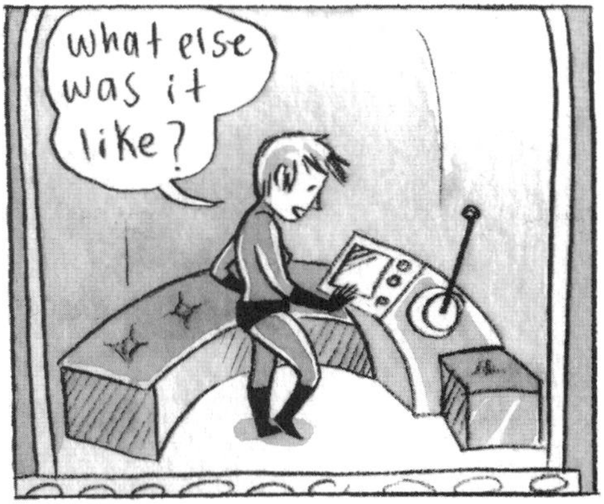
what else was it like?

Family Vacation 1991:

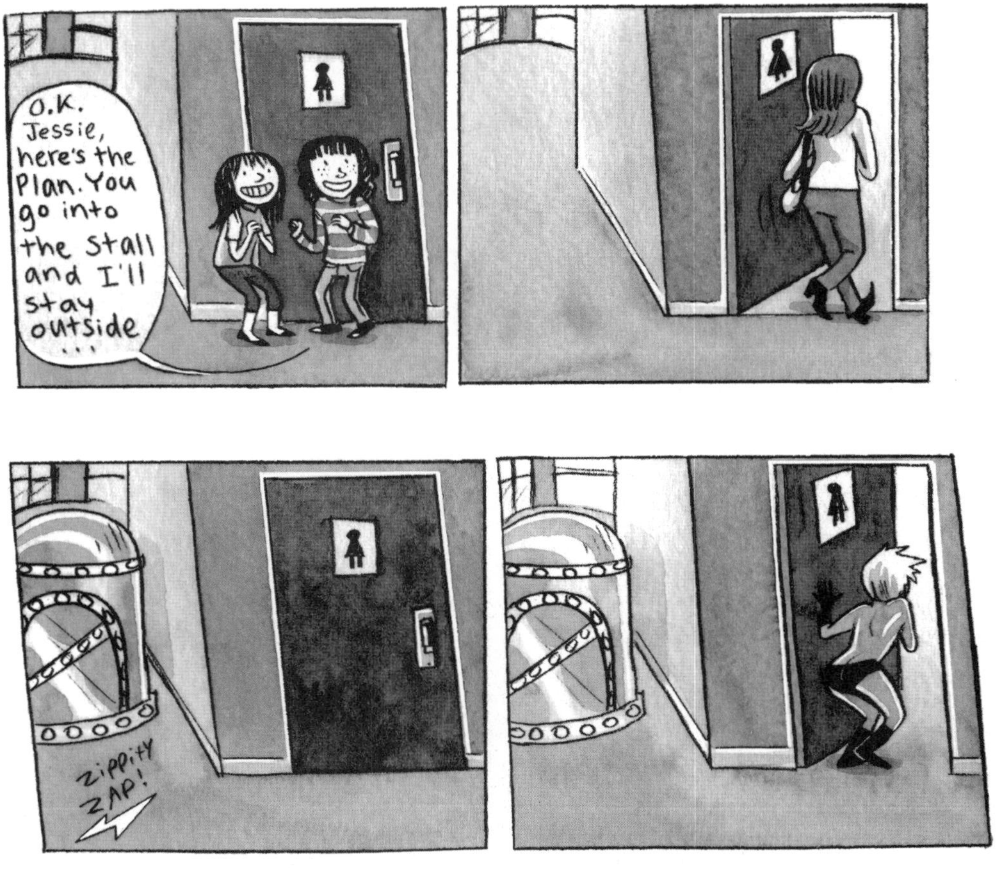
O.K. Jessie, here's the Plan. You go into the stall and I'll stay outside ...
zippity ZAP!

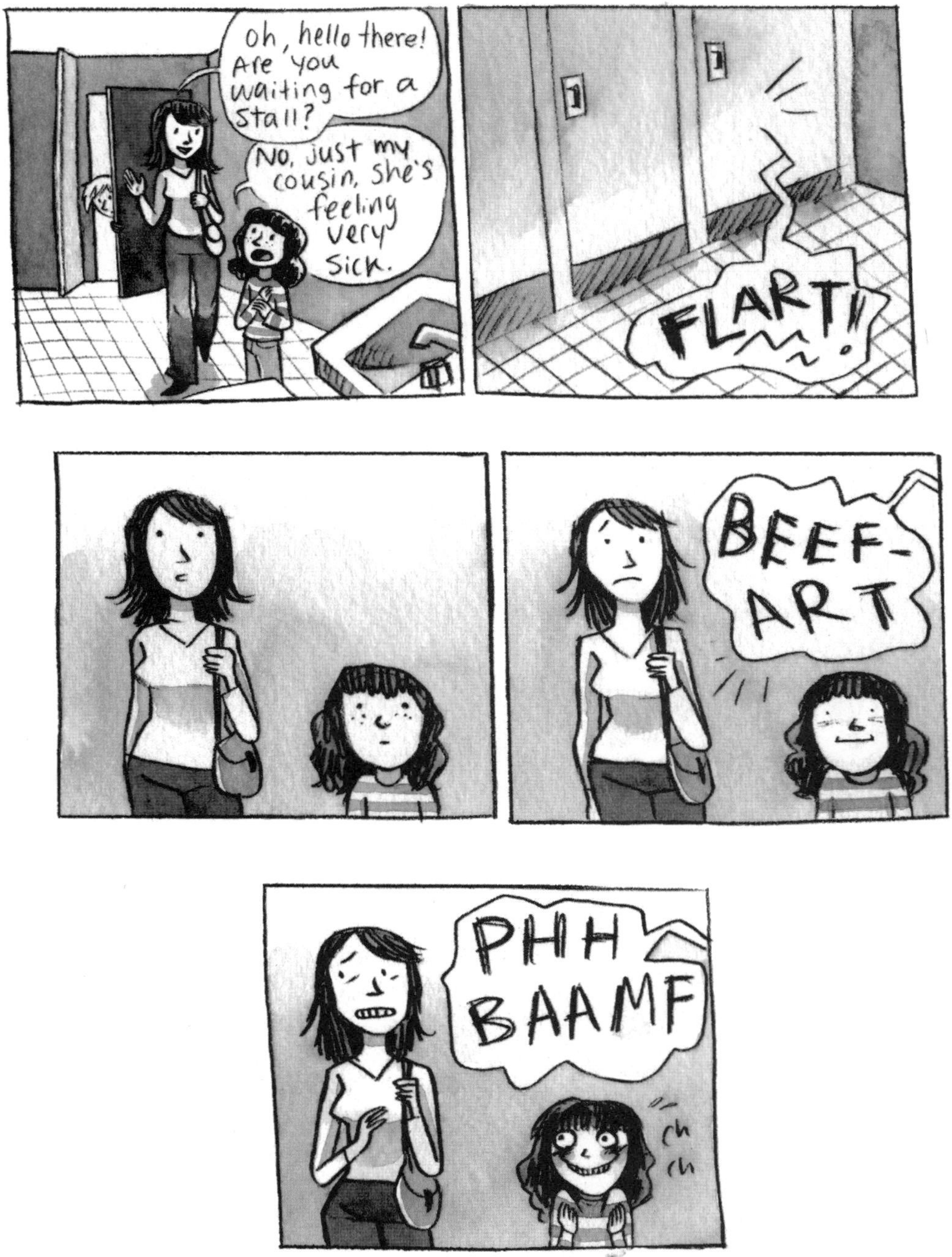
oh, hello there! Are you waiting for a stall?
No, just my cousin, she's feeling very sick.
FLART!!
BEEF-ART
PHH BAAMF
ch ch

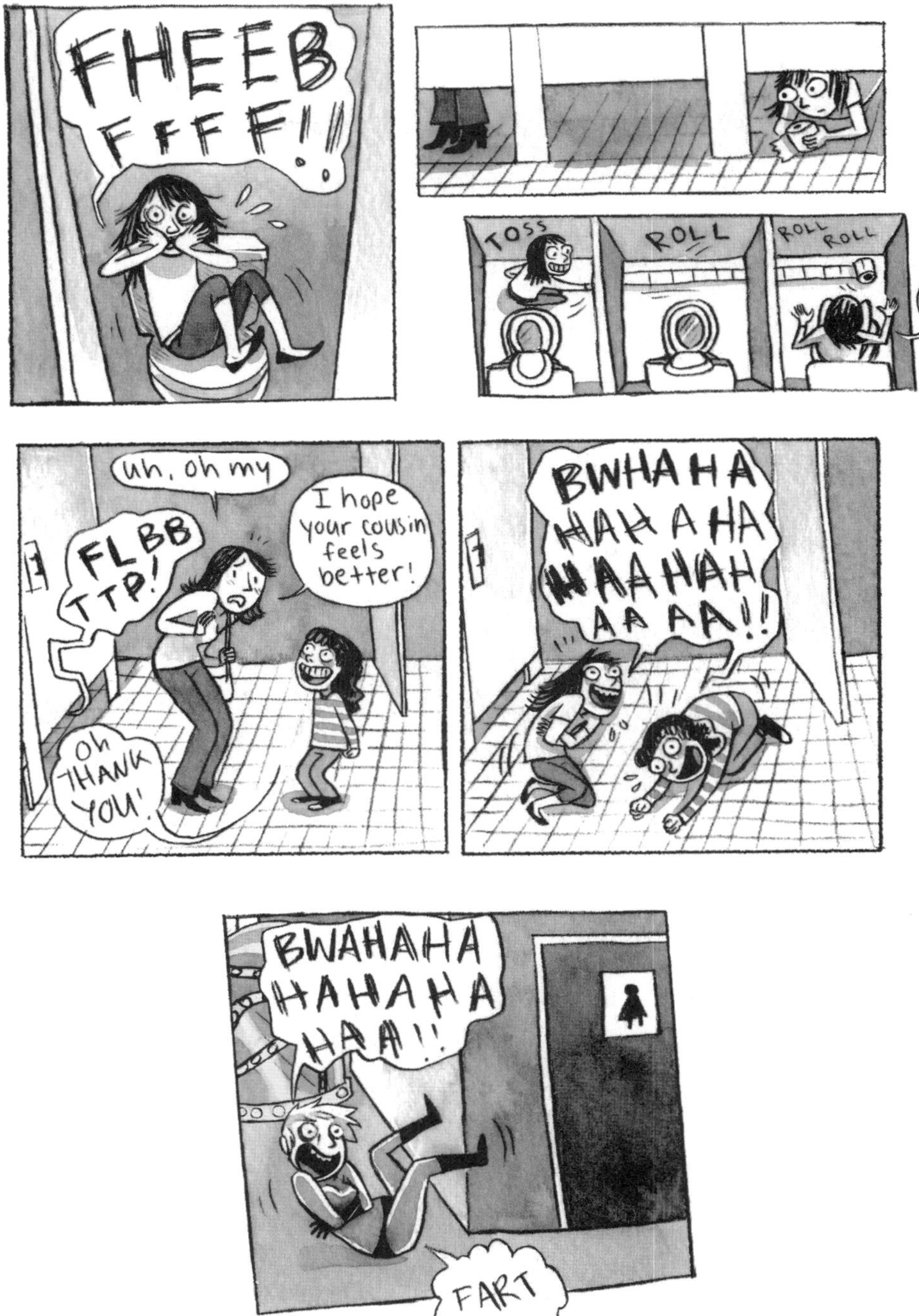
FHEEB FFFF!
TOSS
ROLL
ROLL ROLL
OH!
uh, oh my
FLBB TTP!
I hope your cousin feels better!
Oh THANK YOU!
BWHAHA HAHAHA HAAHAH AAAA!!
BWAHAHA HAHAHA HAA!!
FART

High School - 12th grade

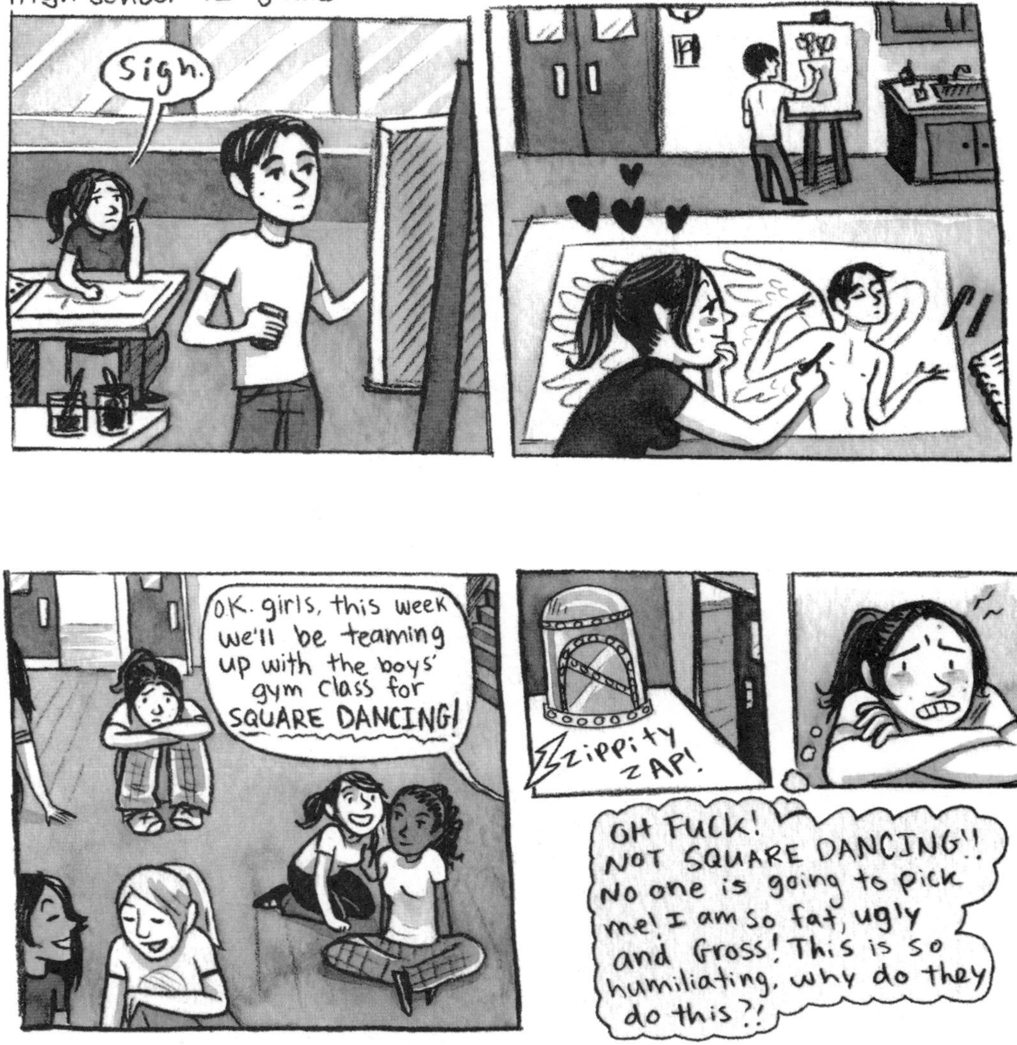

Sigh.
OK. girls, this week we'll be teaming up with the boys' gym class for SQUARE DANCING!
zippity ZAP!
OH FUCK! NOT SQUARE DANCING!! No one is going to pick me! I am so fat, ugly and Gross! This is so humiliating. why do they do this?!

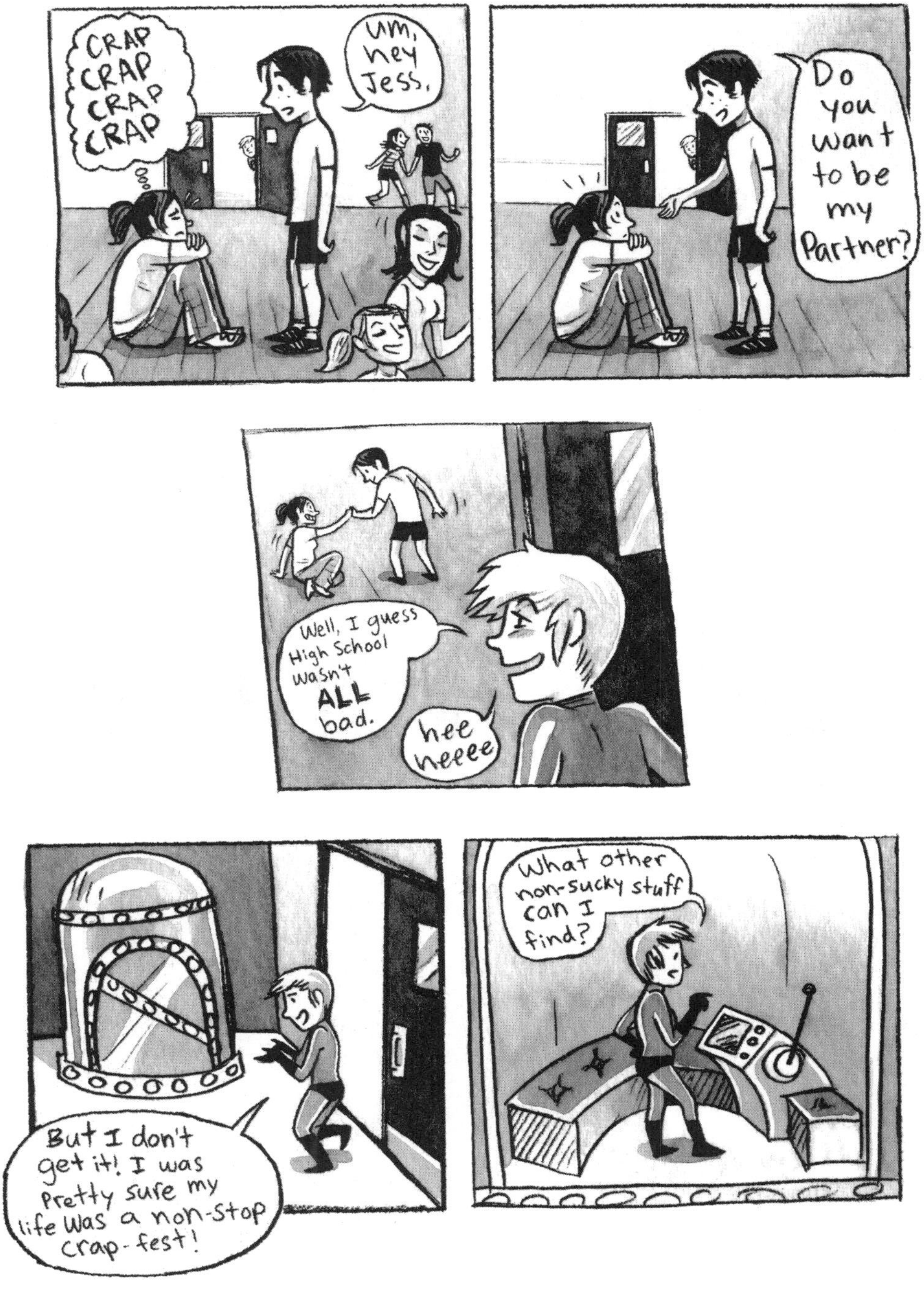
CRAP CRAP CRAP CRAP
Um, hey Jess,
Do you want to be my Partner?
Well, I guess High School wasn't ALL bad.
hee heeee
But I don't get it! I was Pretty sure my life was a non-stop crap-fest!
What other non-sucky stuff can I find?

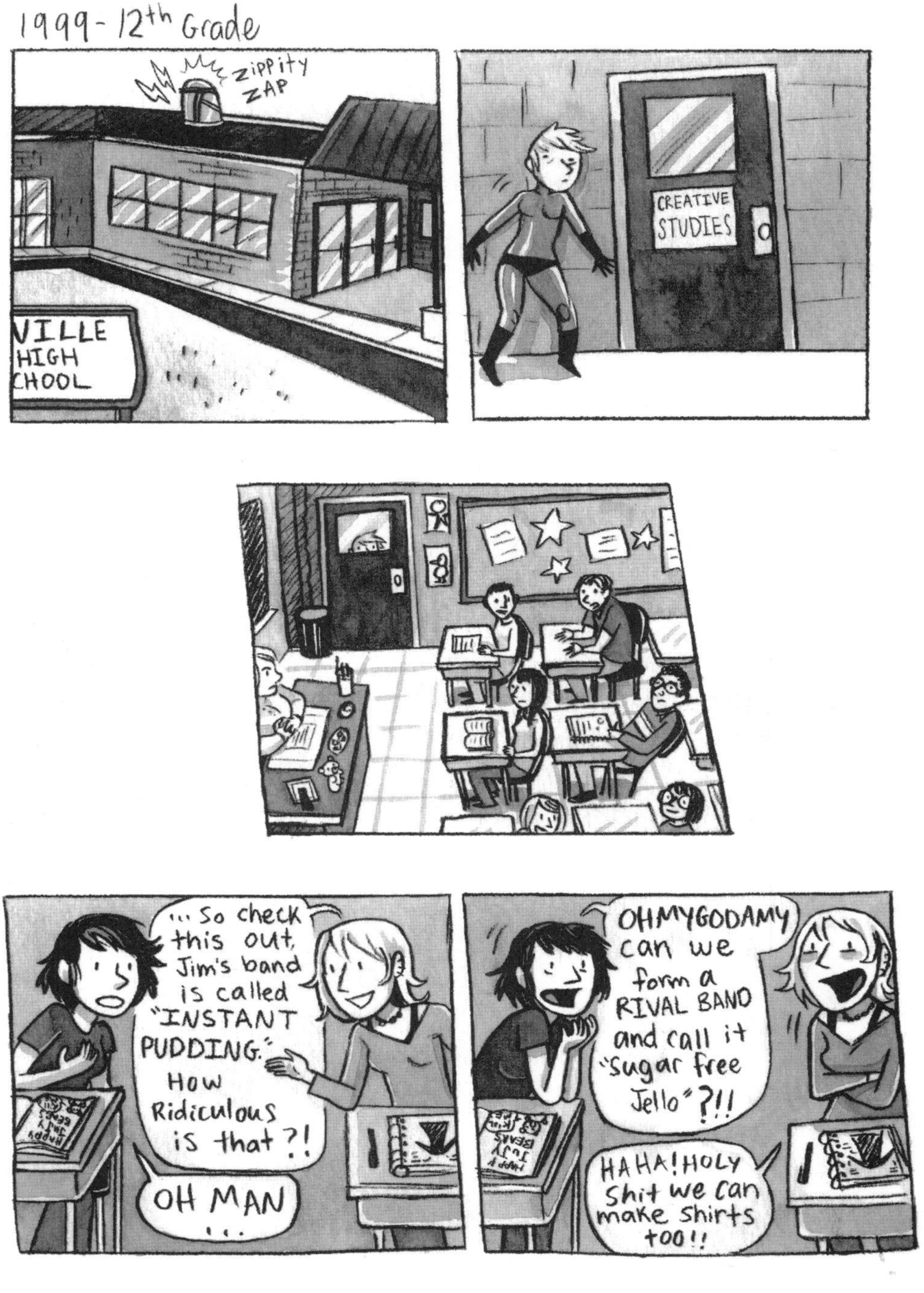
1999 - 12th Grade
ZIPPITY ZAP
VILLE
HIGH
CHOOL
CREATIVE
STUDIES
...So check this out, Jim's band is called "INSTANT PUDDING." How Ridiculous is that?!
OH MAN ...
OHMYGODAMY can we form a RIVAL BAND and call it "Sugar free Jello"?!!
HAHA! HOLY Shit we can make shirts too!!

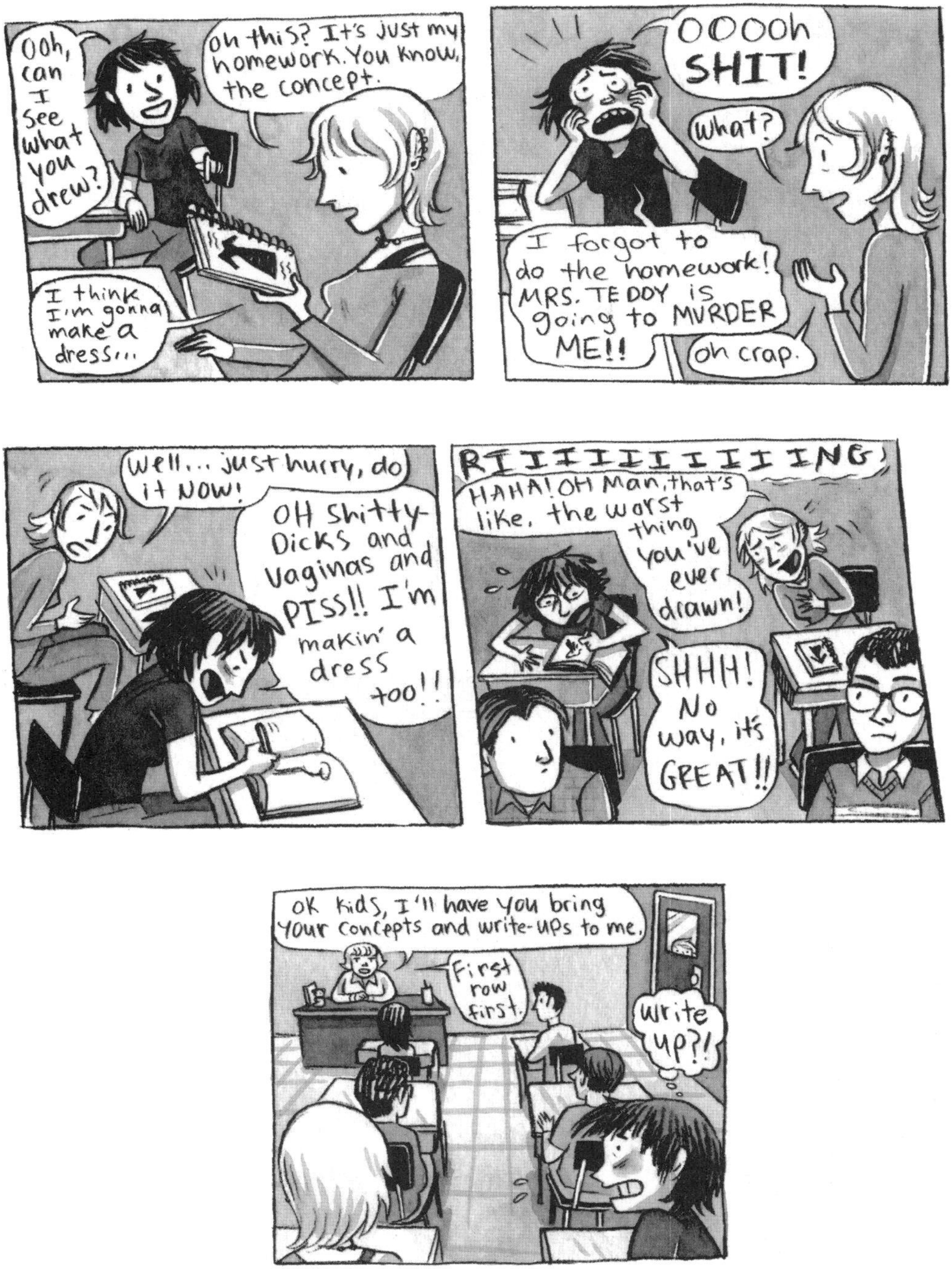
Ooh, can I see what you drew?
Oh this? It's just my homework. You know, the concept.
I think I'm gonna make a dress...
OOOOh SHIT!
What?
I forgot to do the homework! MRS. TEDDY is going to MURDER ME!!
Oh crap.
Well... just hurry, do it NOW!
OH Shitty-Dicks and Vaginas and PISS!! I'm makin' a dress too!!
RIIIIIIIIIING
HAHA! OH Man, that's like, the worst thing you've ever drawn!
SHHH! No way, it's GREAT!!
OK kids, I'll have you bring your concepts and write-ups to me.
First row first.
Write up?!

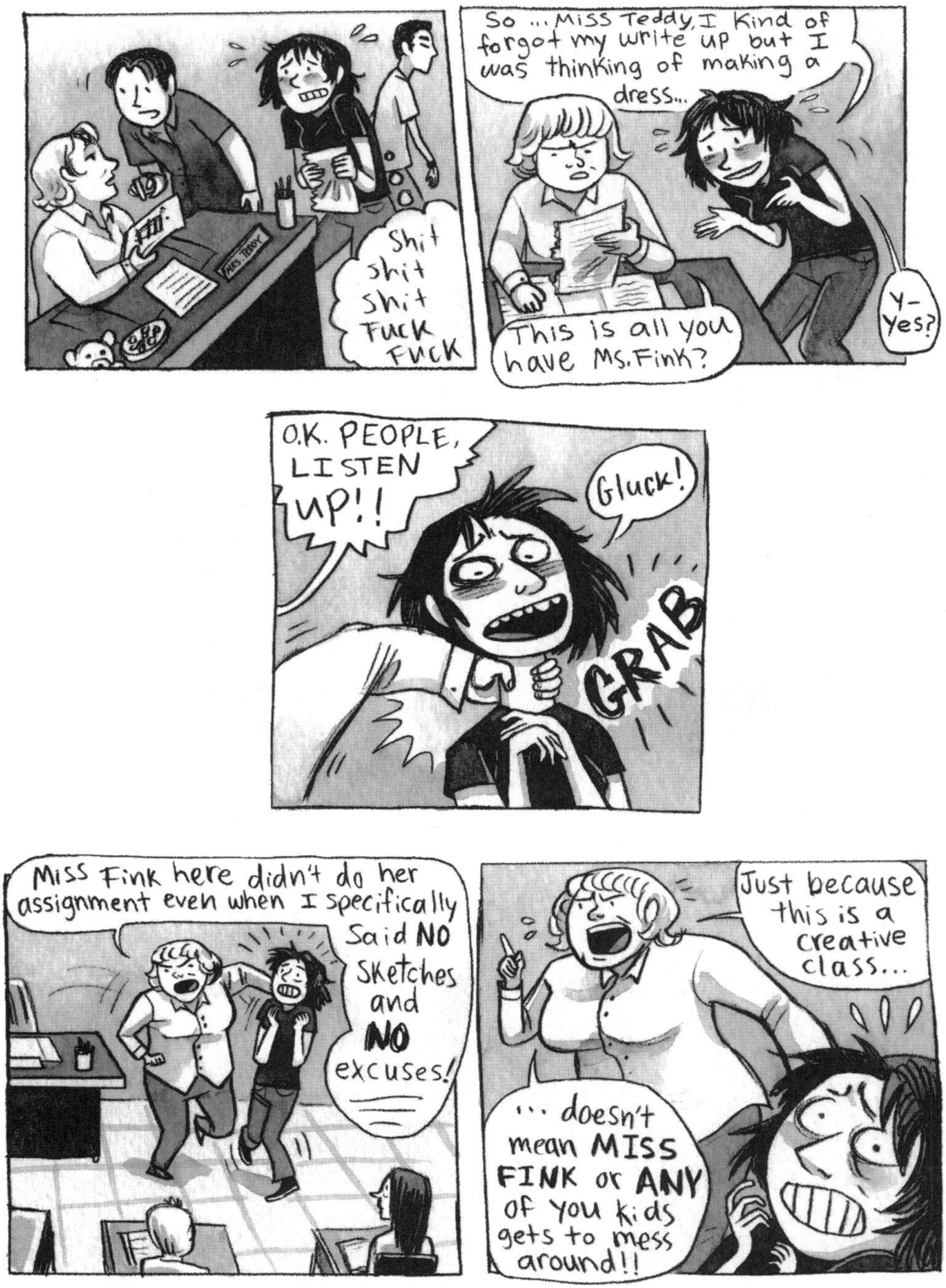
MRS. TEDDY
Shit shit Shit Fuck Fuck
So ... MISS Teddy, I Kind of forgot my write up but I was thinking of making a dress...
This is all you have Ms. Fink?
Y- Yes?
O.K. PEOPLE, LISTEN UP!!
Gluck!
GRAB
Miss Fink here didn't do her assignment even when I specifically Said NO Sketches and NO excuses!
Just because this is a creative class...
... doesn't mean MISS FINK or ANY of you kids gets to mess around!!

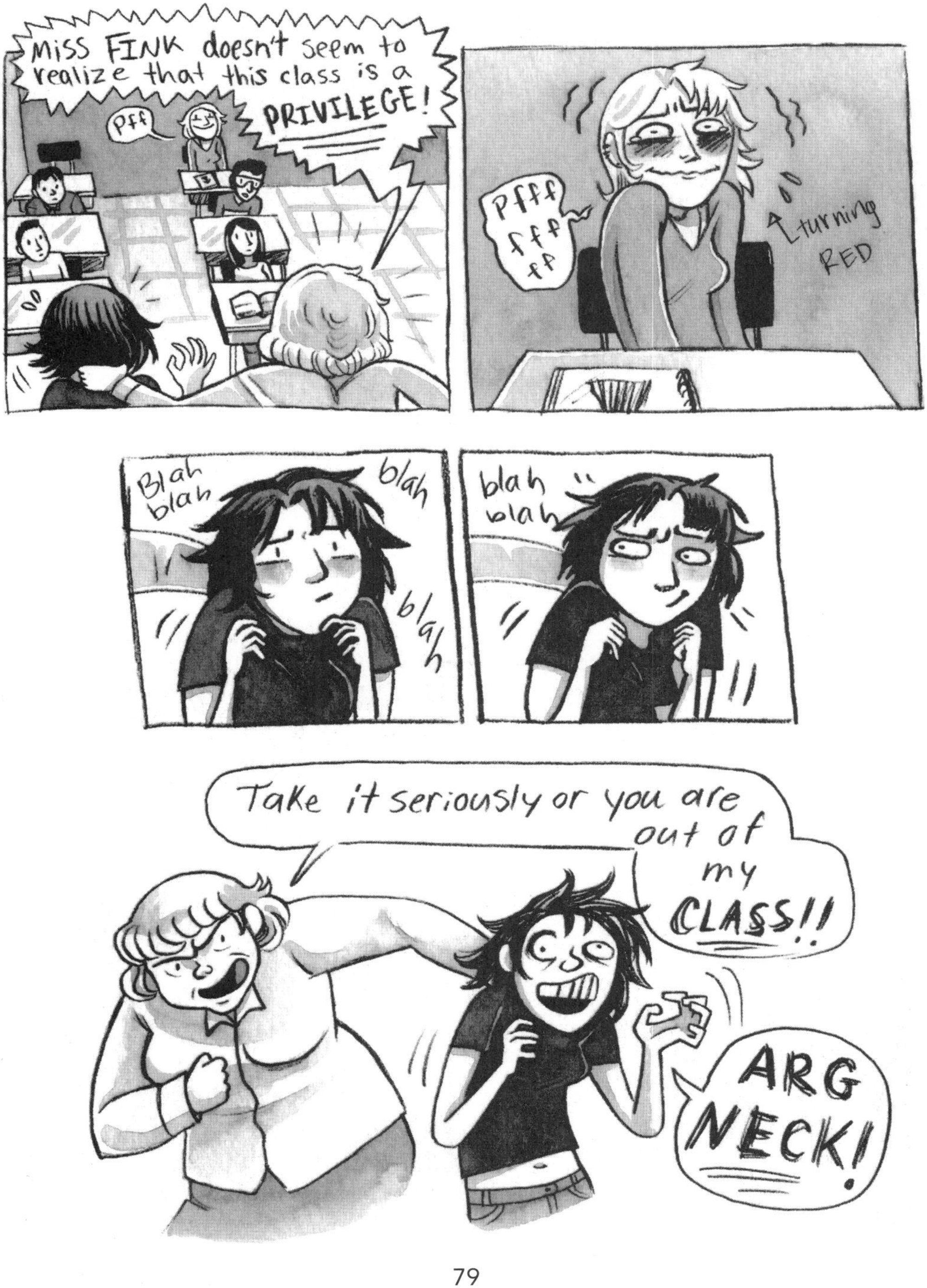
Miss FINK doesn't seem to realize that this class is a PRIVILEGE!
Pff
Pfff fff ff
turning RED
Blah blah
blah
blah
blah blah
Take it seriously or you are out of my CLASS!!
ARG NECK!

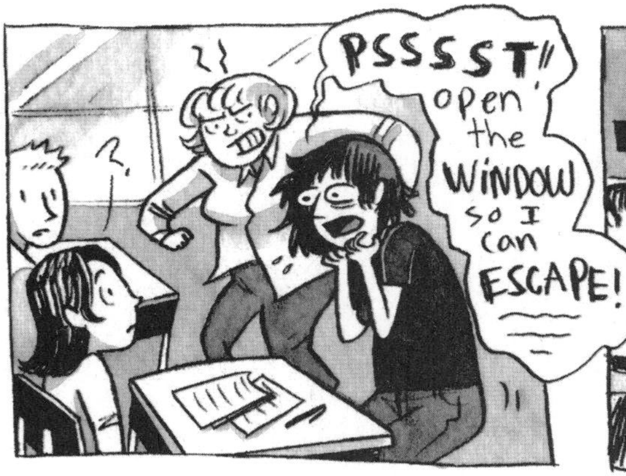
PSSSST!! open the WINDOW so I can ESCAPE!

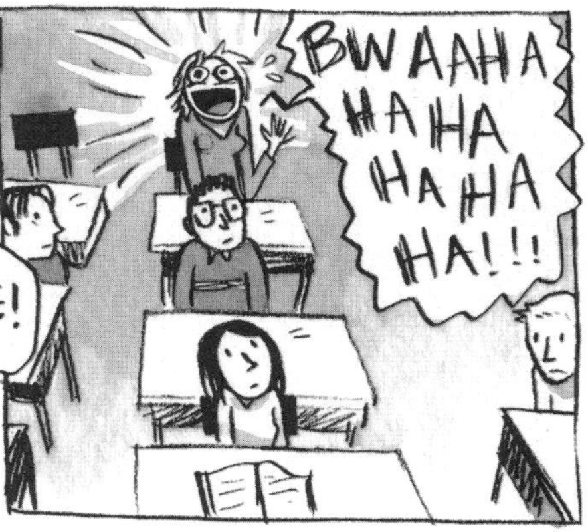
BWAAHA HAHA HAHA HA!!!

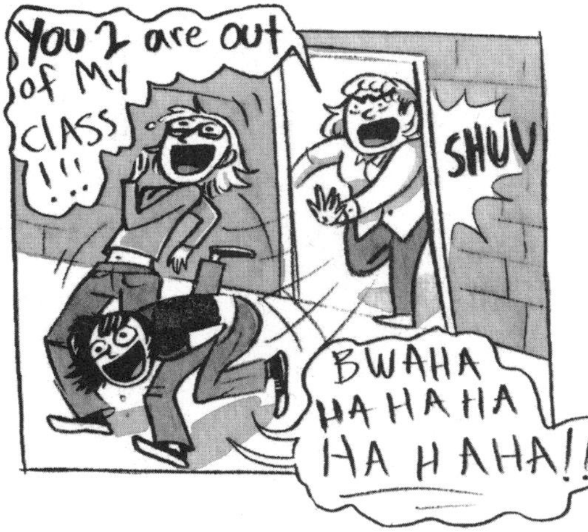
You 2 are out of My CLASS !!!
SHUV
BWAHA HAHAHA HA HAHA!!

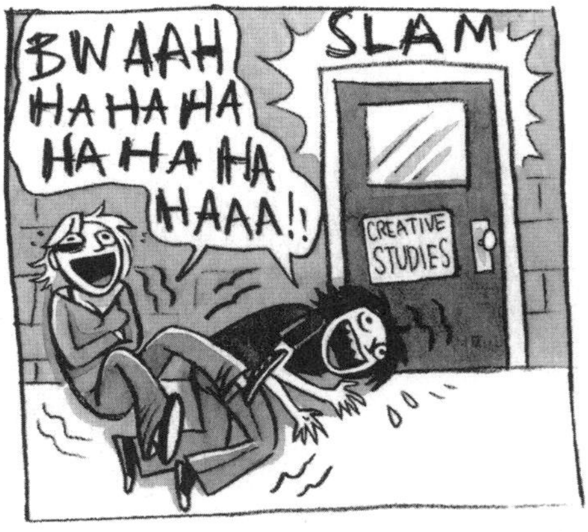
BWAAH HAHAHA HAHAHA HAAA!!
SLAM
CREATIVE STUDIES

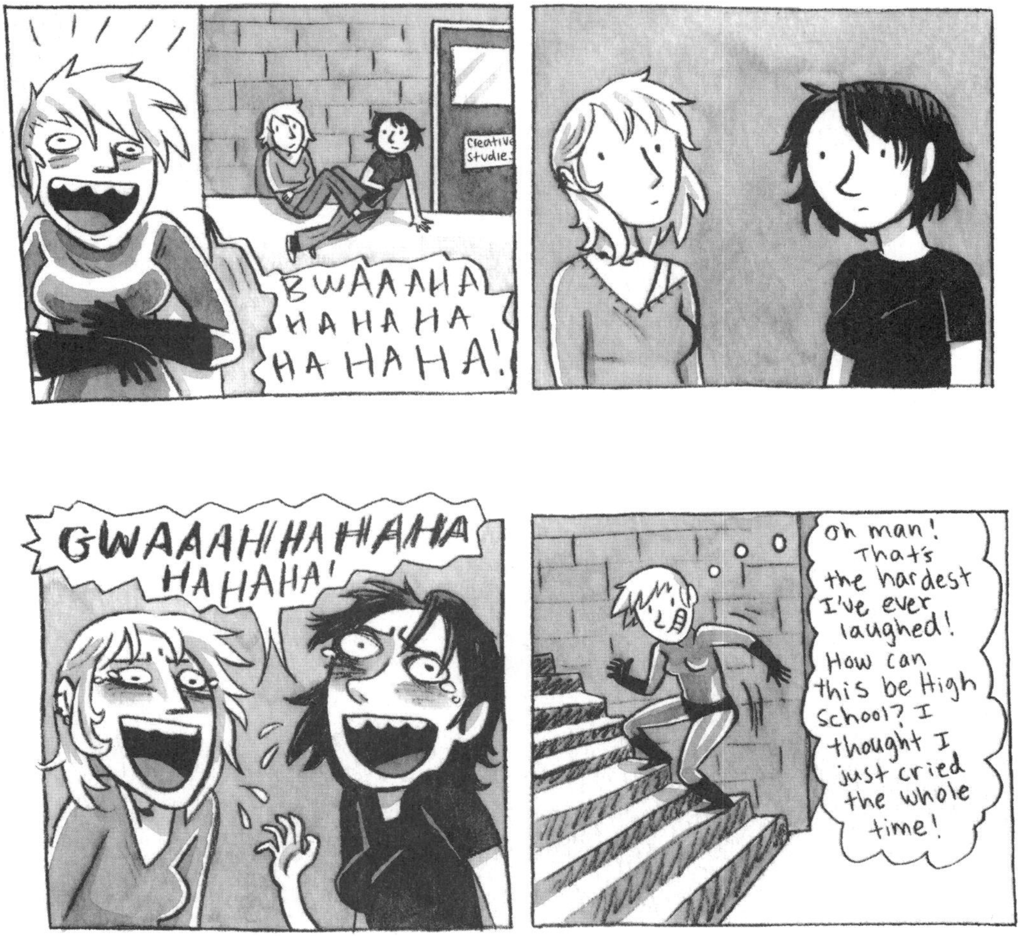
BWAAAHA HAHAHA HAHAHA!
GWAAAHHAHAHAHA HAHAHA!
Oh man! That's the hardest I've ever laughed! How can this be High School? I thought I just cried the whole time!

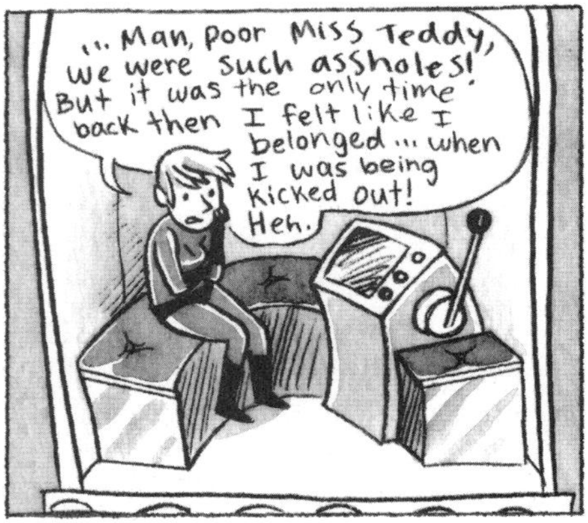
... Man, poor Miss Teddy, we were such assholes! But it was the only time back then I felt like I belonged ... when I was being kicked out! Heh.

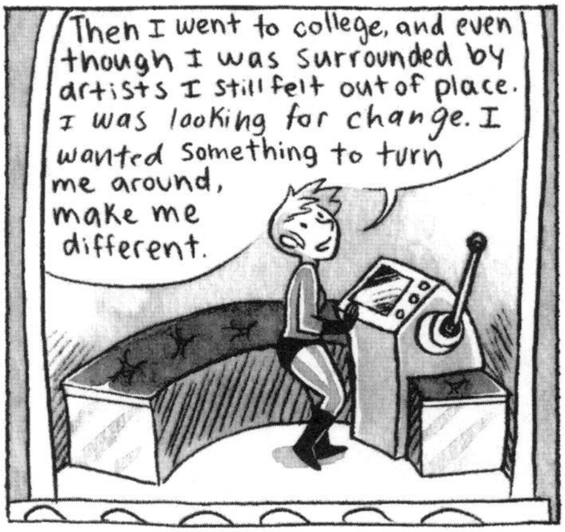
Then I went to college, and even though I was surrounded by artists I still felt out of place. I was looking for change. I wanted something to turn me around, make me different.

School of Visual Arts, NYC, 2001

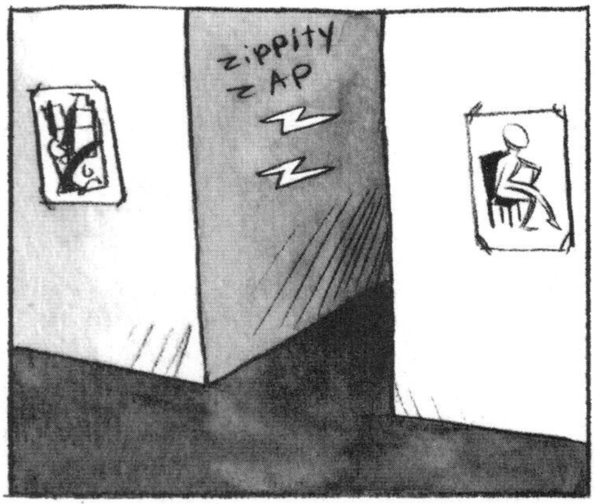
zippity zAP

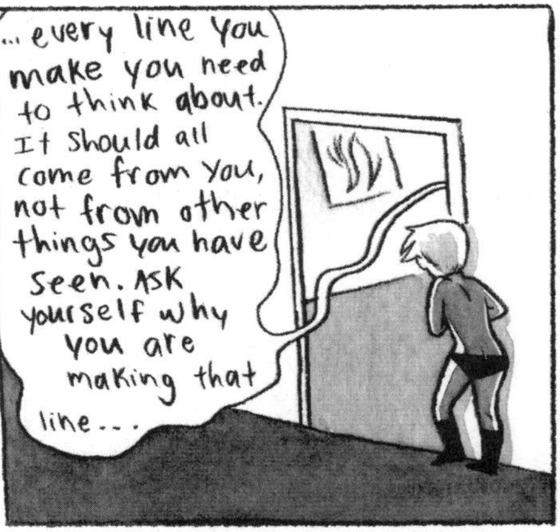
... every line you make you need to think about. It should all come from you, not from other things you have seen. ASK yourself why you are making that line...

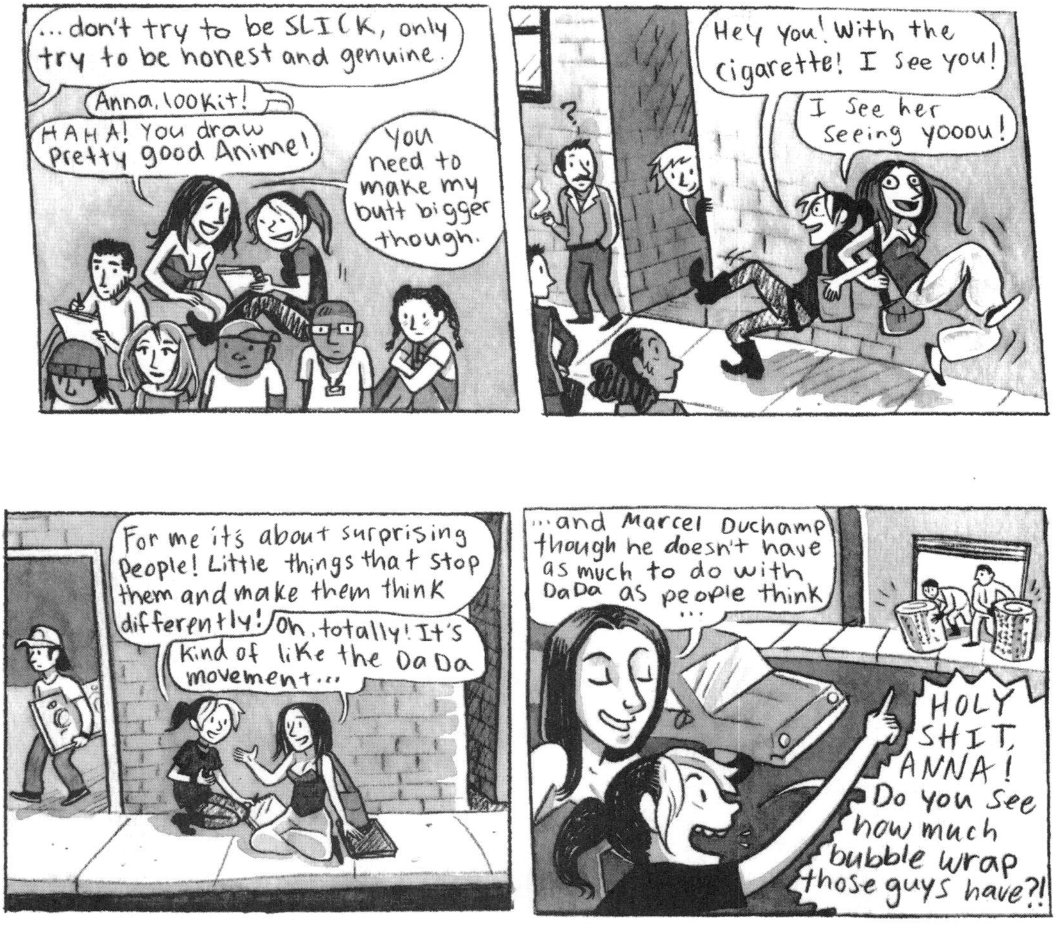
...don't try to be SLICK, only try to be honest and genuine.
Anna, lookit!
HAHA! You draw pretty good Anime!
You need to make my butt bigger though.
?
Hey You! With the cigarette! I see you!
I see her seeing yooou!
For me it's about surprising people! Little things that stop them and make them think differently!
Oh, totally! It's kind of like the DaDa movement...
...and Marcel Duchamp though he doesn't have as much to do with DaDa as people think...
HOLY SHIT, ANNA! Do you see how much bubble wrap those guys have?!

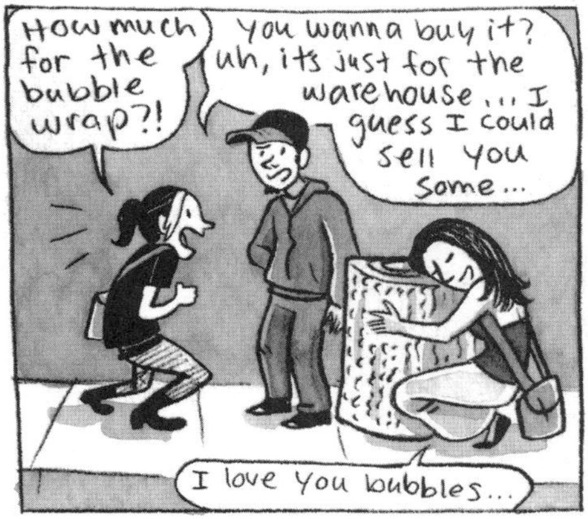
How much for the bubble wrap?!
You wanna buy it? uh, it's just for the warehouse... I guess I could sell you some...
I love you bubbles...
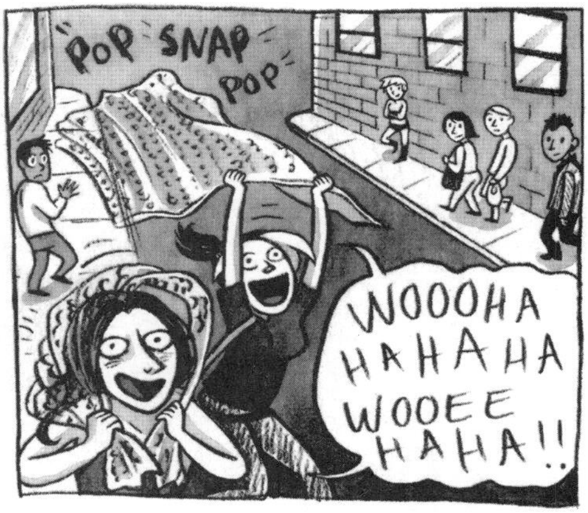
POP SNAP POP
WOOOHA HAHAHA WOOEE HAHA!!
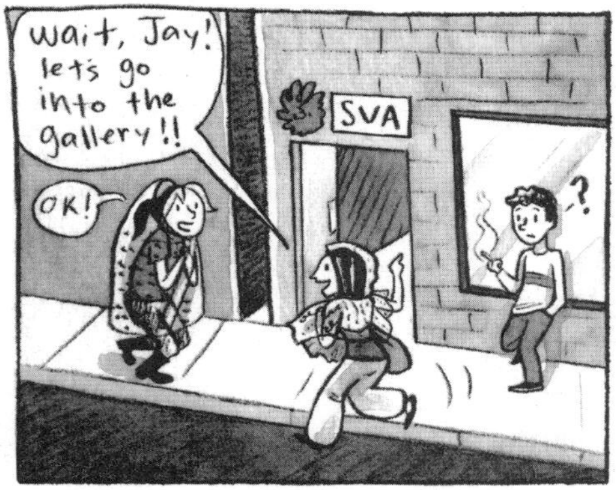
wait, Jay! let's go into the gallery!!
OK!
SVA
?
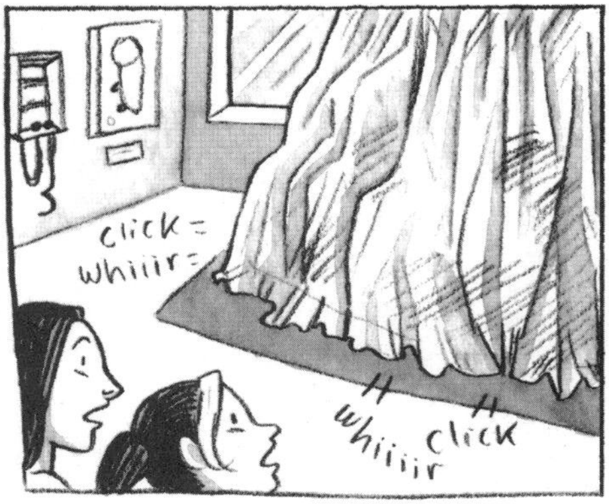
click whiiir
whiiiir click
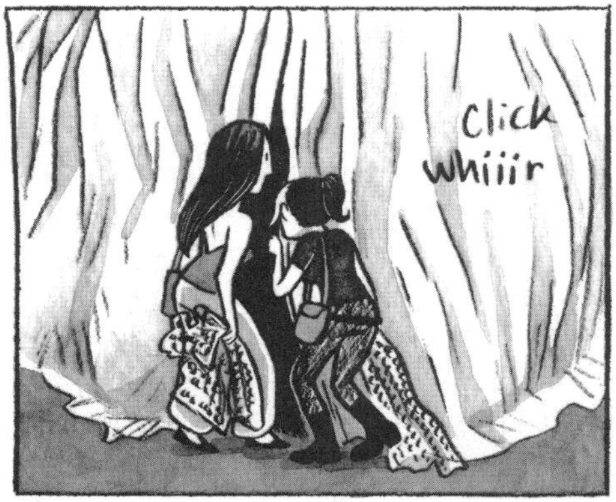
click whiiir

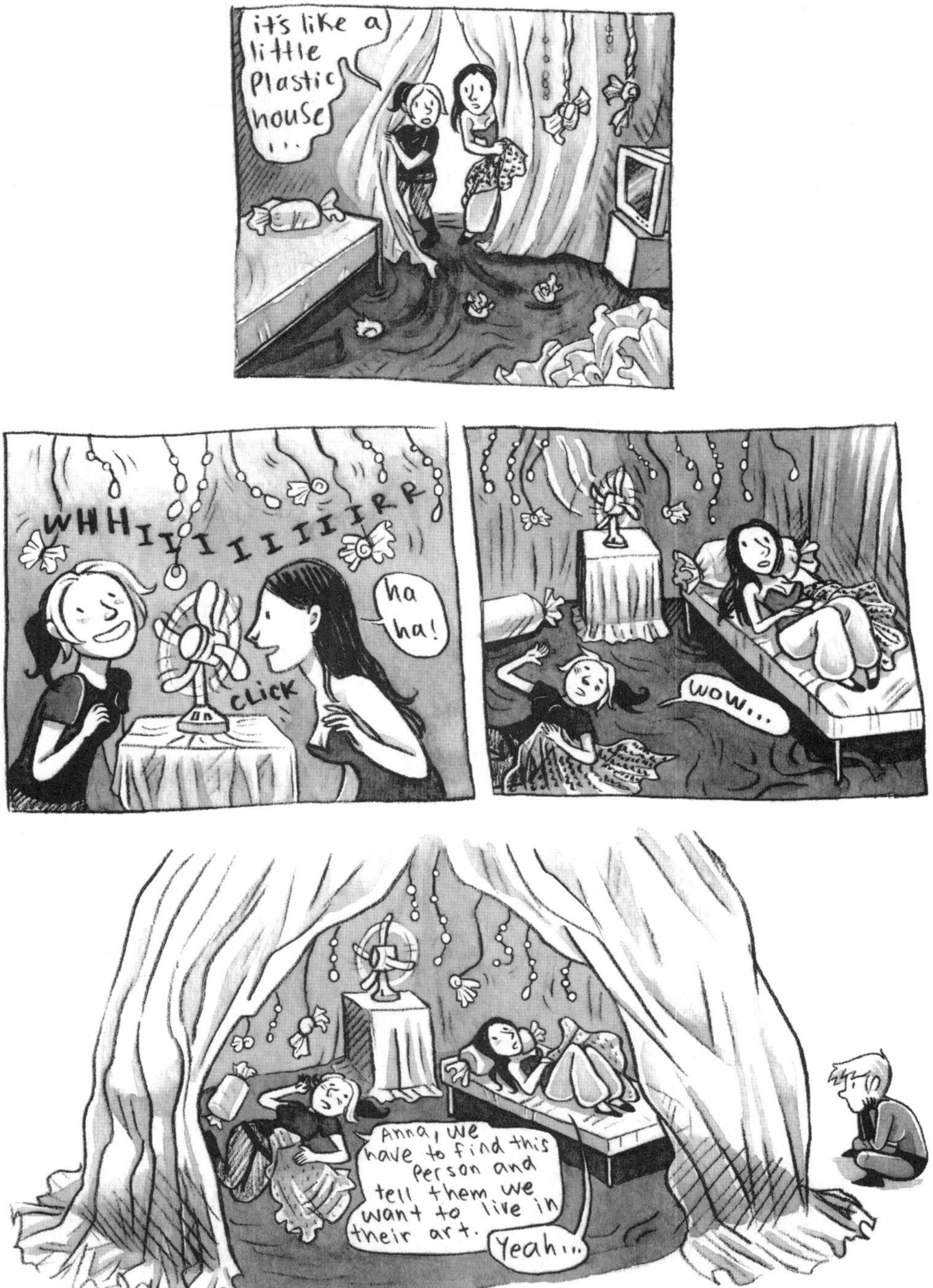
it's like a little plastic house ...
WHHIIIIIIIIRR
ha ha!
CLICK
WOW...
Anna, we have to find this person and tell them we want to live in their art.
Yeah...

Gramercy Park, NYC, 2002

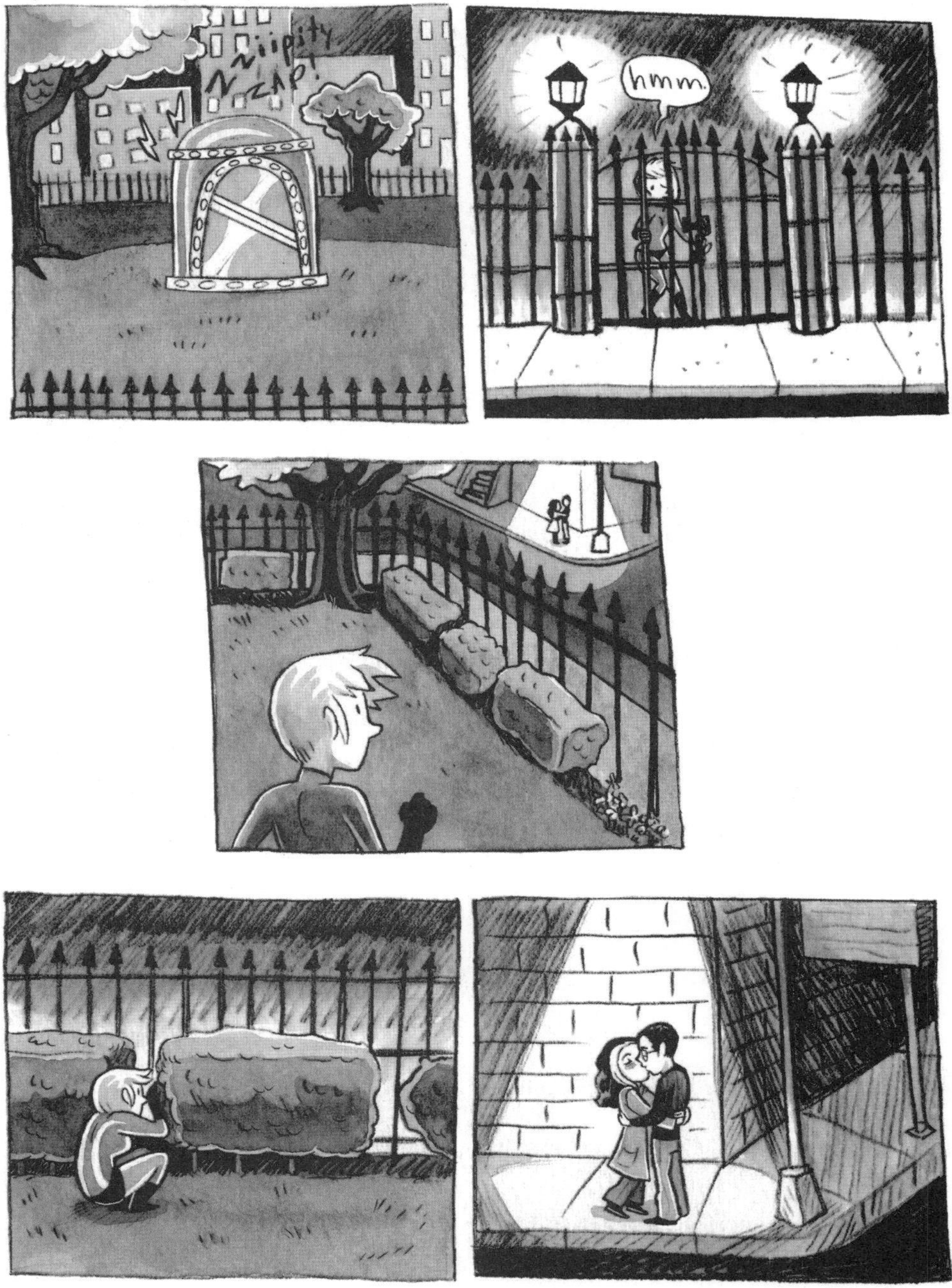
ziiipity
ZAP!
hmm.

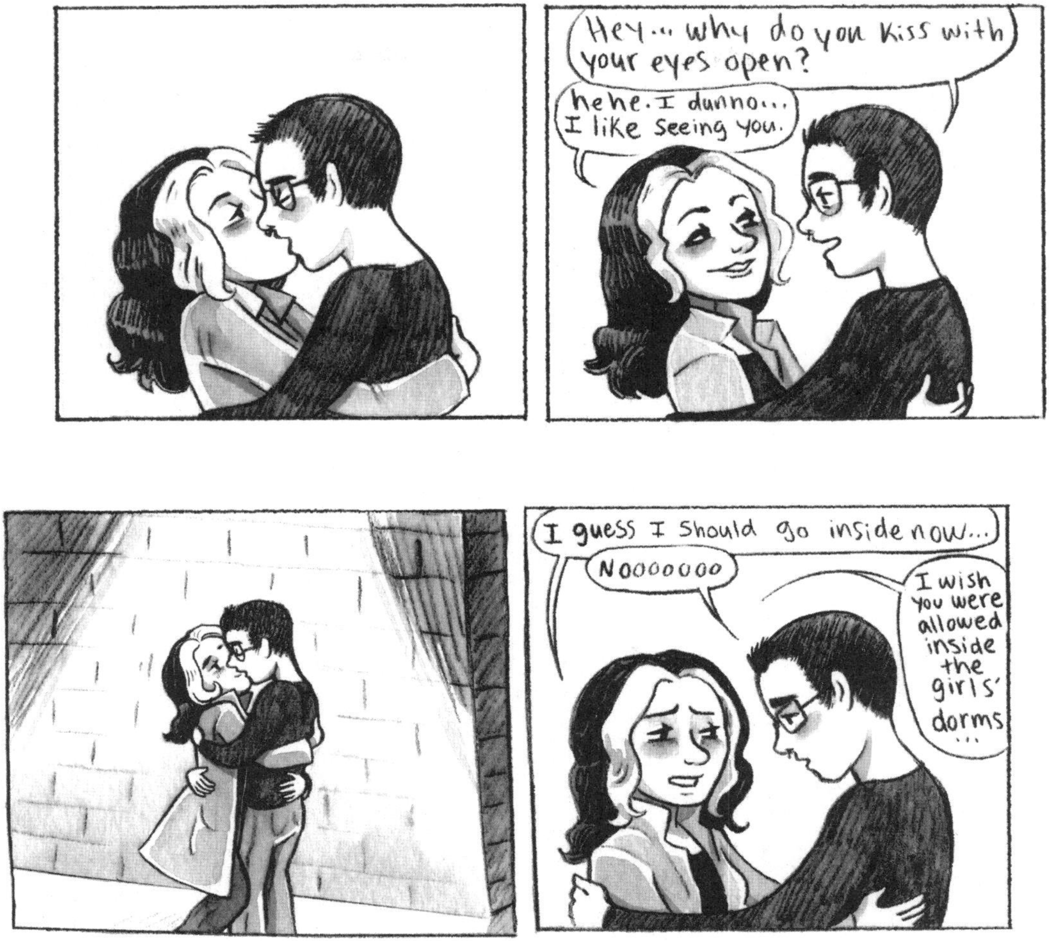

Hey... why do you kiss with your eyes open?
hehe. I dunno... I like seeing you.
I guess I should go inside now...
Noooooo
I wish you were allowed inside the girls' dorms...

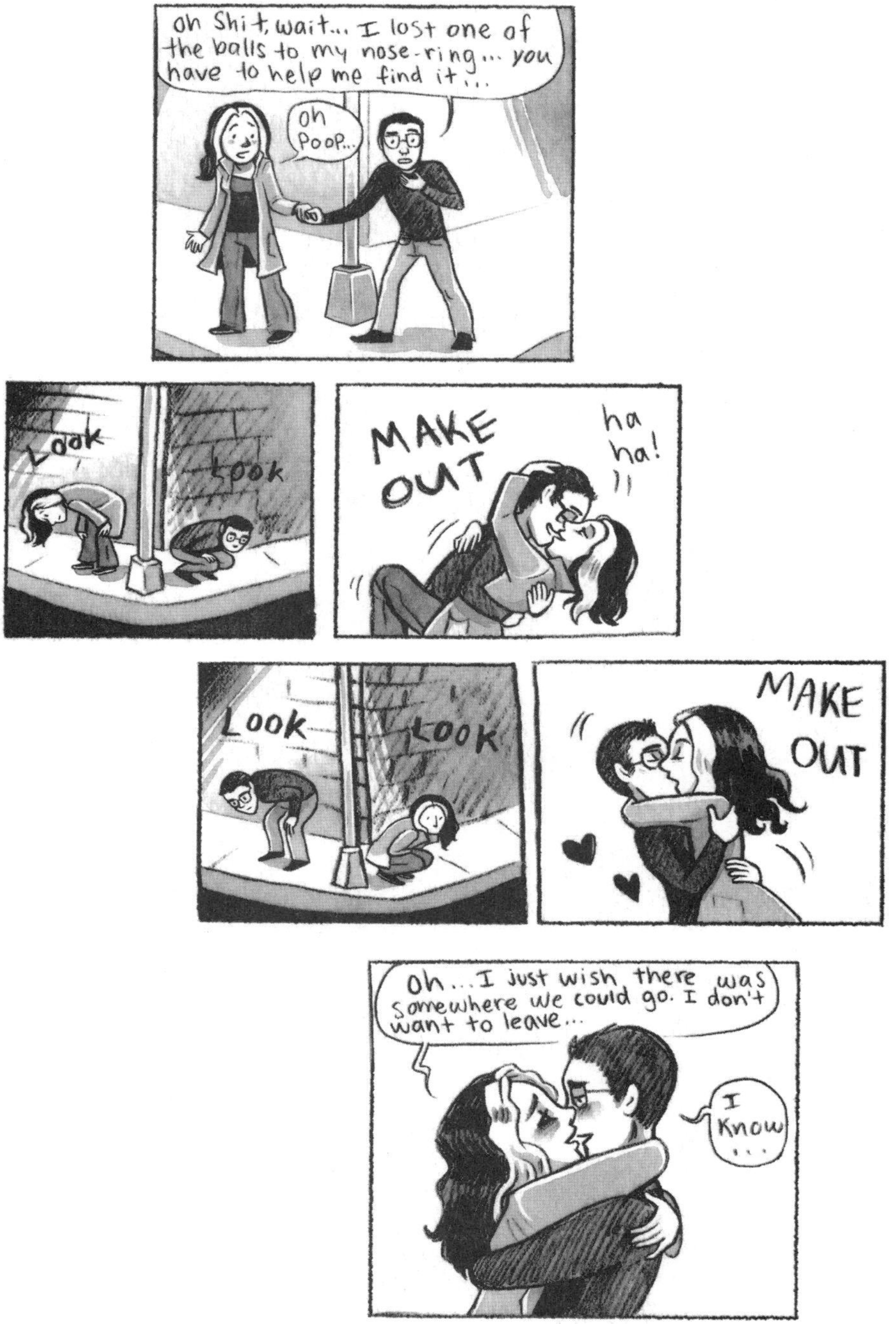
oh Shit, wait... I lost one of the balls to my nose-ring... you have to help me find it...
oh Poop...
Look
Look
MAKE OUT
ha ha!
Look
Look
MAKE OUT
Oh... I just wish there was somewhere we could go. I don't want to leave...
I Know ...

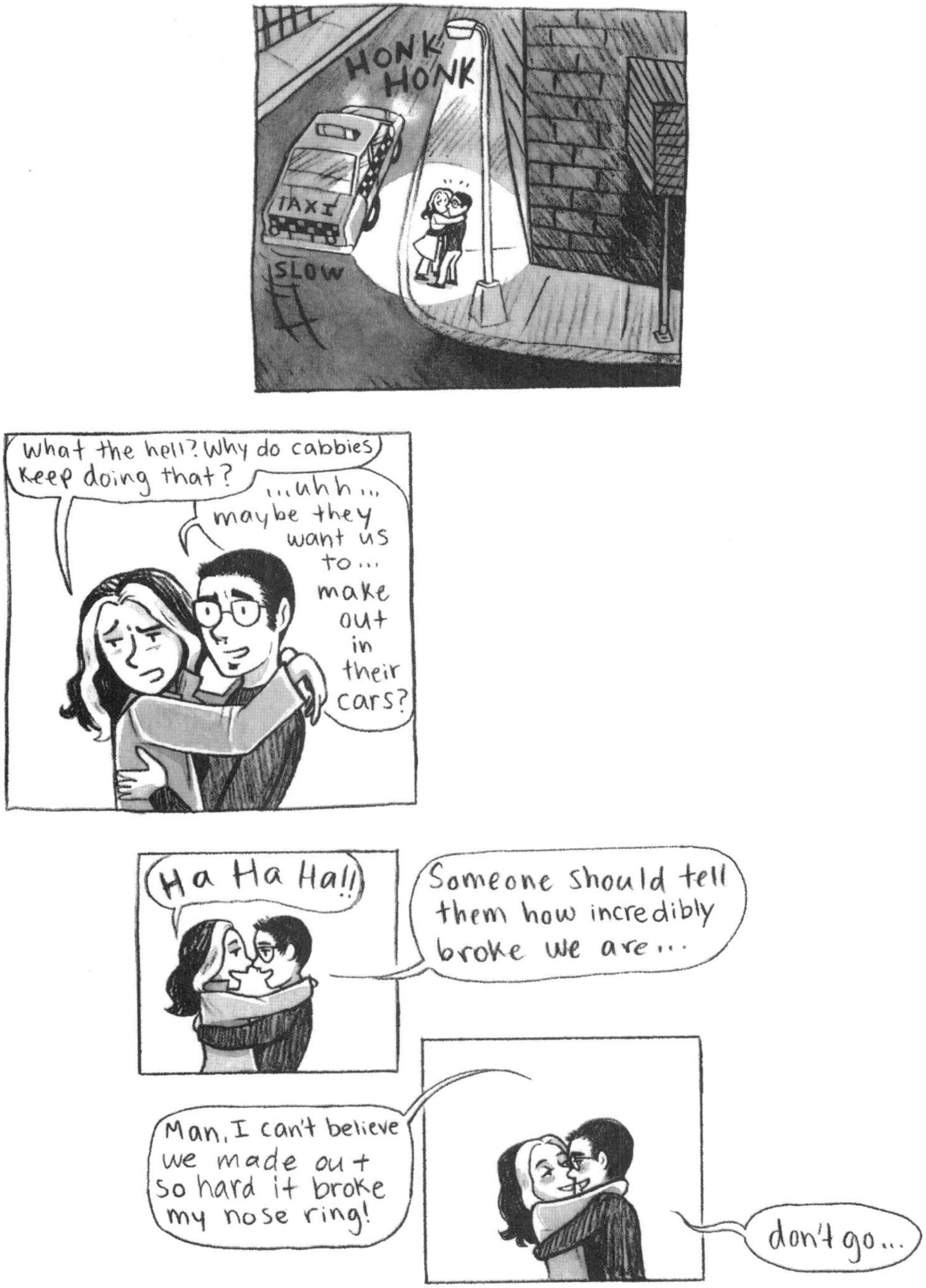
HONK HONK
TAXI
SLOW
What the hell? Why do cabbies keep doing that?
...uhh... maybe they want us to... make out in their cars?
Ha Ha Ha!!
Someone should tell them how incredibly broke we are...
Man, I can't believe we made out so hard it broke my nose ring!
don't go...

1996:

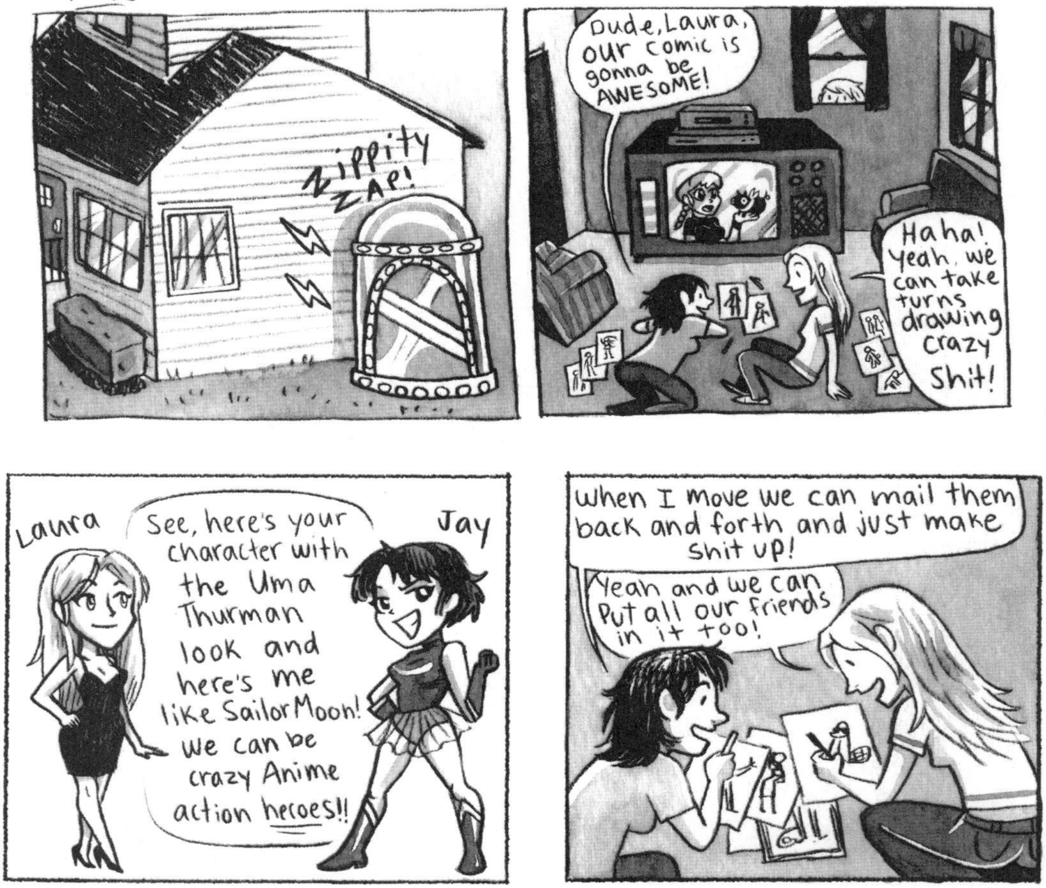
Zippity ZAP!
Dude, Laura, our comic is gonna be AWESOME!
Haha! Yeah, we can take turns drawing crazy Shit!
Laura
Jay
See, here's your character with the Uma Thurman look and here's me like SailorMoon! We can be crazy Anime action heroes!!
When I move we can mail them back and forth and just make shit up!
Yeah and we can Put all our friends in it too!

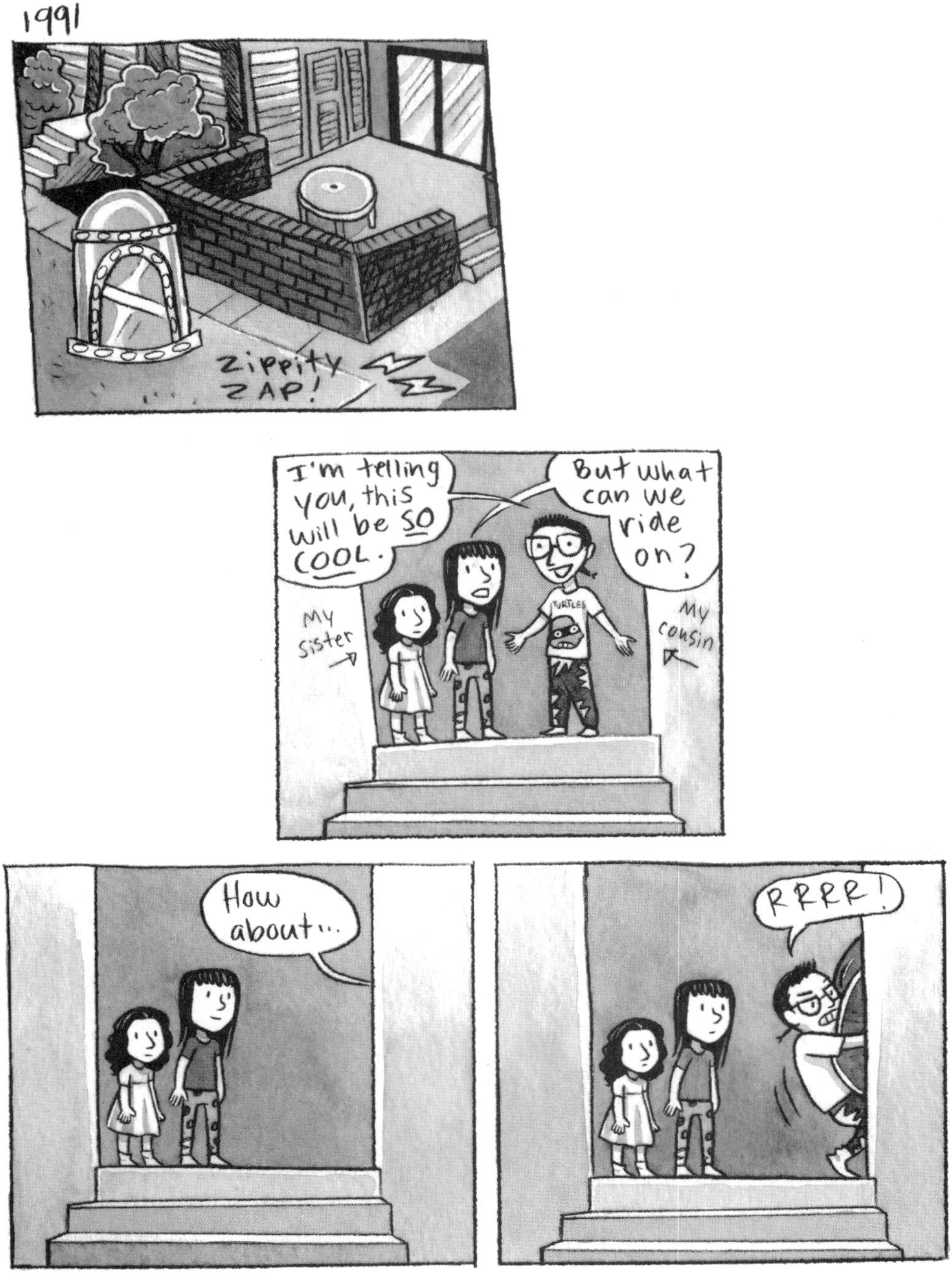
1991
ZIPPITY ZAP!
I'm telling you, this will be SO COOL.
But what can we ride on?
My sister
My cousin
TURTLES
How about...
RRRR!

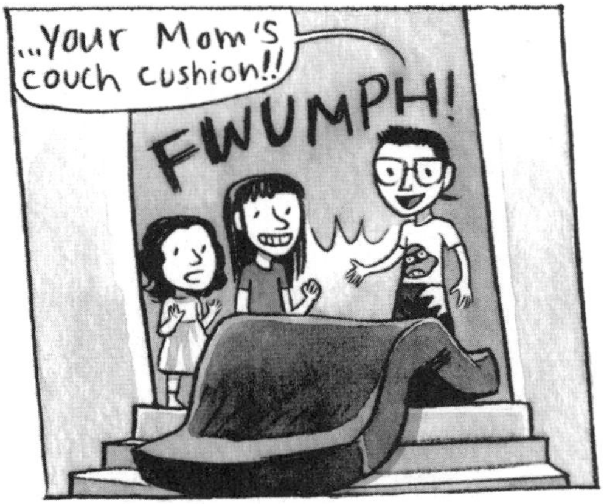
...your Mom's couch cushion!!
FWUMPH!

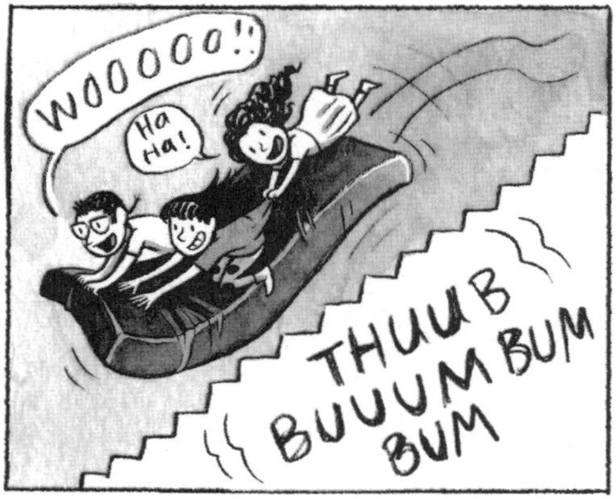
WOOOOOO!!
Ha Ha!
THUUB BUUUM BUM BUM

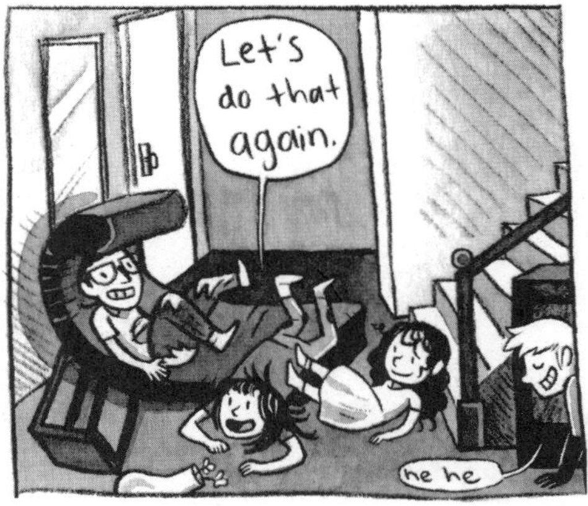
Let's do that again.
he he

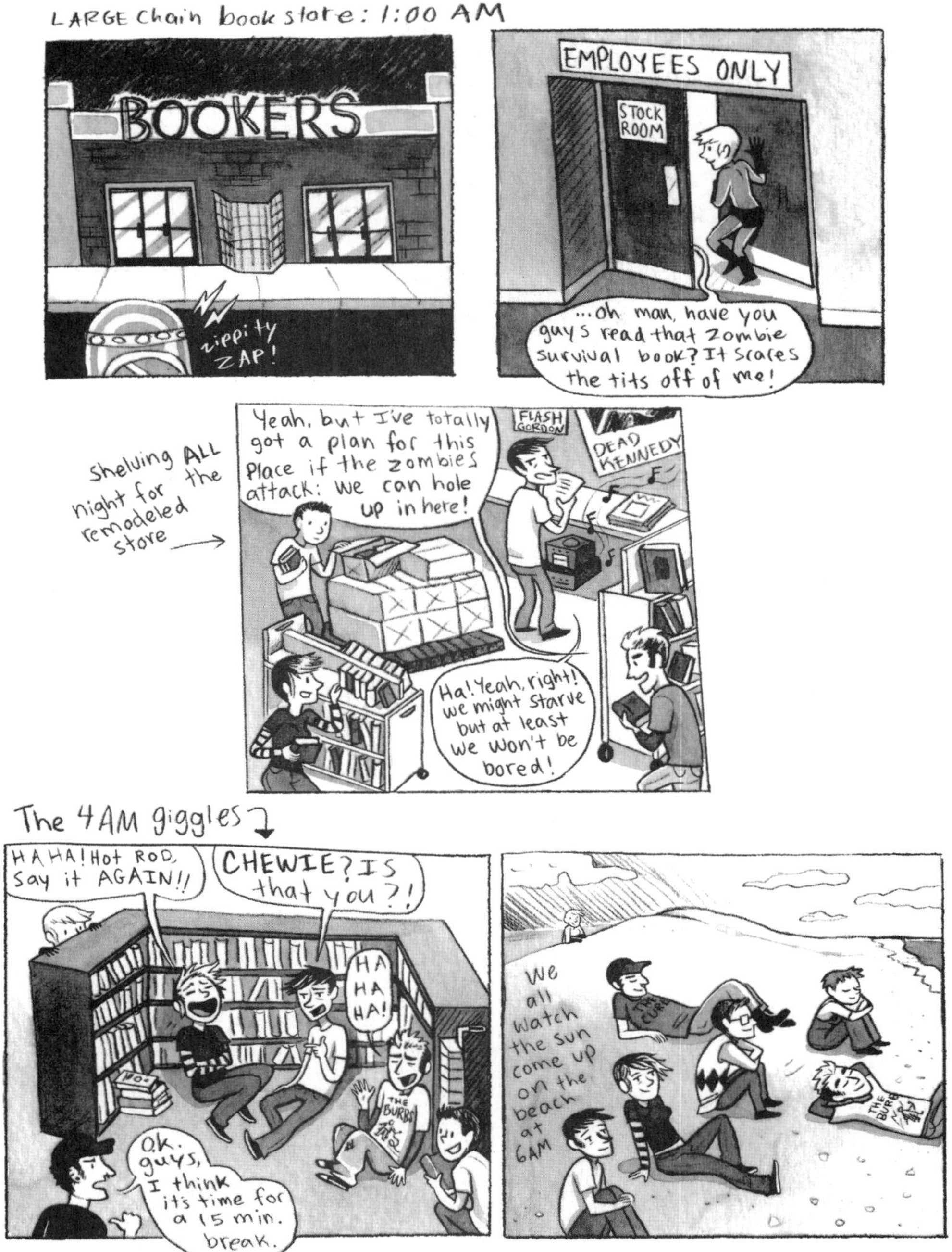
LARGE chain book store: 1:00 AM
BOOKERS
zippity ZAP!
EMPLOYEES ONLY
STOCK ROOM
...oh man, have you guys read that Zombie survival book? It scares the tits off of me!
Shelving ALL night for the remodeled store
Yeah, but I've totally got a plan for this place if the zombies attack: we can hole up in here!
FLASH GORDON
DEAD KENNEDY
Ha! Yeah, right! we might starve but at least we won't be bored!
The 4AM giggles
HAHA! Hot ROD, say it AGAIN!!
CHEWIE? IS that you?!
HA HA HA!
THE BURBS
O.K. guys, I think it's time for a 15 min. break.
We all watch the sun come up on the beach at 6AM
THE CURE
THE BURBS

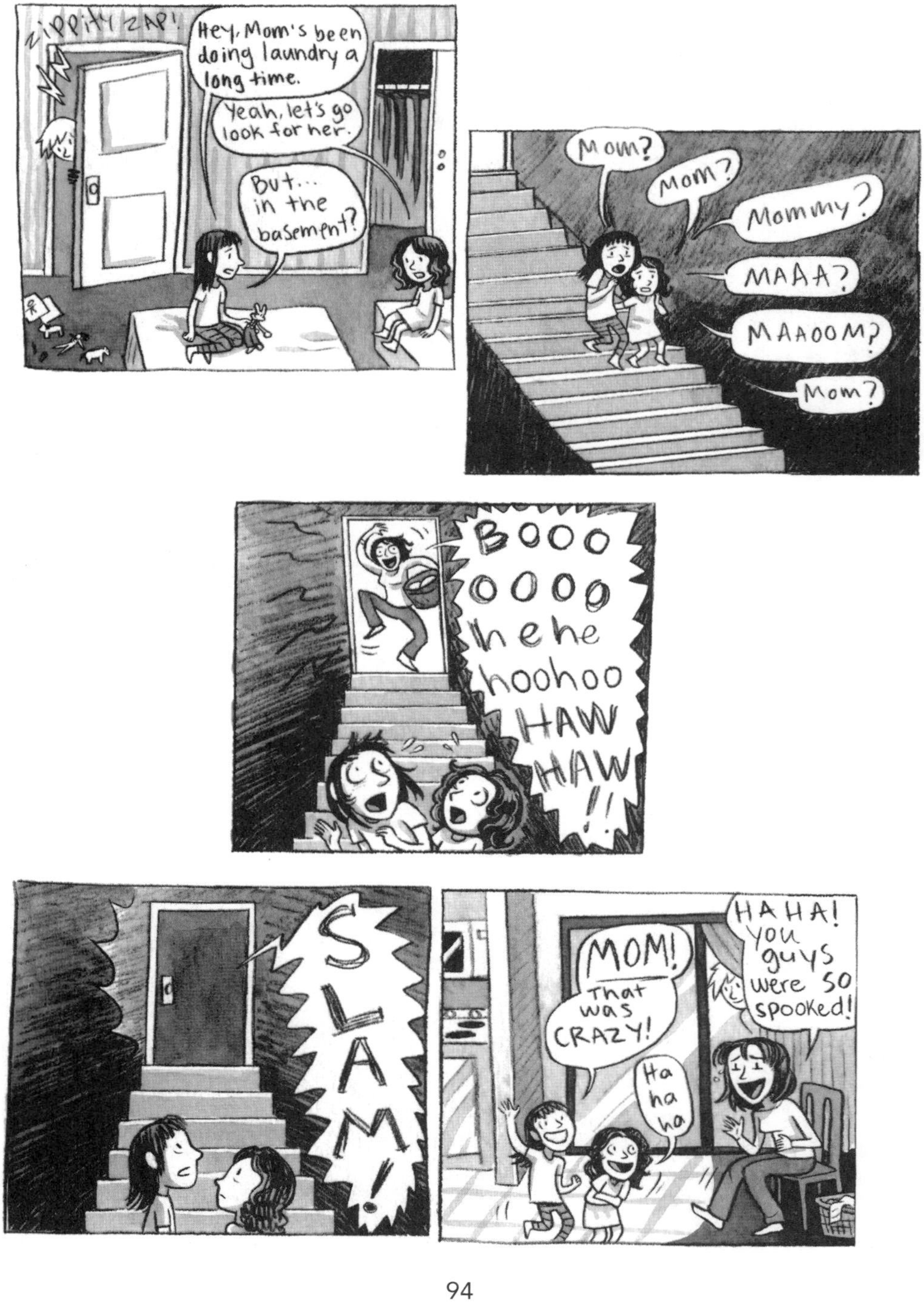

ZIPPITY ZAP!
Hey, Mom's been doing laundry a long time.
Yeah, let's go look for her.
But... in the basement?
Mom?
Mom?
Mommy?
MAAA?
MAAOOM?
Mom?
Boooooooo hehe hoohoo HAW HAW!!
SLAM!
MOM! That was CRAZY!
HAHA! You guys were so spooked!
Ha ha ha

Sayville Theater, 2000

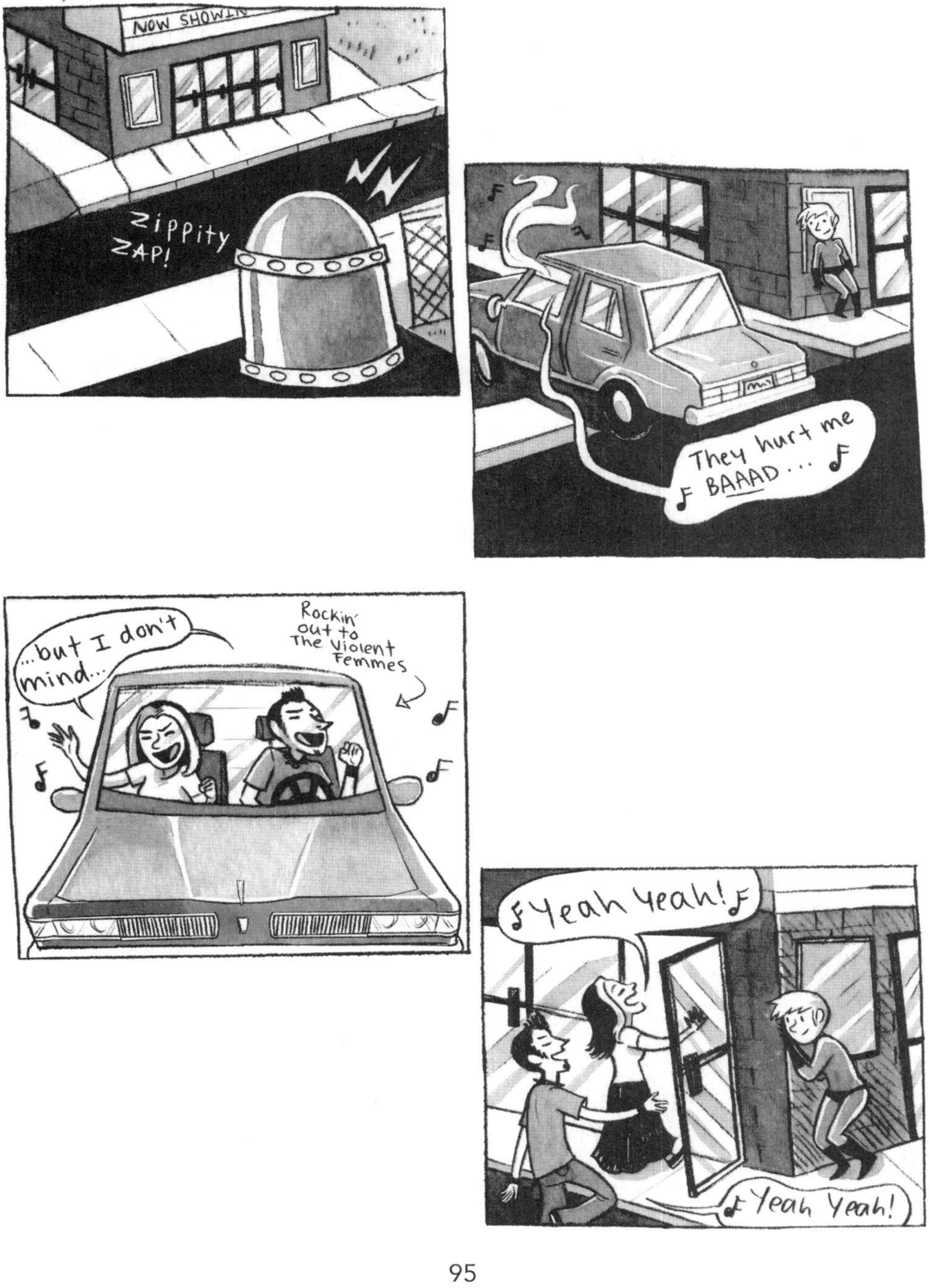
NOW SHOWIN
Zippity ZAP!
They hurt me BAAAD...
...but I don't mind...
Rockin' out to The Violent Femmes
Yeah Yeah!
Yeah Yeah!

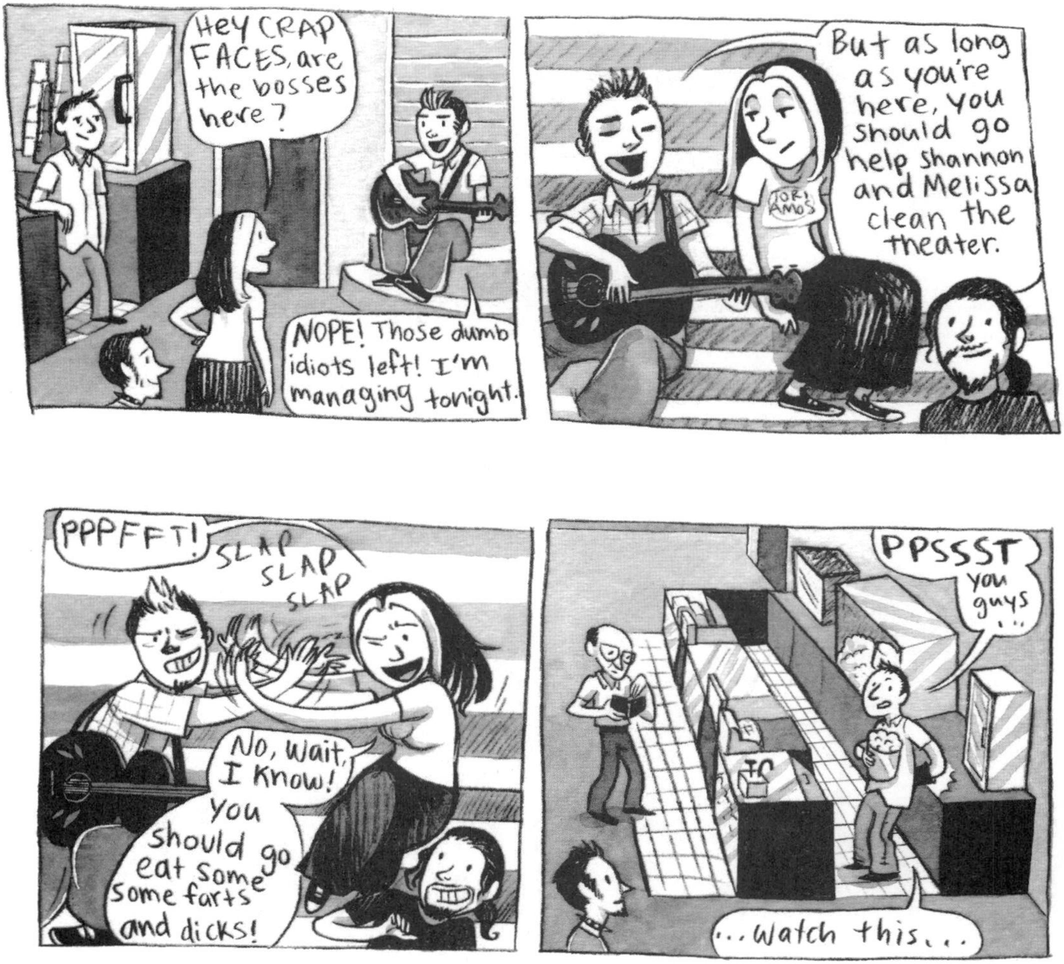
Hey CRAP FACES, are the bosses here?
NOPE! Those dumb idiots left! I'm managing tonight.
But as long as you're here, you should go help Shannon and Melissa clean the theater.
TORI AMOS
PPPFFT!
SLAP SLAP SLAP
No, wait, I know! You should go eat some some farts and dicks!
PPSSST you guys...
...watch this...

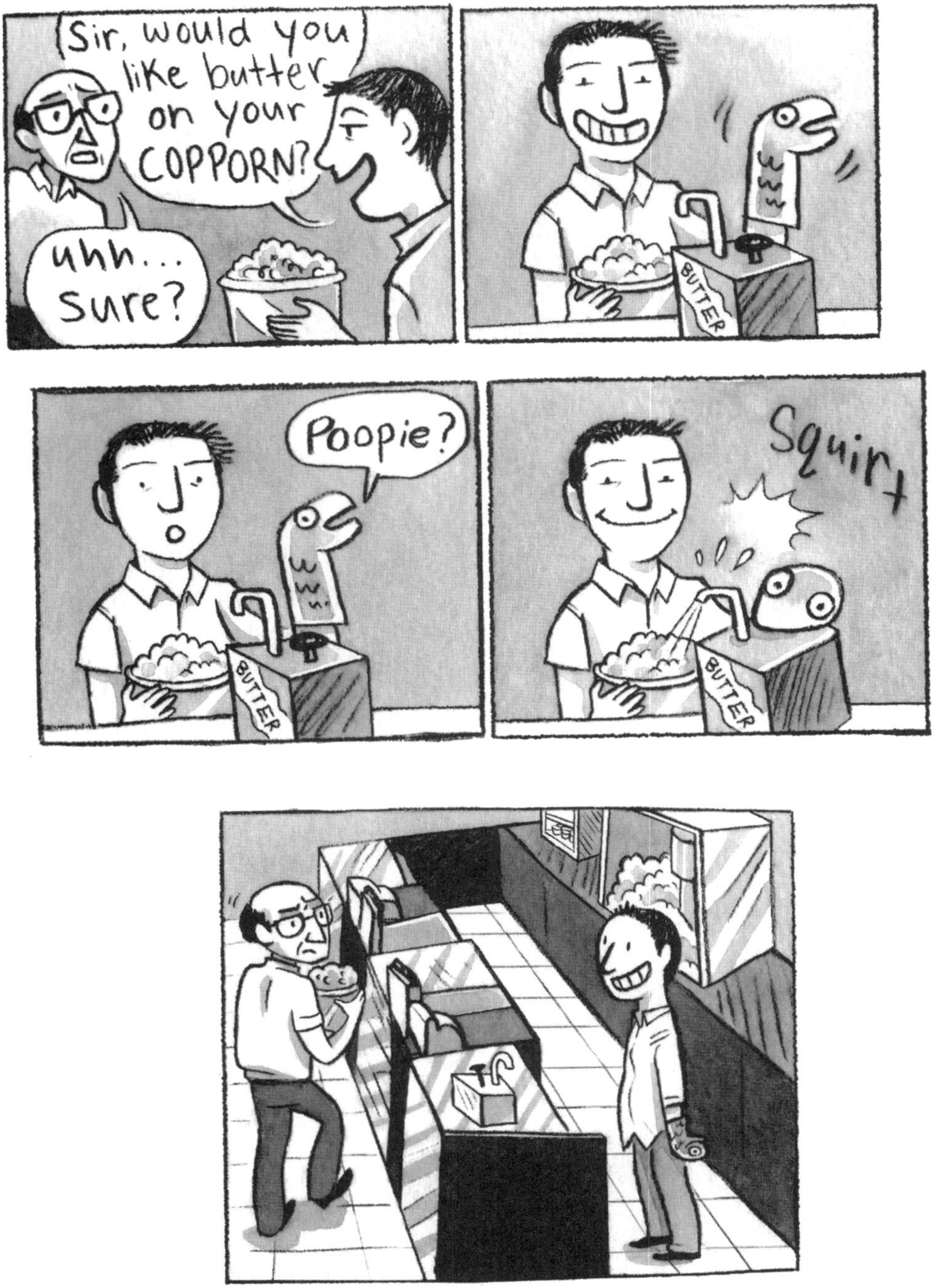
Sir, would you like butter on your COPPORN?
uhh... sure?
Poopie?
Squirt

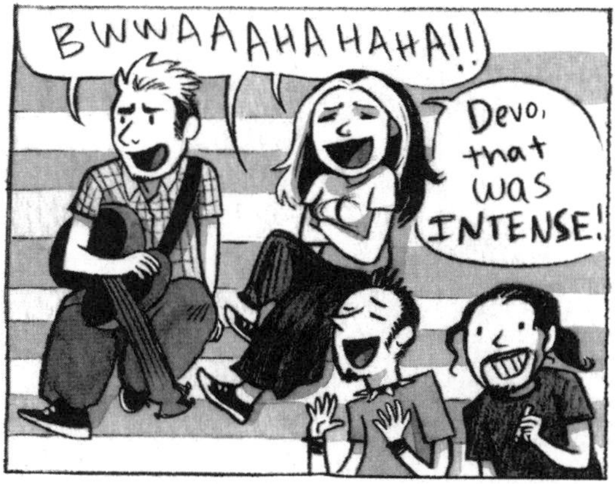
BWWAAAAHAHAHA!!
Devo, that was INTENSE!

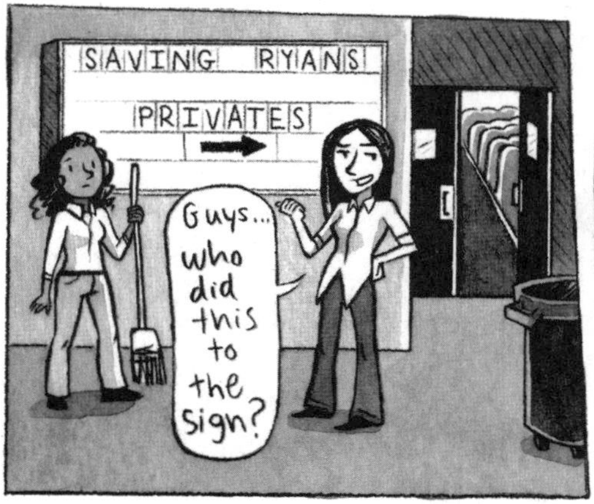
SAVING RYANS
PRIVATES
Guys... who did this to the sign?

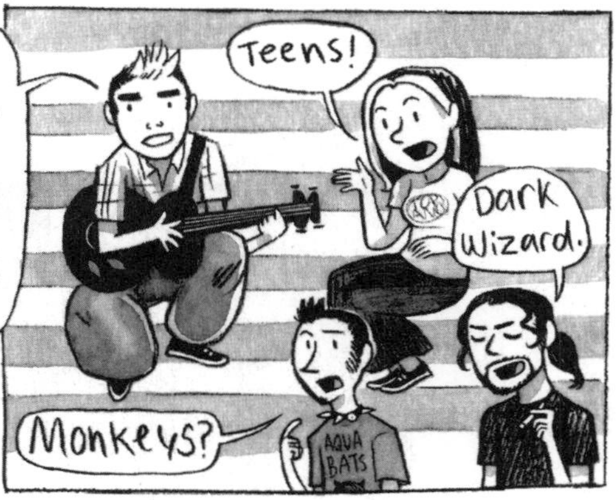
VANDALS
Teens!
Dark Wizard.
Monkeys?
AQUA BATS

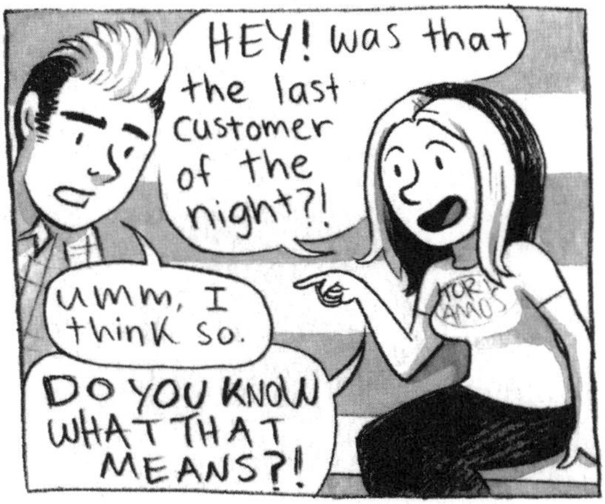
HEY! was that the last customer of the night?!
umm, I think so.
DO YOU KNOW WHAT THAT MEANS?!

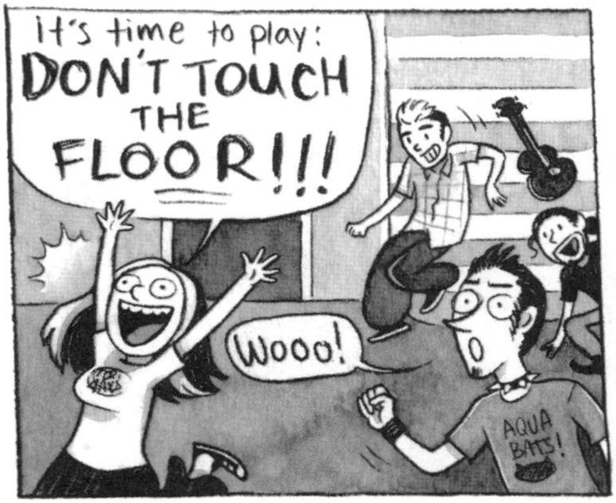
It's time to play: DON'T TOUCH THE FLOOR!!!
Wooo!
AQUA BATS!

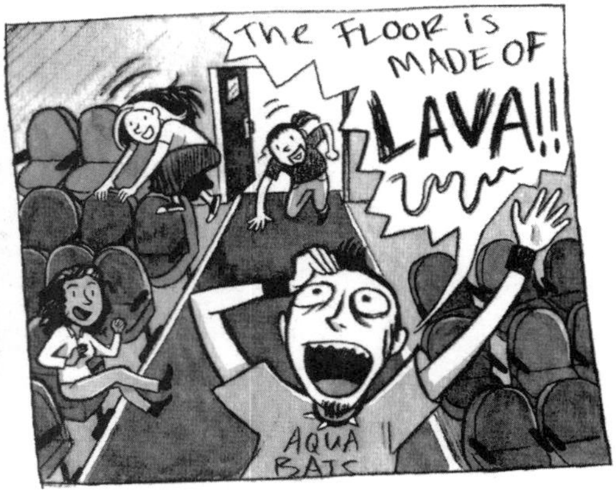
The FLOOR is MADE OF LAVA!!
AQUA BATS

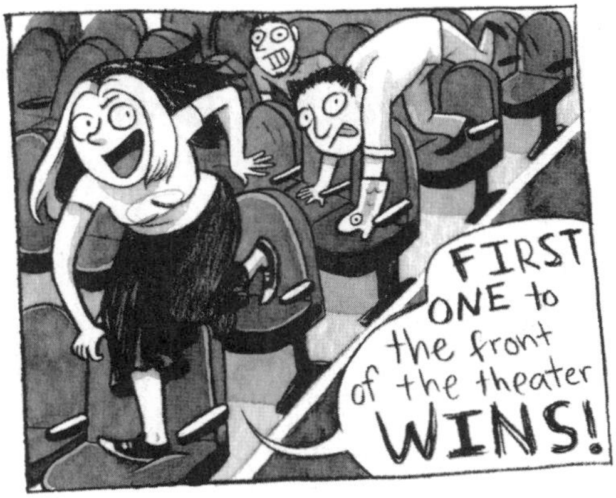
FIRST ONE to the front of the theater WINS!

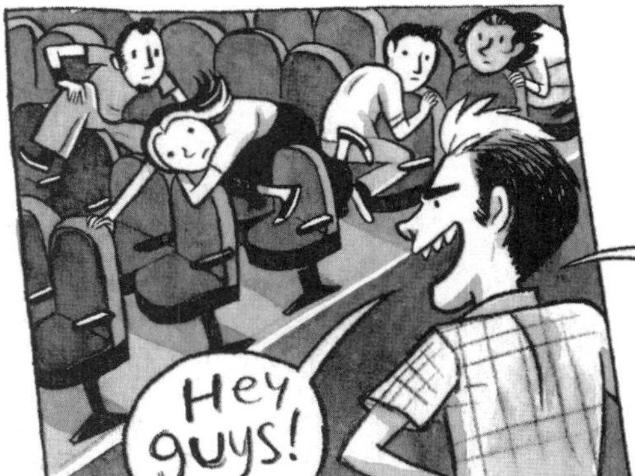
Hey guys!
Check out my ...

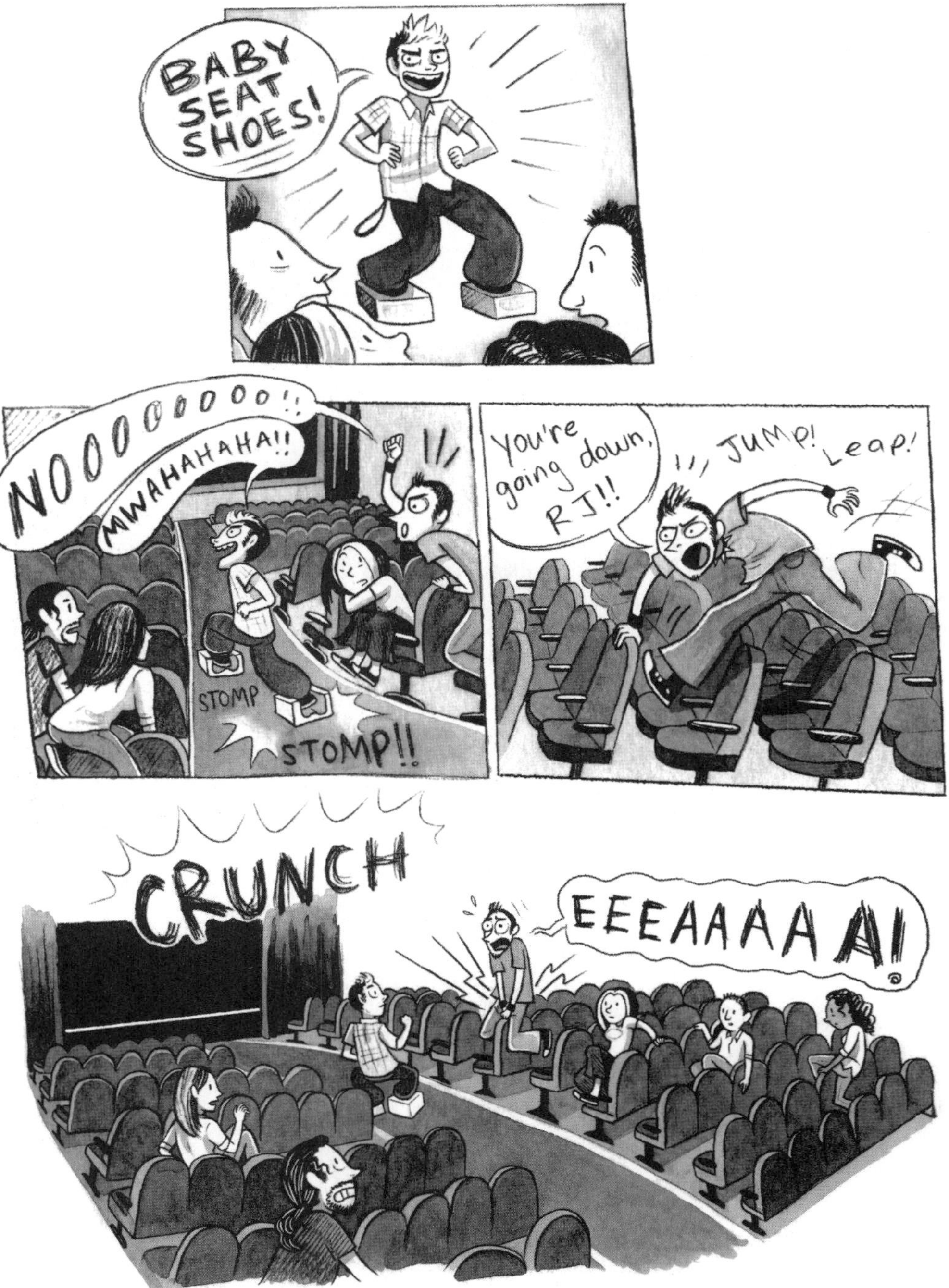
BABY SEAT SHOES!
NOOOOOOOOOO!!
MWAHAHAHA!!
STOMP
STOMP!!
You're going down, RJ!!
JUMP!
Leap!
CRUNCH
EEEAAAAAI!

Later that night...

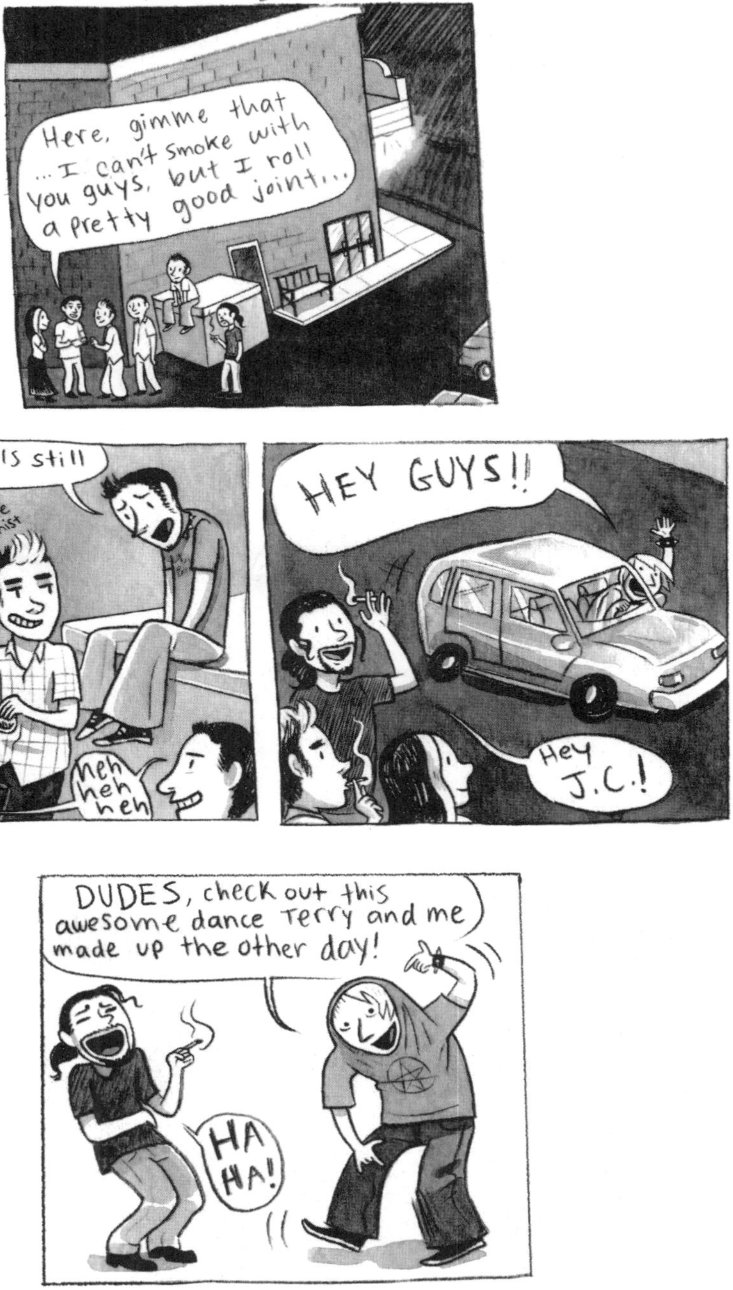
Here, gimme that ... I can't smoke with you guys, but I roll a pretty good joint...
Man...my balls still hurt.
Jay, the Projectionist
neh heh heh
HEY GUYS!!
Hey J.C.!
DUDES, check out this awesome dance Terry and me made up the other day!
HA HA!

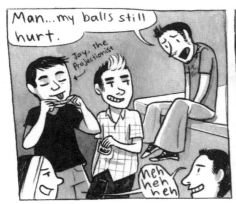

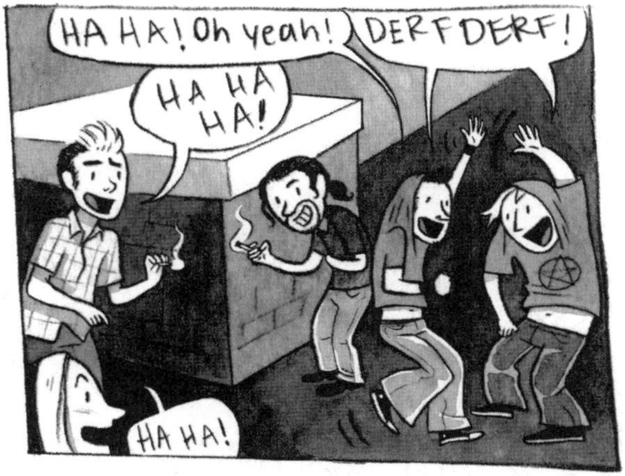
HA HA! Oh yeah!
DERF DERF!
HA HA HA!
HA HA!

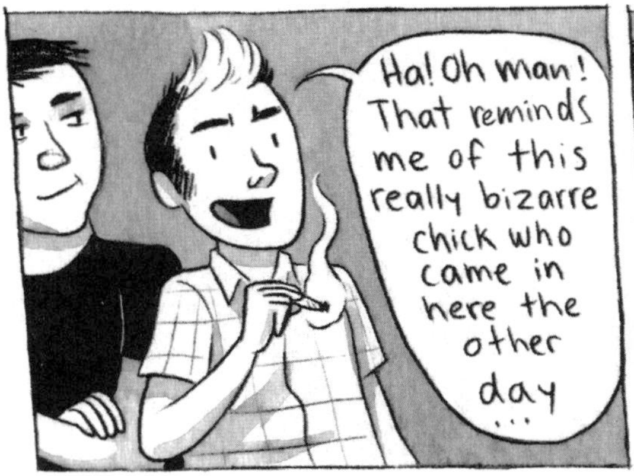
Ha! Oh man! That reminds me of this really bizarre chick who came in here the other day ...

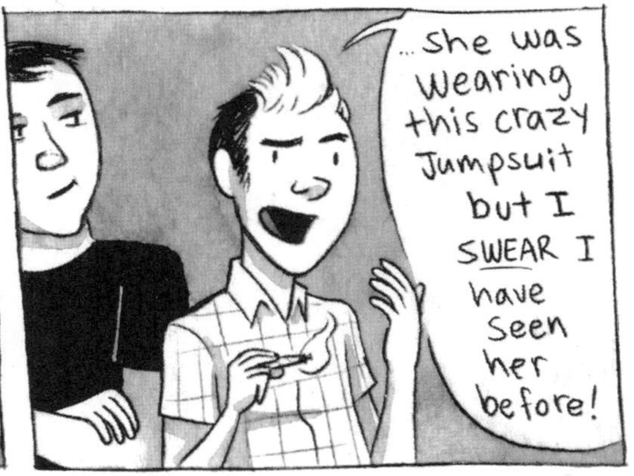
...she was wearing this crazy jumpsuit but I SWEAR I have seen her before!

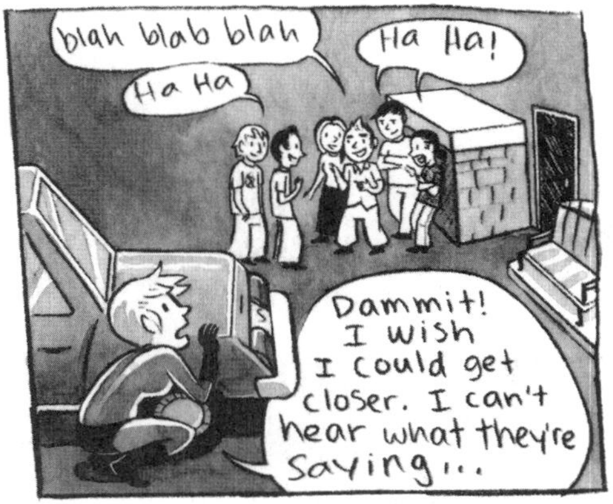
blah blab blah
Ha Ha
Ha Ha!
Dammit! I wish I could get closer. I can't hear what they're saying...

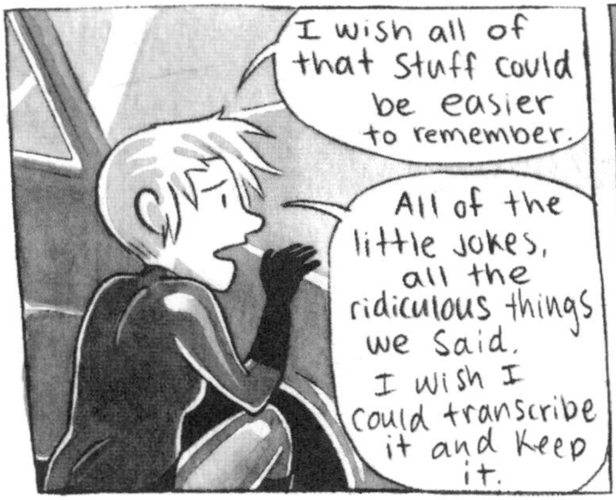
I wish all of that stuff could be easier to remember.
All of the little jokes, all the ridiculous things we said. I wish I could transcribe it and keep it.

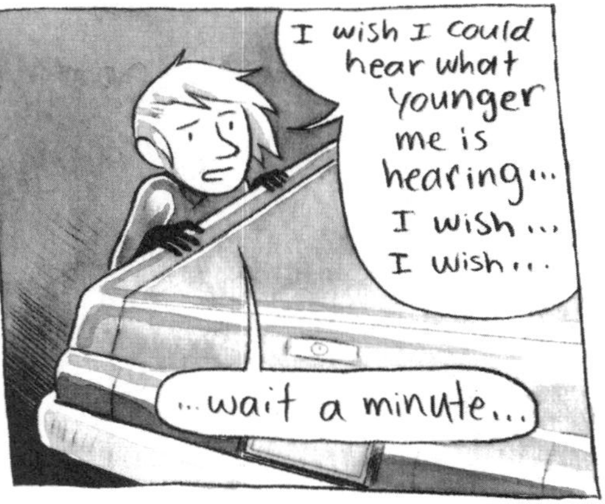
I wish I could hear what younger me is hearing... I wish... I wish...
...wait a minute...

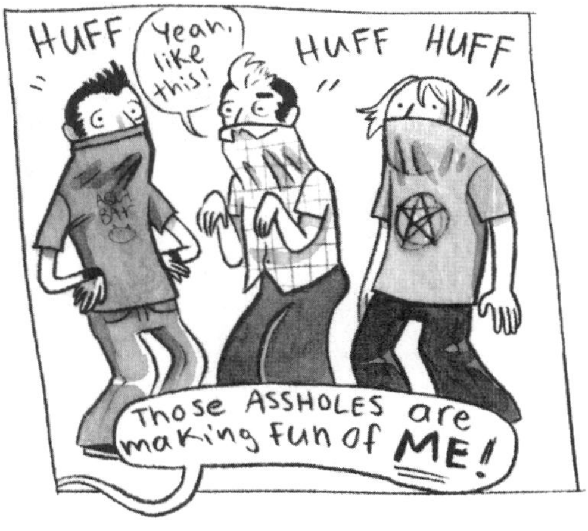
HUFF
Yeah, like this!
HUFF HUFF
Those ASSHOLES are making fun of ME!

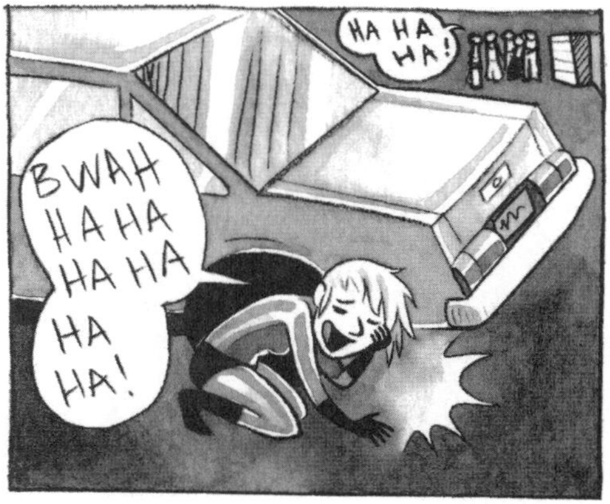
HA HA HA!
BWAH HA HA HA HA HA HA!

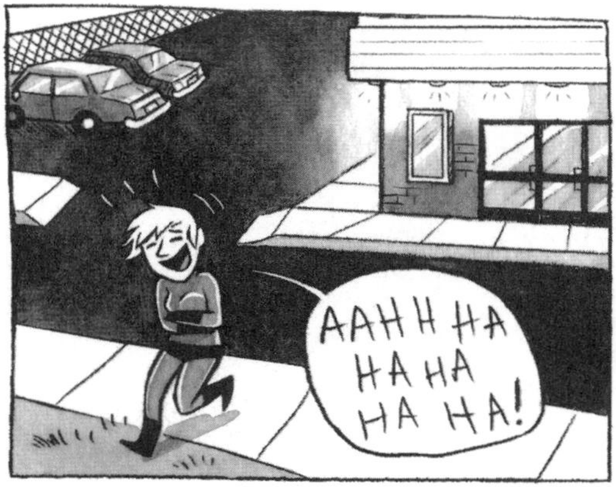
AAHH HA HA HA HA HA!

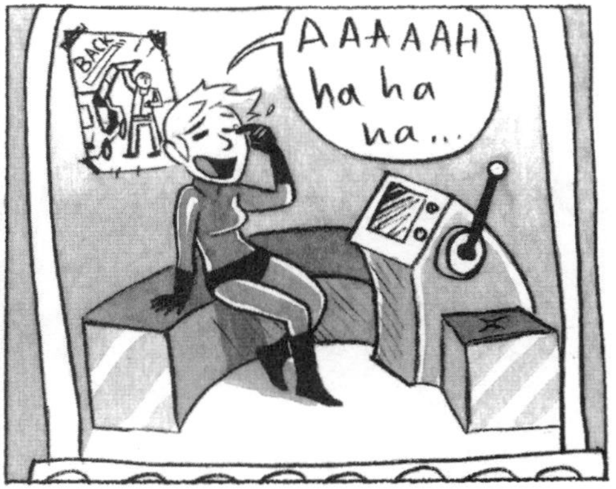
BACK
AAAAAH ha ha ha...

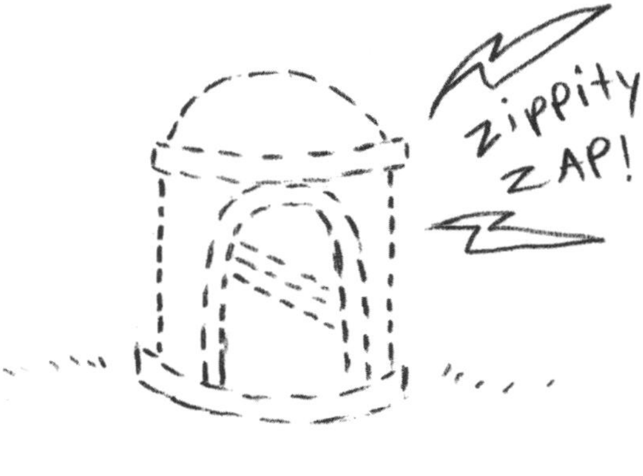
zippity ZAP!

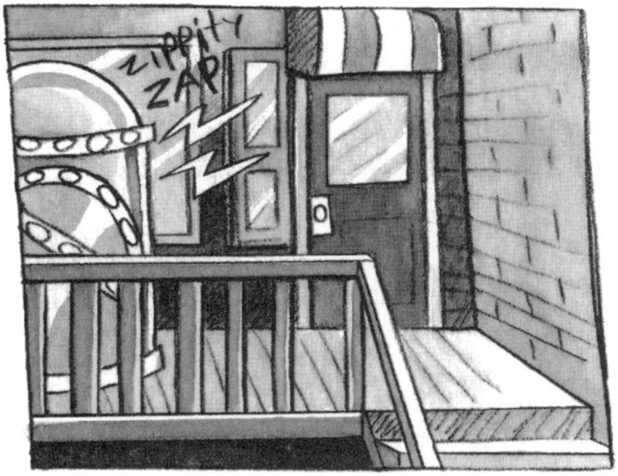
ZIPPITY
ZAP

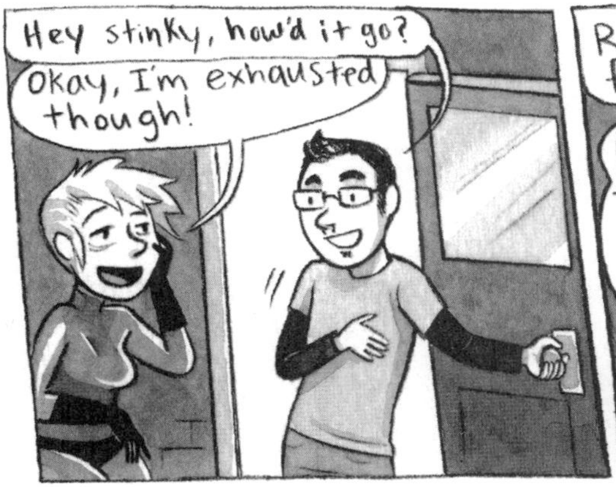
Hey stinky, how'd it go?
Okay, I'm exhausted though!

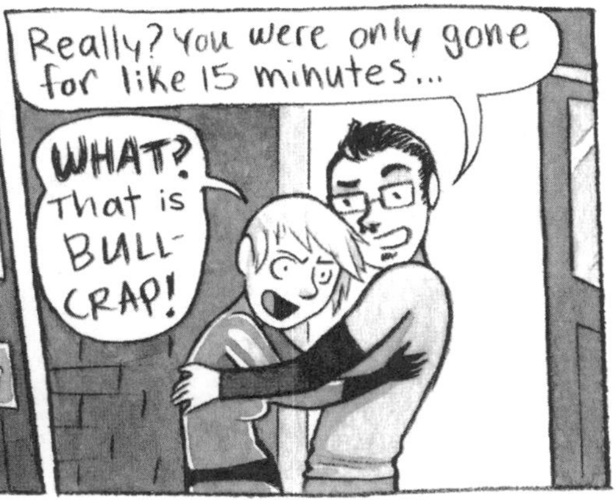
Really? You were only gone for like 15 minutes...
WHAT? That is BULL-CRAP!

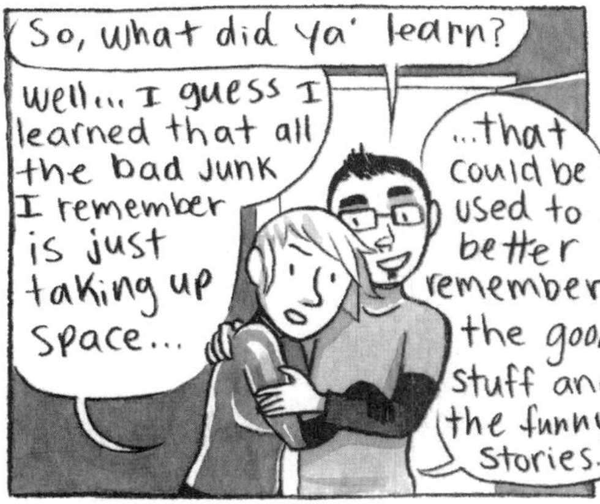
So, what did ya' learn?
Well... I guess I learned that all the bad junk I remember is just taking up space...
...that could be used to better remember the good stuff and the funny stories.

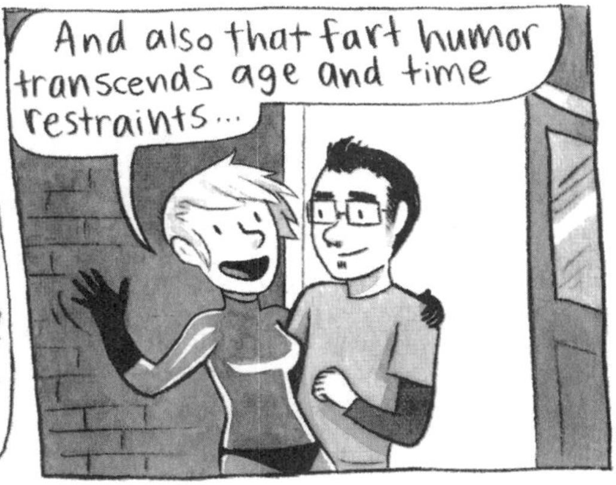
And also that fart humor transcends age and time restraints...

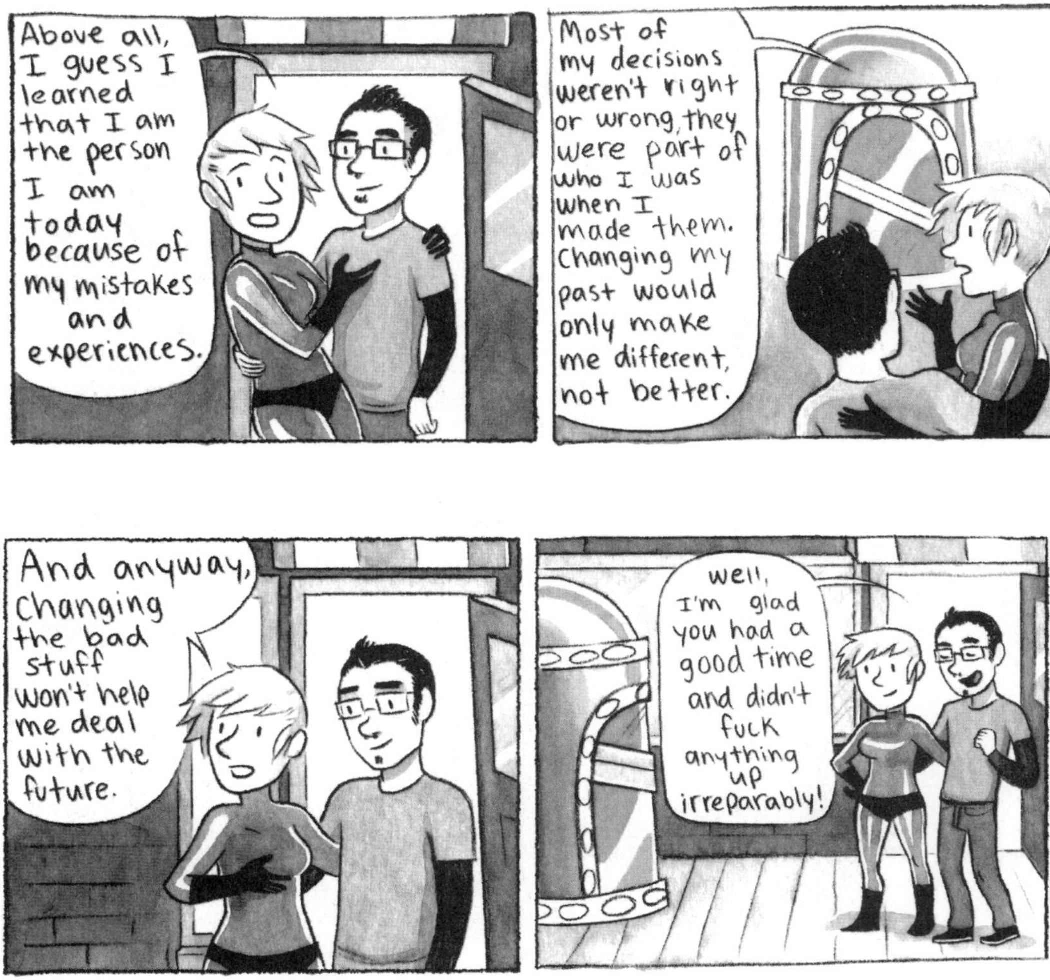
Above all, I guess I learned that I am the person I am today because of my mistakes and experiences.
Most of my decisions weren't right or wrong, they were part of who I was when I made them. Changing my past would only make me different, not better.
And anyway, changing the bad stuff won't help me deal with the future.
Well, I'm glad you had a good time and didn't fuck anything up irreparably!

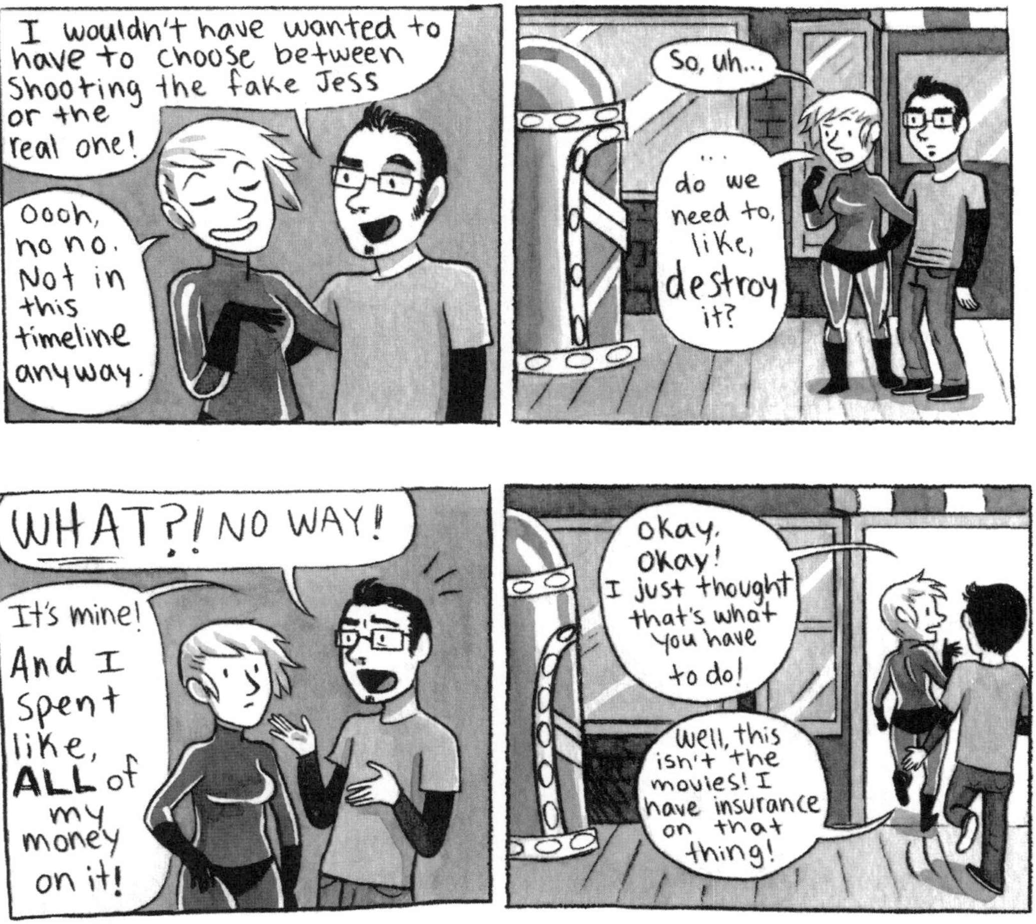
I wouldn't have wanted to have to choose between shooting the fake Jess or the real one!
Oooh, no no. Not in this timeline anyway.
So, uh...
... do we need to, like, destroy it?
WHAT?! NO WAY!
It's mine! And I spent like, ALL of my money on it!
Okay, okay! I just thought that's what you have to do!
Well, this isn't the movies! I have insurance on that thing!

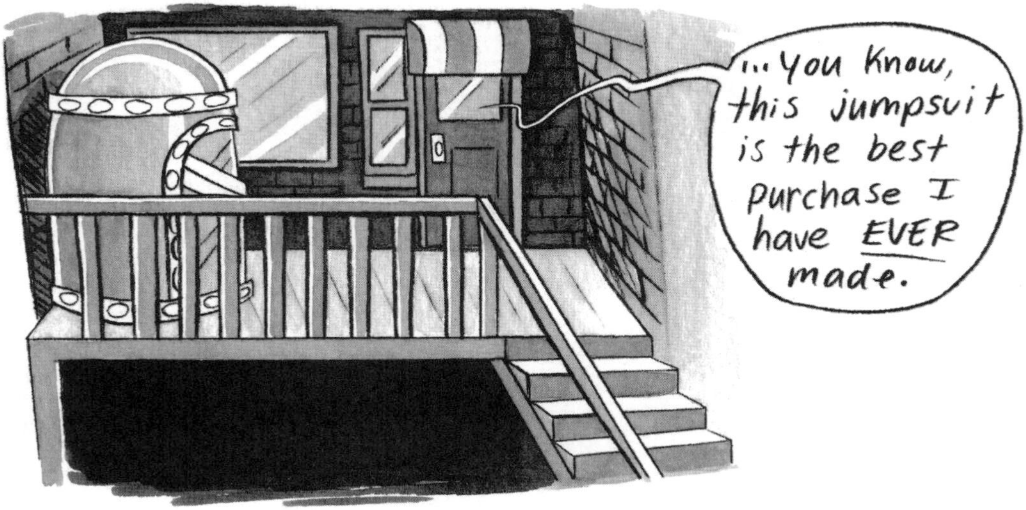
...you know, this jumpsuit is the best purchase I have EVER made.

ABOUT THE AUTHOR

Jess Fink has fornicated with several rainbows, from which she gained her powers.
She graduated from the School of Visual Arts in 2003. Various anthologies have
featured her work, including *SPX* (2002 / 2003), *Best Erotic Comics* (Last Gasp,
2008), *Erotic Comics, Volume 2* (Abrams, 2008), *Popgun Volume 4* (Image, 2010)
and *Smut Peddler* (Iron Circus, 2012). Her erotic comics have been published by
Fantagraphics and featured at the Museum of Sex in New York City.
Her adults-only graphic novel *Chester 5000* is published by Top Shelf Productions.

Her illustration work has been featured in the *New York Times* and *North American
Review*, and she has designed T-shirts and other merchandise available from
Threadless, Hey Chickadee, and Society6.

She is a humanist, she can't ride a bike and she loves marzipan.
She lives in NY with her fella and some cats.
Read her webcomics, *Kid With Experience*: www.jessfink.com/kwe
and *Chester 5000 XYV*: www.jessfink.com/Chester5000XYV
or just drop her a line: JessFinkenstein@gmail.com

 THANK YOU

To Tom Hart for buying Eric and me tickets to see *Amelie* when we were just poor college students, encouraging me to draw "great boobs!," inviting us to awesome comics parties, and overall being an amazing storyteller and teacher.

To Keith Meyerson for being endlessly positive and encouraging your students to take over the world by making it better.

To Kate Beaton, Robert Zemeckis, Audrey Niffenegger, Proust, Terry Gilliam, and my talented boyfriend Eric for inspiring my love of time travel.

To all the artists I admire who have shaped me and still shape me.

To my amazing and hilarious friends and family for making my life interesting and full of love, especially my mother and sister.

To the fine folks at Top Shelf for being excellent.

And most of all, thank you for reading.

Published by
Top Shelf Productions
PO Box 1282
Marietta, GA, 30061-1282
USA

Publishers: Brett Warnock and Chris Staros

Cover Design: Sarah Collins
Art Direction: Brett Warnock

Visit our online catalog at www.topshelfcomix.com.

First printing, May 2013.

Printed in Canada.